MBA

371.   Mnidoo bemaasıng
829   bemaadiziwin reclaiming,
97071 reconnecting, and demystifying
TUR   resiliency as life force energy for
       residential school survivors

Mnidoo
Bemaasing
Bemaadiziwin

Guelph Public Library

371.
829
97071
TUR

Copyright © 2020 Theresa Turmel

ARP Books (Arbeiter Ring Publishing)
205-70 Arthur Street
Winnipeg, Manitoba
Treaty 1 Territory and Historic Métis Nation Homeland Canada R3B 1G7
arpbooks.org

Cover design by Dr. Theresa Turmel with execution by Relish New Brand Experience.
Interior design and layout by Relish New Brand Experience.
Cover artwork by Dayna Rainville.
Printed and bound in Canada by Imprimerie Gauvin on paper made from 100% recycled post-consumer waste.

COPYRIGHT NOTICE

This book is fully protected under the copyright laws of Canada and all other countries of the Copyright Union and is subject to royalty.

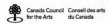   

ARP Books acknowledges the generous support of the Manitoba Arts Council and the Canada Council for the Arts for our publishing program. We acknowledge the financial support of the Government of Canada and the Province of Manitoba through the Book Publishing Tax Credit and the Book Publisher Marketing Assistance Program of Manitoba Culture, Heritage, and Tourism.

Cover image explanation: Some may view First Nations as toppled or broken like the tree on the front cover. This is not true. Our strong roots are firmly attached. We will recover from colonization. We are the tree, standing tall. Our beauty, strength, perseverance and resilience shines through with the assistance of our Ancestors, Traditional Teachings, ceremonies, love of our Mother Earth, and healing through the passion and pride of who we are. Seema leads the way.

LIBRARY AND ARCHIVES CANADA CATALOGUING IN PUBLICATION

Title: Mnidoo bemaasing bemaadiziwin : reclaiming, reconnecting, and demystifying resiliency as life force energy for residential school survivors / Dr. Theresa Turmel.
Other titles: Reclaiming, reconnecting, and demystifying resiliency as life force energy for residential school survivors
Names: Turmel, Theresa, author.
Identifiers: Canadiana (print) 20200241524 | Canadiana (ebook) 2020024289X | ISBN 9781927886359 (softcover) | ISBN 9781927886366 (ebook)
Subjects: LCSH: Indigenous peoples—Mental health—Canada | LCSH: Adult child abuse victims—Canada. | LCSH: Adult child abuse victims—Mental health—Canada. | LCSH: Healing. | LCSH: Resilience (Personality trait) | CSH: Native peoples—Canada—Residential schools.
Classification: LCC E96.5 .T87 2020 | DDC 371.829/97071—dc23

Mnidoo Bemaasing Bemaadiziwin

Reclaiming, Reconnecting, and Demystifying Resiliency as Life Force Energy for Residential School Survivors

Dr. Theresa Turmel

ARP BOOKS   WINNIPEG, MB

TABLE OF CONTENTS

DEDICATION 7

ACKNOWLEDGEMENTS 9

GLOSSARY 13

LIST OF ABBREVIATIONS 15

FOREWORD DR. KATHY ABSOLON 17

ACCEPTING THE LIFE JOURNEY 21

CHAPTER 1 ANISHINAABE THOUGHT: THE BONES AND THE BEDROCK "KANAN MIINWAA NBAGANI- AASMAABKONG" 31

CHAPTER 2 THE WORK PROCESS: RELATIONSHIP AND KNOWLEDGE "NOKIIWIN E-ZHIMAAJIIHKAG: WIIJIKIIWENDIWIN MIININWAA KENDAASWIN" 58

CHAPTER 3 OUR PAST MATTERS "GAA-BI-ZHEWEBAK GCHI-ZHAAZHE GCHI-PIITENDAAGWAAD" 81

CHAPTER 4 UNDERSTANDING LIFE FORCE ENERGY "NSASTAMOWIN MNIDOO BEMAASING BEMAADIZIWIN" 108

CHAPTER 5 "THE TAKEN" ARRIVAL AND LIFE AT THE SCHOOL 137

CHAPTER 6 "THE KNOWING" YOUTH AND THE ROOTS OF RESISTANCE 159

CHAPTER 7 "THE TRANSITION" YOUNG ADULTS RETURNING HOME 186

CHAPTER 8 "THE TRANSFORMATION" SURVIVORS AS KNOWLEDGE HOLDERS *206*

CHAPTER 9 THE PATH OF LIFE CONTINUES *233*

INDEX *262*

REFERENCES *280*

BIO *291*

This work is dedicated to all the residential school survivors and their families everywhere. A special heartfelt dedication goes to the late Susie Jones, the late Vernon Jones, and the Jones family. If you are a survivor reading this work and are in need of support, I encourage you to seek it.

CHI-MEGWEETCH!

I want to acknowledge that I have been privileged and honoured to work alongside Walpole Island First Nation as they are the members who invited me into their community to complete our community project. The acceptance I received and more importantly the wonderful sense of belonging I felt was exactly what we all crave in our lives. I must acknowledge my immediate family. I most sincerely thank my husband, Mike, for his understanding and support. Forever—I will hear his words, "Get your work done!" and lament at my sadness of having to leave him yet again and travel one more time to either Walpole Island or Peterborough. It was my wish to not be gone for so long and explained that I might be gone even longer if I encountered bad weather that it may delay my return, and then hearing him say, "I'd rather miss you for one night than for the rest of my life." His reply gives me a warm, happy feeling.

I must acknowledge my beautiful adult children, John, Danielle and Chantal for their unwavering support while listening to my complaints. John, my son, on hearing these complaints would say, "Ma, did you think that they were just going to hand you that paper?" My daughter Danielle who shares my love of books, remarked that she was recently promoted at work and must oversee co-workers' grammar and spelling mistakes and blamed me for her gift of literacy. My daughter, Chantal, is probably the most beautiful and resilient person I know. I am most proud of my children and grateful to the Creator in that we were chosen to have them bestowed onto my husband and I. My adult children are the bright lights in my life. My grandchildren, Ariel, Alexandra, Dylahn, Emma-Leigh and Benjamin are my Northern Lights that shimmer and glow. They are young ones, precious beings who nurture and feed my soul with their spirit and joy. I drink from their happiness and silent beauty. I also must acknowledge the love and encouragement I received from my late mother, Angeline and my best bud, Mac. Forever I will be especially grateful to know Mac and to have her in my life. I have been truly blessed.

I must acknowledge many others who have been generous with their precious time. The wonderful friends such as the late Susie and Vernon Jones, Michael Cachagee, and Elders Doug Williams, and Shirley Williams have greatly assisted me during my learning journey, and I owe them a great debt of gratitude. I must also give a very special chi megweetch to the late Leonard Kicknosway, the late Patrick Isaac, the late Billy Blackbird, the late Louis Johnson, the late Buster DeLeary, Sylvia Deleary, Una Day, Joanne Day, Geraldine Robertson, Mary Gilbert, and Eric Isaac. I could not have completed my final narrative without their understanding, bravery and honesty.

In addition, I must sincerely thank my brothers, Joseph Buckell and the late William Buckell and my cousin the late Veronica Nicholson for their support and encouragement. I could not have completed my doctoral work without the assistance of the late Carol Sanders in her role as Band Manager of Michipicoten First Nation.

I would also like to thank my editor, Irene Bindi, and her colleagues at the ARP Books publishing company for their thoughtfulness and careful work on my manuscript. I appreciated Irene's insight and effective wordsmithing. A special acknowledgment goes to Dr. Kathy Absolon who wrote the foreword to this book. When I asked her if she would consider doing this, I was overjoyed that she had consented immediately. I must be mindful and sincerely thank Dr. Maggie Kovach whose work sparked my life force energy, and I also say chi megweetch to Dayna Rainville for her beautiful understanding in her artistry in her work for my book cover. I would also like to thank Madeline Whetung for her feedback. It was so much appreciated! This book is a dream come true that has been on my mind, an important obligation, a promise I made to survivors for over twenty-five years. It is certainly a commitment that I embraced and worked hard to fulfill. It is now complete.

GLOSSARY

Anishinaabemowin – Ojibway language
Anishinaabe-kwe – human being woman
Anishinaabe mino-bimaadiziwin – everybody getting along, harmonious
Anishinaabe mino-bimaadiziwin – the way of a good life
Anishinaabe mnidoo bemaasing bemaadiziwin – Anishinaabe life force energy
Anishinaabe-naakgonigewin – Natural Law
baawaamin – animal helper
bskaabi-miigwewin wiijkiiwendiwin – reciprocal relationships
doodem – clan
Epingishmok – where the sun sets in the west
gaa-bi-zhewebak gchi-zhaazhe gchi-piitendaagwaad – our past matters
gchi-mikinaak – the great turtle
gchi nookmis – Great Grandmother
Giizhigo-kwe – Skywoman
kanan – bones
kanan miinwaa nbagani-aasmaabkong – bones and bed on the rock
kendaaswin – knowledge
kookum – Great Grandmother (Northern Ojibway language)
maawndoobiigegin kendaaswin – gathering knowledge
miigweyan neyaab – giving back
miigwech/megweetch – thank you
miinwaa – and/again
mino-bimaadiziwin – the way of a good life

mnidoo bemaasing bemaadiziwin – life force energy
Nanaboozhoo – the trickster
nbagani-aasmaabkong – bed on the rock
Nimkii-Bineshiinh – the thunderbird
nokiiwin e-zhimaajiihkag – process
nookmis – Grandmother
nsastamowin – understanding
odeh – heart
Waabnoong – east
Waabnoong noodin – east wind
Wasakajec – the trickster (western) (*Wesakejig* in Anishinaabemowin)
weedjeewaugun (western Ojibway) or *wiijiiwaagan* – companion; he who goes with or she who walks with
wiijkiiwendiwin – relationship
wiikaa-giizis – the moon or late sun
zhaaganaash – white people (those that came in a sail boat)
zhichigan zhiitaang – project preparation
Ziiqwan – south wind
zongwaadiziwin – the strength of life (resilience)

LIST OF ABBREVIATIONS

AHF	Aboriginal Healing Foundation
CSAA	Children of Shingwauk Alumni Association
NAIA	North American Indian Assoiciation of Detroit
RCAP	Royal Commission on Aboriginal Peoples
RCMP	Royal Canadian Mounted Police
TRC	Truth and Reconciliation Commission
WDSS	Wallaceburg District Secondary School
WIFN	Walpole Island First Nation
WIRSSG	Walpole Island Residential Schools Survivors Group
YMCA	Young Mens Christian Association
YWCA	Young Womens Christian Association

FOREWORD

Dr. Kathy Absolon, MSW, PhD

I am honoured to offer the foreword to this book. Anishinaabe-kwe, Dr. Theresa Turmel has written a book of beauty, spirit and resilience. This is a much-needed book. It is a book to bring balance to the legacy of trauma Indigenous children and families experienced from the Indian residential schools in Canada. Theresa brings balance and shares the other side of the children's gifts and spirit.

Important works have been published to date revealing the harm and crimes against Indigenous peoples' humanity in the Indian Residential School projects in Canada. In the early 1900s, Dr. Peter Bryce wrote a report, The Bryce Report, that disclosed the travesty of medical and health conditions of Indigenous children in the schools. Later, in 1922, he published his findings in a book called *The Story of A National Crime: An Appeal for Justice to the Indians in Canada*. Further, in Canada national commissions such at the Royal Commission on Aboriginal Peoples (1996) and more recent Truth and Reconciliation Commission (2015) have unveiled the traumas, policies and acts of cultural genocide committed by the Federal government of Canada against Indigenous peoples. Gross atrocities, inhumanities and abuses that children experienced and endured at the residential schools are the roots of much pain and suffering. The emotional, spiritual, mental and physical traumas that have occurred at the residential schools are documented through courageous survivor and witness testimonies. Families of survivors needed to know what happened in order to understand their loved ones. Society needs to know to understand the socio-political oppression that Indigenous peoples and families have been marred with. Indigenous people also need to understand that we carry gifts of spirit, heart, mind and beauty. This book is a tribute to unveiling those gifts.

We are people that have inherited a legacy of trauma from the residential school projects. Theresa shows that we are so much more. We are also people that have inherited a legacy of resilience and resistance. We are a people who have survived. We are a people who come from thousands of years of people who lived with spirit. We come from people who know of spirit. We are descendants of people who understand a life energy rooted in spirit in all of creation. Our ancestors lived with this knowledge and lived in a manner that honoured this knowing. In this book, Dr. Turmel moves into a story of unveiling a spirit of life force energy and resilience within the survivors. These stories matter. They are stories of how the children endured and what within them sustained their life presence. How is it that children lived through such tumultuous circumstances and survived?

The healing medicine of life force energy is embedded in what the Anishinaabek call Anishinaabe Mino Bemaadiziwin (the good way of life). Gifts. In the Anishinaabek Creation story teachings, the elders affirm that every spirit who enters into this earth lodge carries with it gifts. All Anishinaabek children carry their gifts from infancy into adulthood and our hope is that their life is a manifestation of their gifts in creation. Indian residential schools and the cultural genocide of these inhumane projects against Indigenous peoples' identity existed to annihilate those beautiful spirited gifts that the Indigenous children carry. Some children survived, despite the inhumane conditions within the residential school projects and despite the attempts to resocialize and colonize their minds, spirits, hearts and bodies.

The focus on "mnindoo bemaasing bemaadiziwin" or life force energy is a unique contribution to Indigenous scholarship. This focus has been missing in the re-search on the stories and experiences of survivors of the Residential School system. Theresa, in this book, has done an exquisite job trying to capture something that is phenomenological, and spirit based. The stories are rich and full of resilience.

Not only does Dr. Turmel present beautiful stories of resilience, she makes another meaningful contribution to the field of Indigenous methodologies. Through her work she practices and models ways of engagement that demonstrate relational accountability. She illustrates traditional teachings and protocols. She models how knowledge gets revealed when the sacredness of process is honoured. Other ways of coming to know include acknowledging a genealogy of knowing that emerges from literature, journaling and by giving back. This work is wholistically approached and nicely articulated.

As an Indigenous re-searcher I am interested in how other Indigenous knowledge keepers articulate Indigenous ways of searching for knowledge. The articulations of the many ways in which we come to know is necessary for others seeking models and examples. Theresa offers such an example through the stories she has gathered and shared in this book. All stories matter and all stories contain knowledge. Knowledge emerges from relational accountability. What I mean by relational accountability is attending to the relationships within the stories and honouring the storyteller, story maker and the story itself. Because relationships were violently disrupted in the residential school projects of cultural genocide, relational accountability and relational healing has to be central to story gathering with survivors. Dr. Turmel builds on her relationships. She models a deep respect and integrity for the survivors and their life experiences. Indigenous research projects that focus on resiliency, restore and represent the strength and beauty of people.

The book is wholistically organized using the Medicine Wheel and ending each section with identifying "mnidoo bemaasing bemaadiziwin." Each section of the medicine wheel is pivotal to gaining a whole perspective of the resiliency and spirit of the survivors.

In the east, there is a focus on children and how they kept the fire of life alive within through acts of resistance. The south shares strong stories of youth at times of growth and change where they learned to be on guard. She lifts up how youth were revolutionary heroes in resourcefulness and life force energy. In the western direction, she brings attention to transitions, transformations and returning home to families and communities. The northern direction is a time of change where she moves into stories that tell of courageous journeys of recovery, reclaiming identity, transformation and restoration, reclamations, recovery, relearning and resilience.

This book is thorough, engaging and respectfully representative of survivor stories. I enjoyed all the inclusion of voice and accompanying commentaries. The beginning story by Shirley Williams is especially powerful and touching. I like the flow of the survivors' quotes on survival, the life path teachings, survivor accounts from the interviews, all followed by extractions of "mnindoo bemaasing bemaadiziwin." If anything, this book tells stories that are much needed and will leave readers with inspiring legacies of resiliency, life force, spirit and strength. Our people, and youth, need to hear these stories and see the legacies of resistance and resilience all survivors have gifted to us. We are strong because they were.

Miigwech Theresa for offering up this side of our peoples' beauty and resilience!

Accepting The Life Journey

In 1991 I experienced an important turning point in my life. First, I came to understand a dark part of Canadian history, namely the reality of Indian[1] residential schools which operated between 1830[2] and 1996. Because of the horrendous circumstances in which these schools operated, the children of these schools are now seen as survivors of this tragic time and there could be as many as 80,000[3] still alive. Second, as a student at Algoma University College, I was asked to volunteer and be the registrar at the second reunion of the Shingwauk Residential School[4] survivors. As the life experiences of the survivors of the residential school were revealed to me, I remember feeling shocked about what I heard, then angry about what had

1. The term "Indian" has its origin within the Indian Act of 1876. The term is used by the federal government to define those who are recognized as having Indian status under the Indian Act. Status Indian refers to individuals who meet the criteria for and are registered as an Indian in accordance with the Canadian Indian Act. For more information see http://laws-lois.justice.gc.ca/eng/ acts/I-5. Today, many consider the term to be derogatory, although it is still used by Indigenous people in certain contexts. Indian is used in this text only in reference to the residential schools, historical references to government agents and if used in a quote.
2. Truth and Reconciliation Commission of Canada, *Canada, Aboriginal Peoples, and Residential Schools: They Came for the Children* (2012), 5.
3. "The TRC estimates that 80,000 survivors of residential schools live in all regions of Canada today..." Retrieved from http://www.trc.ca/websites/trcinstitution/File?pdfs/Backgrounder_E.pdf.
4. This residential school was located in northern Ontario.

happened to my ancestors. For me, it brought forward an understanding, a peaked sensitivity toward residential school survivors and their needs. It also brought forth a commitment to see that the survivors, Shingwauk Alumni, and their families would always be treated with respect. I didn't know then that I would develop a very special relationship with the survivors of the Shingwauk Indian Residential School. This work, also called the 'project' is my dissertation which is the truth telling of a group of thirteen survivors from Walpole Island First Nation[5] who tell their life experiences in order to understand their resiliency.

I am an **Anishinaabe-kwe**[6] (woman) who has come through the waters of Angeline who came through the waters of Mary. My mother's territory is Michipicoten, which is situated on the shores of Lake Superior twenty minutes south of Wawa, Ontario. Growing up in the city of Toronto, I knew little of life on a First Nations community or of my own Anishinaabe identity including my original language **Anishinaabemowin**. I was different, not **zhaaganaash** or white, as the children at my elementary school repeatedly pointed out. Around age 30, I was enveloped with a hunger to know about my culture and it was during my undergraduate years at Algoma University that I discovered a beautiful, different worldview. I remember asking why Anishinaabe danced. I did not receive an answer, leaving me to find out for myself. When attending my first powwow, I did not know the

---

5   I use "First Nation" when referring to a relatively small group of Indigenous people residing in a single locality who also may be part of a larger Indigenous nation or people. This term gained popularity in the late 20th Century in Canada and while it has no legal definition it generally replaced the word "Indian" although it did not include Inuit or Métis.

6   Anishinaabe-kwe means human being woman. Elder Shirley Williams (Migizi ow Kwe, Eagle Woman), a member of the Bird Clan of the Ojibway and Odawa First Nations of Canada who was born and raised at Wikwemikong, Manitoulin Island, has acted as the translator for this book. The Anishnaabemowin dialect reflects her home territory. The words are bold and italicized however, the word Anishinaabe is not.

meaning of "Grand Entry" but the beauty was intriguing. It was not until after my first sweat lodge ceremony that I felt enormous pride for what was to become a huge part of my life and eventual maturation process. The powerful transformation instilled in me a positive internal core, a keen sense of identity and pride in finding out about the history of our people, and soon I was debating university students and professors alike, challenging their words and viewpoints in classes concerning Indigenous[7] issues. Upon graduation in 1992, I felt transformed, happy in my Anishinaabe identity, confident in my being, and ready to take on the world!

For the past twenty plus years I had been in an ongoing relationship with the Shingwauk residential school survivors. From 1991 to 1998, I worked as a volunteer in different capacities. One of the responsibilities was as a helper and/or coordinator of the Shingwauk Reunions of 1991, 1996, 2000, and 2002. In 1999, I was hired as the Office Administrator/Healing Coordinator of the Children of

---

7   The term "Indigenous" is used when referring to original peoples inhabiting North America including the Anishinaabe. The word Indigenous also includes terms such as Aboriginal, Indian, Inuit, and Métis which are only used within quotes. However, the focus of this work is on First Nations people who attended residential schools, although the Inuit and some Métis people also attended residential schools. I refer to Anishinaabe specifically in discussing our teachings, the survivors who were interviewed, and our literature. According to Dr. Erica-Irene Daes, chair-rapporteur of the United Nations Working Group on Indigenous Populations, there is no one precise definition of Indigenous peoples. She established four relevant factors that inform the concept. They are:

(a) Priority in time, with respect to the occupation and use of a specific territory; (b) The voluntary perpetuation of cultural distinctiveness, which may include the aspects of language, social organizations, religion and spiritual values, modes of production, laws and institutions; (c) Self-identification, as well as recognition by other groups, or by State authorities, as a distinct collectivity; and (d) An experience of subjugation, marginalization, dispossession, exclusion or discrimination, whether or not these conditions persist. Marie Battiste and James Youngblood Henderson, *Protecting Indigenous Knowledge and Heritage: A Global Challenge* (Saskatoon: Purich Publishing Ltd, 2000), 64.

Shingwauk Alumni Association (CSAA). The office was located at Algoma University in Sault Ste. Marie, the very site of the old Shingwauk Indian Residential School which closed in 1970.

For the next four years, my job consisted of maintaining both the office and member database which originally had 365 names. By 2003, the number had grown to over 1,300. The duties within the scope of my position included recording meetings, making travel arrangements for the Alumni Council, giving tours of the building and grounds, welcoming visitors, survivors and their families to the site, locating archival material and answering questions from and about the former students.

By 2003, nearing the end of available funding for the CSAA, I was asked by survivors to listen and tell their story. I was first invited to participate in a community-based partnership with the Walpole Island Residential Schools Survivors Group (WIRSSG), an affiliate of the parent group, CSAA. The WIRSSG formed as an official group in 2000 after a residential school survivor conference.

Second, this work builds on the experiences and education of the legacy of Canadian residential schools. The WIRSSG proposed this collaboration for a number of reasons. They believe everyone needs to learn the history of Canada from a survivor's perspective. Until recently, the current Ontario curriculum had not acknowledged and/or fully explained the Indian Act or the treaty relationship between Canada and the First Nations, including the associated treaty obligations and the fiduciary responsibilities to Indigenous peoples. Therefore, Canadians grow up not fully understanding the relationships between Canada and the Indigenous peoples or Indigenous peoples' relationship to the land.

Third, the survivors voiced to me that they believe people need to be made aware of what happened in the Indian residential schools. Canadians need to know that the children were taken from their homes and lifestyles. Many children, who were as young as three years of age were traumatized by this experience. In many instances their caretakers and educators, the very people who were supposed to be nurturing them, actually physically and sexually abused them.[8] They were forbidden to speak their original First Nation language and forced to learn English, which for them was a foreign language. They were told that their culture and traditional ceremonies were taboo, devil's work.[9]

Fourth, it was very important to the former residential school students that they were able to tell their stories as this is an essential part of the healing process for them and their families. In order to reclaim their identity that was left unbalanced by the residential school experience, they needed to heal holistically with a healthy coming together of the mind, body, heart and spirit. They must be allowed to "unfold the lessons of colonization"[10] and live with a centred soul.[11]

Fifth, they wanted to ensure that such an episode never happens again. This means that we should all learn from past mistakes and respect Indigenous traditions and culture and practices, which foster a respect for diversity. For example, some non-Indigenous people are unfamiliar with the Anishinaabe smudging ceremony and are afraid of it. Some non-Indigenous people incorrectly assume Indigenous people smoke marijuana because of the smudging—the smell of the sacred medicines burning. Finally, the most important reason was that with the open acknowledgement of these experiences, survivors can move forward, and resolve their experiences. The resolution could include the decision to heal through whichever

---

8 Roland Chrisjohn, Sherri Young, and Michael Maraun, 2006. *The Circle Game: Shadows and Substance in the Indian Residential School Experience in Canada*. Penticton: Theytus Books Ltd., 2006), 51-52, 93.
9 Assembly of First Nations, *Breaking the Silence: An Interpretive Study of Residential School Impact and Healing as Illustrated by the Stories of First Nations Individuals* (Ottawa, Ontario: First Nations Health Commission, 1994), 26.
10 Marie Battiste, ed., *Reclaiming Indigenous Voice and Vision* (Vancouver: UBC Press, 2000), xvi.
11 Susie Jones, personal communication, November 5, 2008.

non-traditional practices of faith-based or traditional Indigenous practices chosen.

In working with the Shingwauk Residential School survivors for twenty plus years, I have been struck by their strength. They are a hardy group of focused individuals that work together as a very goal oriented tight-knit group. Many individuals who have endured a difficult childhood may be bitter and angry. This is not the case with the former residential school students I encountered. They are active members in their First Nations, taking on leadership roles. I have seen them come together for meetings and reunions with one purpose: to heal and take care of each other and their communities. These observations were central to the development of this work.

The survivors at Walpole Island have asked me to be their partner because of my relationship and history with the CSAA. They know I have an appreciation for their history, and their cultural and spiritual essence. This relationship which began with the CSAA and extended to its sibling, the Walpole Island Survivors Group, is based on trust, and continues today. For example, I was asked by the CSAA to act as a support person on Parliament Hill in Ottawa, Ontario during the June 11, 2008 apology by the Government of Canada,[12] as well as in May, 2015 when the Truth and Reconcilation Commission completed their wrap-up in Ottawa, Ontario. This was both an honour and an enormous responsibility that I had undertaken with humility and strength. Although, it was difficult to remain strong while others around me were crying during the apology.

Although I am **Anishinaabe-kwe** and have worked closely with residential school survivors, I am not a survivor of the residential school experience nor a member of Walpole Island First Nation. As

---

12   The apology to Aboriginal peoples for the Indian Residential School system across Canada was made by Prime Minister Stephen Harper on behalf of the government of Canada and said, "…Today, we recognize that this policy of assimilation was wrong, has caused great harm, and has no place in our country…" Retrieved from http://www.pm.gc.ca/eng/media.asp?id=2149.

Anishinaabe-kwe, I chose to be guided by the Seven Grandfathers Teachings as I did this work. These teachings are discussed further in the next section and concern working and living with wisdom, love, respect, bravery, honesty, humility, and truth. Our traditions also hold that I cannot speak for another person, so in the writing of this book, the quotes are exactly what the survivors said without paraphrasing, and the interpretation is mine.

Recall that the purpose of this work was to listen to 13 Indian residential school survivors from Walpole Island First Nation tell their life experiences in order to understand their resiliency. I used an Anishinaabe process which was experiential and personal, and worked closely with the WIRSSG.

As you the reader accepts this journey, we embark on learning about Anishinaabe Thought, Anishinaabe ways of being or what I like to call the bones and the bedrock or **kanan miinwaa nbagani-assmaabkong** for this work. I begin with The Creation Story[13] because for me that is the foundation of Anishinaabe Knowledge. The Original Instructions are part of the Creation Story that tells the role and responsibility of Anishinaabe people in the context of our role as caretakers of Mother Earth. This also includes a discussion about the gifts (i.e. Seven Grandfather Teachings) from our ancestors, and an introduction to the Anishinaabe Medicine Wheel. The intent is to offer a deeper penetration into the nature of how we view our relationship and responsibilities to all Creation.

The Anishinaabe ways of being are followed by our approach for gathering and interpreting knowledge. This gathering of knowledge represents my life long learning of Traditional Teachings from all the Elders, Traditional teachers, and medicine people I have come to know. I speak to the sacredness of relationship and how I developed

---

13 For this work capitalization of these terms are used for the particular purpose of identifying Anishinaabe thought and concepts. This includes the Original Instructions, the Creation Story, Creation, Medicine Wheel, Sky Woman, Water Beings, Natural Law, and Traditional Teachings.

a relationship with a group of residential school survivors and the respectful process I followed to complete this journey.

Our Past Matters follows and offers you a brief overview of the policies and legislation of the Canadian Indian Residential School system. This is necessary to understand and capture the link between the past and the present. This section outlines the historical background of the development of the Shingwauk Indian Residential School including Chief Shingwauk's vision and the formation of the CSAA, and I introduce the WIRSSG as the younger sibling of the CSAA and the backbone of this work. Since the WIRSSG grew out of the CSAA, I would be remiss in not including CSAA in this journey. For Anishinaabe, this would be like forgetting half your family. I also acknowledge the underlying relationship and spirit that resides there.

Understanding Life Force Energy helps readers to learn the concept of resiliency, and its relevance to Anishinaabe peoples. In order for me to understand resiliency, I looked at the existing literature on resiliency in Canada and the United States. I also looked at the views of Indigenous residential school survivors in print and video in North America. Particularly important were the publications of the Royal Commission on Aboriginal[14] Peoples (RCAP)[15] and the

---

14 The word "Aboriginal" in Canada dates to section 35(2) of the Constituion Act, 1982 and was used to include First Nations, Inuit and Métis. The Commission used "the term Aboriginal people to refer to the Indigenous inhabitants of Canada when we want to refer in a general manner to Inuit and to First Nations and Métis people, without regard to their separate origins and identities" Royal Commission on Aboriginal Peoples, *Report of the Royal Commission on Aboriginal Peoples Volume 1: Looking Forward, Looking Back* (Ottawa: Canada Communication Group, 1996a),iii. Within this work, this term is only used when found within organization titles, commission reports and in quotes.
15 The Report can be accessed at https://www.bac-lac.gc.ca/eng/discover/aboriginal-heritage/royal-commission-aboriginal-peoples/Pages/final-report.aspx.

Aboriginal Healing Foundation (AHF).[16] Finally, and most importantly, the interviews with WIRSSG residential school survivors form the heart of the discussion.

With this understanding, the next four sections use the Anishinaabe Medicine Wheel for telling the stories of the survivors. The four quadrants are used to identify the stages of life, which are similar to the cycles of nature. Each quadrant offers a perspective of Anishinaabe *mino-bimaadiziwin* (the way of a good life), for the particular stage of life, followed by the actual experiences of the survivors and concludes with the nutrients of their life force energy or ***mnidoo bemaasing bemaadiziwin***. Each quadrant begins with a story, a gift from the survivors. The Taken begins with their arrival at residential school. The Knowing continues with the students' journey into youth and their acts of resistance in order to survive. The Transition examines their transition from residential school to adulthood. The Transformation describes their lives and their activities in present day and documents their contributions to community as a time of reclaiming and victorizing their spirit.

Our journey comes full circle, with The Path of Life Continues which takes us back to the bones and the bedrock or ***kanan miinwaa nbagani-aasmaabkong***, including how the former residential school students nurtured their life force energy or ***mnidoo bemaasing bemaadiziwin*** and continued on their life path. The section concludes with the learnings on this journey and my interpretation of

---

16 The federal government of Canada funded, as part of its Gathering Strength–Canada's Aboriginal Action Plan, this Aboriginal-managed, national organization for eleven years (March 31, 1998-March 31, 2009) "to encourage and support, through research and funding contributions, community-based Aboriginal directed healing initiatives which address the legacy of physical and sexual abuse suffered in Canada's Indian Residential School System, including inter-generational impacts" (retrieved from http://www.ahf.ca/faqs). See http://www.ahf.ca/.

coming to know as an **Anishinaabe-kwe**. By accepting this journey, we will now travel the Anishinaabe road. Our first experience is to learn something about Anishinaabe thought and worldview.

CHAPTER 1

Anishinaabe Thought:
The Bones and the Bedrock "*Kanan miinwaa nbagani-aasmaabkong*"

> Worldview is important because it is the filter system behind the beliefs, behaviour, and actions of people. It is the tacit infrastructure people use for their beliefs, behaviour, and relationships. Two persons with differing worldviews can look at or experience the same event and come away with very different interpretations.
>
> —LEROY LITTLE BEAR[1]

My endeavour in this first section is to invite you to take this learning journey with me. In order to do this I want to explain how I understand Anishinaabe philosophy and worldview. Embedded within this worldview is the Anishinaabe paradigm or ontology and epistemology that life and spirit is found in everything on Mother Earth. Balance and good health (emotionally, spiritually, physically and mentally) can be achieved holistically within self. The Anishinaabe paradigm is

---

1 Leroy Little Bear, "Aboriginal Paradigms: Implications for Relationships to Land and Treaty Making," *Advancing Aboriginal Claims*, ed. Kerry Wilkins (Saskatoon: Purich Publishing Ltd., 2004), 26.

like the sacred tree.² It is rooted in relationships, family, the language, traditions, ceremonies, spirituality, storytelling (morals), healing work and counselling (guidance) which act as nutrients that feed and nurture our Anishinaabe life force energy or *mnidoo bemaasing bemaadiziwin*. Anishinaabe life force energy or *mnidoo bemaasing bemaadiziwin* is difficult to understand if you have never experienced the feeling. Elder Herb Nabigon describes it as an inner " fire [which] is seen as a spark that lives in all human beings."³ He further explains that this fire is situated within the "Hub" which he refers to as the dynamics of human behaviour and offers an excellent understanding of life force energy as an inner fire. He asks us to "imagine three circles, one inside the other. The outer circle represents the negative side of life. The middle circle represents the positive side, and the centre circle represents one's inner fire."⁴

I have titled this chapter "Anishinaabe Thought: The Bones and the Bedrock" or **kanan miinwaa nbagani-aasmaabkong** because an Anishinaabe worldview encompasses the bones and the bedrock or **kanan miinwaa nbagani-aasmaabkong** which means much more than skeletons and concrete. Bones, to me, conjures up images and gifts of knowledge of the ancestors and from the ancestors. The bedrock for Anishinaabe and perhaps for other Indigenous peoples is relationship. This cement is the foundation on which we carry on through the bones and blood memory of our ancestors.

---

2   The Creator planted a Sacred Tree where the people of the earth would gather under and "... find healing, power, wisdom and security." Phil Lane Jr., Judie Bopp, Michael Bopp, Lee Brown, and Elders, *The Sacred Tree* (Lethbridge, AB: Four Worlds International Institute, 2004), 7.
3   Herb Nabigon, *The Hollow Tree: Fighting Addiction With Traditional Native Healing* (Montreal: McGill-Queen's University Press, 2006), 116.
4   Ibid., 46.

The Bones "*Kanan*"

The bones or ***kanan*** are gifts of knowledge of the ancestors and from the ancestors. This includes all Indigenous ancestors and not solely Anishinaabe, and acknowledges the wisdom and the knowledge of the ones whose bones we walk on every day. They are our strength and we have come to rely on what they have learned. "Knowledge is shared with all of creation,"[5] and the bones and bedrock or ***kanan miinwaa nbagani-aasmaabkong*** are the firm foundation created by our ancestors as our survival tools.[6] As Anishinaabe people, we honour and acknowledge the gift of knowing, re-discovering and uncovering the information from the ones who have gone before us. The information they have placed before us is meant to nurture growth and goodness and seeks to connect "what is old to what is new."[7] I have heard that at one time every person on Mother Earth was Indigenous, but for many this mindset has changed with Western ways and its systems of progress and development. Expressed through the bones are three foundational teachings; the Creation Story, Original Instructions and the Seven Grandfather Teachings. All are connected and offer guidance and remind us of our responsibilities for living each day. A brief discussion of each follows.

An Anishinaabe Creation Story

My experience has been that before we proceed, it is important to know who we are and how we are made. I have learned that we come from the spirit world with a pre-destined life, in that our life path is already laid out before us. We are born into clans

---

5   Shawn Wilson, *Research Is Ceremony: Indigenous Research Methods* (Halifax: Fernwood Publishing, 2008), 74.
6   Manu Aluli Meyer, "Acultural Assumptions of Empiricism: A Native Hawaiian Critique," *Canadian Journal of Native Education* 25, no.2 (2001): 188-200.
7   Ibid.

whereby traditional knowledge is transmitted to us while in the womb. Our journey from the spirit world and in becoming an earth being means we become part of a circle. We become part of something bigger—Creation. As babies we become part of a family, a circle of beings that teach us and love us. Along our life path we come with tools or gifts that we are born with and there are several tools we have on the trail. Through the oral tradition of storytelling we come to learn the Original Instructions and the Seven Grandfather Teachings and we are reminded by the Creation Story that we are situated within a context and we are the last ones to be created on Mother Earth.

The Original Instructions and the Grandfather Teachings convey to us the ethics and protocols for our behaviour for living within the cosmos. They are sacred teachings that tell us that the animals are our brothers and that the moon is our grandmother and the sun is our grandfather and we are all related. If we are not respectful of this relationship, then the animals will not give themselves up to us for food. I have learned that everything on Mother Earth has a spirit, and in this knowledge, we must be respectful of our world. As an *Anishinaabe-kwe*, I always start with our Creation Story and worldview. I was given the following Creation Story teaching by an Anishinaabe Elder:[8]

Aaniin, my name is *Kitiga Migizi*, Pike *doodem*, a member of the Mississaugas of Curve Lake First Nation, my English name is Doug Williams.

> A long time ago, way back in time, it was total darkness here. There was nothing but the Creator had a dream and,

---

[8] An Elder is a specific type of person who holds certain qualities and maintains a certain lifestyle and knowledge base: Jonathan Ellerby, *Working with Indigenous Elders: An Introductory Handbook for Institution-Based and Health-Care Professionals Based on the Teachings of Winnipeg-Area Indigenous Elders and Cultural Teachers* (Winnipeg: Aboriginal Issues Press, 2005), 7.

in that dream, Creator saw the world as we know it today. The Creator saw the mountains, saw the plains, saw trees, saw rocks, saw desert, saw the great rivers, saw animals, saw birds flying and he saw humans. That dream kind of stuck with Creator. Just let me say that, if I say Creator it's him, it's because you're translating into English and in *Anishinaabemowin* you don't have personal pronouns like that. Just to fit it into English, we'll say him but Creator had no sex, could be woman, could be it, that's important to remember. That's a big distinction in *Anishinaabemowin*. So anyways because it was a Creator's dream and then it became a wish of the Creator, therefore because it was the Creator, it had to be. It had to come about.

So anyway, sure enough, the earth happened and everything was created instantly and everything was beautiful. This went on for a long time, everybody was getting along, what we call translated harmonious—*Anishinaabe-kwe mino-bimaaziwin*, lived in an ideal environment. Everybody was kind and lived in peace with each other including the animals. So that went on until one day things started to go bad, things did not work out and then everything died off is the one story and nobody knows why that happened. It could be that life is actually not that easy to keep. The Creator wanted this to be so good but when things started to happen even with the Creator's creation, things went wrong so everything kind of died off, a few things were safe. Apparently, the elements were saved. There was still the sun. There are still great waters and still the land but everything living had died off and this bothered Creator. Creator was upset.

So, the spirits that lived up in the sky went to Creator and said, "Can we help you? We know you feel bad because the place you created has gotten into trouble." The Creator said, "yes, why don't you go down there and see if you can fix things?" So this spirit is called **Giizhigo-kwe** means Sky Woman. **Giizhigo-kwe** decided to come to Earth and had a spirit partner. We're not sure exactly who that partner was because she asked Creator for a partner so that they could create humans, and also other animals but in this particular instance, she wanted to create humans. So, she came. She came from the sky and always remember that the Haudensaunee also have this story in some form. And remember that it was us who were the peacemakers and I'll tell about why we're peacemakers later on in the story and it was us who travelled all through northeastern North America delivering peace and we would have told that story to the Haudensaunee.

So anyway, **Giizhigo-kwe** came and tried to have humans, in fact had a form of a human and they soon died off. She had two kids apparently and they soon died off again. Something was just not working right so the Creator's dream just wasn't gellying. **Giizhigo-kwe** went back to the spirit world and said to Creator, "I really can't—this didn't work out." Another thing that happened at this point was a great flood and there were all other things happening physically on Earth. The Creator said to **Giizhigo-kwe**, "Well, you can't give up! You have to try. You have to keep trying and make this dream a reality." This is the theory of creation and re-creation that we talk about so **Giizhigo-kwe** came back again and one of the animals that survived from the first creation was the turtle cause it could live in this water. So, when the flood happened, only the fishes, and the water animals survived, the ones that could swim like the beaver, the turtle, all the fishes survived. So, the land was flooded when **Giizhigo-kwe** came down again and apparently **Giizhigo-kwe** went around and couldn't settle on anywhere because **Giizhigo-kwe** couldn't swim. Water was a strange element to her because she's from the sky.

The turtle comes up and said, "You want a place to land —land on my back." The turtle is called **Gchi-mikinaak**, in other words **gchi**-mackinac like the place in the Northern Michigan is called Michilimackinac that's a corruption of "**Gchi-mikinaak**," the great turtle. The Haudenosaunee had called this great place here Turtle Island[9] but we call it the Great Turtle. Now when the turtle came up, it said to **Giizhigo-kwe**, "Land on my back and you can stay here— so do what you have to do." **Giizhigo-kwe** noticed all the designs on the turtle's back and she thought it was beautiful and actually from there came the thirteen moons that are depicted on the turtle's back and the other twenty-eight days are depicted of the month around the rim. So **Giizhigo-kwe** ran her finger around the rim and said, "This is some meaning—you must be carrying something." The turtle said, "yes, I also want to help you create the earth again as it was before because I remember as a turtle going way back how it was beautiful here at one time but we have to get some earth."

So, she's sitting there on the turtle's back and the water beings including all the water animals were around there watching **Giizhigo-kwe** because they are curious. So, it was the loon, the bird because the bird could swim and float and could survive the great flood, who said to **Giizhigo-kwe**, "Well I can dive. I'll dive to the bottom and I'll try to get some earth and I'll bring that up to you because the turtle said if you put that on my back and because of the teachings on my back, the earth will grow and that will be called the great Turtle Island." The loon went down. It took a long time. Finally, the loon came up, but it was drowned.

---

9   Through the telling of creation stories Turtle Island is known to many Indigenous peoples as the land created on the back of a turtle. Settlers would later create boundaries and refer to it as North America.

Floated, and it got drowned because it tried so hard to get down to land, the earth, so it drowned. The next one who came was the otter and the otter said, "I think I can do better than the loon" and he goes down. The same thing happened to the otter, couldn't do it, floated up dead and nothing.

So, the next to step up was the beaver, he said, "I can go further than the loon and the otter. I think I can get you some earth." So, the beaver went down. The same thing happened with the beaver eventually after a long time, it floated up despite the Creator giving the beaver a special trait in that the beaver could keep oxygen in its tail and that's why the beaver has a big tail. But again nothing, the beaver had passed, floated up in the water. So **Giizhigo-kwe** was very disappointed because she needed this earth to be able to again create this vision of Creator. So the muskrat comes along and they told the muskrat the story of what they were trying to do. **Giizhigo-kwe** and the turtle said, "No one has been able to give us earth, they have all died trying to do it." So the muskrat says, "I can go further than them. I'm really good at this. I can also keep oxygen in my tail." So the little muskrat dove, he was gone for a long time. Gone longer than any of the other animals and they waited—it seemed like days. Finally, the muskrat came to the surface but the muskrat had drowned but clutched in its little paws was some earth so they took that earth and put it on the turtle's back, as it was prophesied, and sure enough it started to grow, and with that little bit of earth, it started to become big—become an island—it became a big land with all of the characteristics of what was in the original creation. It began to have mountains, and streams and lakes and so on as we know it. Anishinaabe country was created with the Great Lakes. They're all created. There were clouds, there was rain, there was wind, all again those beautiful animals that lived that couldn't swim for long periods of time—they were created. The deer, the moose, the elk, caribou, bears—all kinds of beautiful animals as we know them were all created.

So **Giizhigo-kwe** said, "I'm going to go back and think about creating humans" because at this point, human wasn't created—just all the animals, all the trees had come back, all the rocks as we know them had reappeared on the turtle's back and she went back to the sky. In fact she went back and became the moon, at least we know her as the moon and some people, instead of calling the moon **wiikaa-giizis** which is late sun, we call her **kokum** or **nookmis** or **gchi nookmis**, great grandmother but today, when she said, "I'm going to give the power of giving birth to humans once they are created, because I know they are going to be created" but what happened was she said to the Creator, "I think you should ask another spirit to do something about creating humans." So again, out of nothing, Creator asked **Epingishmok**. Some people say **Epingomook**. **Epingishmok** means where the sun sets in the west, "Can you see what you can do?"

Epingishmok picked a partner and this partner apparently—this is actually a debate with Anishinaabe, the older Anishinaabe, did he **Epingishmok**, in male form, pick a woman from earth and how did that woman survive the great flood? We really don't know or was it a spirit? Some people said they tried also, a couple of times because two spirits were trying to make an earth being. The first time, one of the stories says that the first time **Epingishmok** and this woman tried to have kids. Again, they had two kids, but they fought each other and literally got rid of each other, because the essence of what we know today of man and woman was not there. It just wasn't clicking. So, they tried again. The second time, the woman, it's a big debate that he picked another woman. The woman we know is called Winona or Winonan. So *Epingishmok* and Winona tried again to have kids and they had a boy and a girl as we know them today. Now, the boy and the girl had subsequent kids, but it is said—that is not incest because what was created by the spirits is an essence of male and the essence of female. Hence earth humans were created![10]

The Creation Story tells me about my place in the world and teaches the responsibility that I have been given as a human being. As humans we learn from nature and the Creation Story teaches that we are connected to the land and that there is a specific order to Creation. Humans were the last to be created. In addition to knowing my place as part of Creation, the Creation Story reminds us that Sky Woman and the Water Beings worked together as a collective to bring about the Creator's vision. In embracing the vision, the Water Beings sacrificed themselves because of their caring obligation to the well-being of future humans. Highlighted for me is the determination showed by our brothers, the Water Beings.

At one time our hearts were so pure that we could talk with the animals and think of them as our brothers and sisters. The animals and plants gave themselves up for maintaining the well-being of the people. We must "express your gratitude to what sustains us"[11] Our service, duty and responsibility are to care for them and to care for ourselves. This responsibility is manifested in our relationship to Mother Earth and to all Creation. "We need to help our young people maintain this relationship and these teachings, because that connection is the umbilical bond to all of Creation."[12]

10 Personal communication November 30, 2011.
11 Dan Longboat, lecture at Trent University, October 1, 2008.
12 Leanne Betasamosake Simpson, *Dancing On Our Turtle's Back* (Winnipeg: Arbeiter Ring Publishing Ltd., 2011), 37.

The Original Instructions

The Original Instructions[13] remind me of being responsible—they are ingrained in me and may resonate with other Indigenous peoples; they teach that we are the responsible stewards of Mother Earth. "The relationship to all things in creation is understood to be one of kinship. The human relationship to mother earth is in all respects the same relationship to one's own natural mother."[14] As Lewis Cardinal says:

> Indigenous peoples with their traditions and customs are shaped by the environment, by the land. They have a spiritual, emotional, and physical relationship to that land. It speaks to them; it gives them their responsibility for stewardship; and it sets out a relationship.[15]

Eva Marie Garroutte, an American Indian member of the Cherokee Nation and an Associate Professor at Boston College adds that:

> These *"Original Instructions"* (sometimes called "First Instructions," or a similar variant) usually concern coming into relationship with other beings—human and nonhuman—in the natural world in particular ways... The Original Instructions by which many Native people still live have never been revoked, as my own elders frequently remind me.

---

13   The Original Instructions "... is based on standards of respect and sustainability... [that] outline that our primary responsibility is not for the survival of the people currently alive but for continuation of all life so that the future generations will be adequately provided with all they need to survive. Leanne Betasamosake Simpson, *Lighting the Eighth Fire: The Liberation, Resurgence, and Protection of Indigenous Nations* (Winnipeg: Arbeiter Ring Publishing Ltd., 2008), 29.
14   Robert Antone, Dianne Miller, and Brian Myers, *The Power Within People: A Community Organizing Perspective* (Brantford: Hurryprint, 1986), 22.
15   Lewis Cardinal, "What is an Indigenous perspective?" *The Canadian Journal of Native Education* 25, vol. 2, 1 (2001): 80-183.

A definition of identity that acknowledges this spiritual heritage will recall each tribal community to its Original Instructions—to its specific teachings about the nature of the world and how its members are to live in it... But Indian people who remember themselves within the framework of their Original Instructions will be looking for a definition of identity that allows them to determine who they will invite to join them in their sacred work. Who will properly be part of their daily lives, their communities, as they go about the fulfillment of their Original Instructions?[16]

I accept and acknowledge that the Creator has bestowed this stewardship responsibility upon us and that we must nurture Mother Earth and feed her as she does us. This is the nature of our reciprocal relationship.

Seven Grandfather Teachings

The Seven Grandfather Teachings are our values and morals. According to Edward Benton-Banai, a special baby was chosen as a messenger by the spirit beings, the Seven Grandfathers, to receive sacred teachings to teach us about how to live in harmony with Creation. The baby, now growing older into a boy, returned to Earth and shared the Seven Grandfather Teachings[17] with the people.

He told them that the nee-zho-day' (twin) of physical existence was spiritual existence. In order for the people to be completely healthy they must seek to develop themselves spiritually and find a balance between the physical and the spiritual worlds.[18]

16 Eva Marie Garroutte, *Real Indians: Identity and the survival of Native America* (Berkeley: University of California Press, 2003), 115-116. Author's emphasis.
17 See Edward Benton-Banai's *The Mishomis Book: The Voice of the Ojibway* (Minneapolis, MN: University of Minnesota Press, 1988), 64.
18 Ibid., 66.

Those seven teachings, expressed succinctly by Benton-Banai are:

1. To cherish knowledge is to know **WISDOM**.
2. To know **LOVE** is to know peace.
3. To honor all of the Creation is to have **RESPECT**.
4. **BRAVERY** is to face the foe with integrity.
5. **HONESTY** in facing a situation is to be brave.
6. **HUMILITY** is to know yourself as a sacred part of the Creation.
7. **TRUTH** is to know all of these things.[19]

These teachings are the fundamental principles for living *mino-bimaadiziwin* (A Good Life). Children learn these teachings through storytelling by the Elders and extended family. They learn the rules of behaviour without judgment or blame. Many Elders have said that children are our future and will lead the next generations. They are to be revered and always included in all activities, loved and guided to accept their responsibility. We believe that everything is for the children.

Next, I discuss these relationships and introduce a visual teaching tool, an Anishinaabe Medicine Wheel. I use the Medicine Wheel as a framework in discussing what I learned from the survivors. This circle sparked me and it ignited the sacred fire, or *mnidoo bemaasing bemaadiziwin*, within me.

The Bedrock "Nbagani-aasmaabkong"

As previously mentioned, the bedrock for Anishinaabe is relationship. From our teachings we learn everything is interconnected and our Anishinaabe life force energy or *mnidoo bemaasing bemaadiziwin* connects within the constant flux. As Leroy Little Bear says:

> Constant flux results in a 'spider web' network of relations, out of which arises a very important part of Aboriginal

---

19 Ibid., 64.

philosophy: interrelationships. Because of the constant motion and flux, everything mixes, combines, and recombines with everything else. The flux gives rise to the belief that all creation is made of energy waves. If all is animate, then all must be somewhat like humans: awareness with energy forces that we call spirit. If all have spirit, then all of creation – including animals, rocks, the earth, the sun, the moon, and so forth – are 'all my relations.' Another important outcome of the notion of constant flux is the idea of transformation. Again, the flux results in constant mixing, combining, and recombining of energy waves resulting in new combinations.[20]

The bedrock or **nbagani-aasmaabkong** is the relationship that enables information to be transmitted both orally and spiritually from generation to generation. As an *Anishinaabe-kwe*, I am now aware of my cultural identity and continue to learn more during my adult life. I am my mother. I am my grandmother. I am the face of my ancestors. Being Anishinaabe is steeped in my heritage, thrives and rests in my spirituality and springs from the land. Being **Anishinaabe-kwe** is organic, my lived adult experience is deeply rooted in my being—the essence of who I am which cannot be externally dictated with labels such as "Canadian Indian." Shannon Thunderbird, a Coast Tsimshian First Nations songwriter, artist and author, elaborates:

> First Nations Ancestors were often accused of having a rather cavalier attitude toward death. Nothing could be further from the truth. Native ceremonies allowed for a time of keening for the dead, but the prophetic words of the great Nimii-puu (Nez Percé) Leader, Chief Joseph resonates

---

20 Leroy Little Bear, "Aboriginal Paradigms: Implications for Relationships to Land and Treaty Making," 29-30.

through most tribes. He remarked that his Ancestors were not dead but merely 'living in another world.' In this way they would always be kept alive in present day realities. Moreover, the Ancestors are always the first ones called to a ceremony.

Native people simply accepted that the essence of a person would remain an integral part of everyday life even though the physical body had been returned to the Earth Mother. Tribal survival also did not allow for extensive grieving because it was a harsh environment and life had to plough on. Therefore, it was a comfort to those who were grieving that their loved-one(s) really never left them.

Ancestors are the first family members we call to ceremony, and they always come. They love a good get together! In most traditional ceremonies to this day, the Ancestors are usually at the top of the list to be called to the dance. It was simply unheard of to conduct a ceremony without the presence of the entire family, both Seen and Unseen.[21]

As bedrock is relationship and those relationships are interconnected, a visual and narrative description follows using the Medicine Wheel.

The Medicine Wheel

In 1990, I recall a time during my undergraduate years when a professor drew a circle on the blackboard with white chalk. He asked a student to draw another circle on the blackboard. The student drew another circle beside the first circle. The professor then asked me to draw a circle.

21 Retrieved from http://www.shannonthunderbird.com/symbols_and_meanings.htm.

I went up to the blackboard and drew a circle within the first circle; at the time I didn't know why. Perhaps it was cellular memory or intuition. I will never forget the stirrings felt inside me when first viewing this circle on the blackboard. The circle was a simple circle; a white line on a black setting but it had enormous power! I felt so happy to see this circle. This circle had invoked tremendous feelings inside; it spoke to me, like it was reaching out, enveloping me. One could say that seeing the circle awakened something deep inside me. The visual stirred my Anishinaabe life force energy or **mnidoo bemaasing bemaadiziwin** and made me feel good. I felt a level of comfort, like an energy that had laid dormant inside of me was now standing up inside me! The circle had called my Anishinaabe life force energy or **mnidoo bemaasing bemaadiziwin** to attention!

Since that special first time in that university classroom, I have experienced this sensation, this wonderful feeling several times. The feeling comes when I am asked for advice about life situations. At first it was scary but in speaking with Elders, I have accepted the sensation, and now happily embrace the essence of my being. It was not too long after that first time that I started to draw Medicine Wheels. I see Medicine Wheels intuitively, automatically, as they speak to me much like the water that I feel calls to me and that is why I put tobacco in the water whenever possible.

For me, the Teachings of the Medicine Wheel come through flashes and sparks within me: revealed knowledge. I see the groupings, threads, and themes automatically. The Medicine Wheel teachings are holistic. They speak to me. The Medicine Wheel is a natural process and that is why I have chosen to use this visual teaching tool to guide my learning journey. The intricate design of the Wheel makes sense to me.

The Medicine Wheel (see Figure 1) best represents my feelings of responsibility in fulfilling my obligation. My obligation is first to my family as wife, mother, grandmother, sister and auntie.

We are all part of that is beneath us, all that is around us, and all that is above us. Our past is our present, our present is our tomorrow and our tomorrows are the seven generations, past and present.

Figure 1. *Medicine Wheel – Identity.* Reprinted with permission from the Aboriginal Healing and Wellness Program at the Timmins Native Friendship Centre, Timmins, Ontario.

Please note that the colours that make up the Medicine Wheel are a crucial part of its extended meaning. The versions used in this text use the following colour formation: the North quadrant is white, the Eastern quadrant is yellow, the Southern quadrant is red, and the Western quadrant is black. The Medicine Wheels presented in this book have been approved by the Elders consulted for this work.

The Wheel reflects my development as an individual while manifesting my maturation in fostering a sense of belonging while acknowledging duty and role modeling as serious aspects of respect towards family, community and myself. My obligation to my community,

Michipicoten First Nation, will continue through loyalty of being a Band Member and role model, and is reflected in my work and responsibility to the generations of our people. The expectation can be overwhelming in accepting an enormous task such as this. Respect is entrenched in my core being and uppermost in my mind. This respect also reflects within my clan. As stated earlier, clan teachings are manifested in the womb and as a member of the eagle clan, our members are known for courage and preknowledge.[22]

While the precise origin is unknown, the Medicine Wheel "is an ancient symbol used by almost all the Native people of North and South America"[23] and is utilized "to show the many different ways in which all things are interconnected."[24] The Anishinaabe express this interconnectedness and movement through concepts in sets of four. For example, the four Earth directions, north, east, south, and west or the four elements, earth, air, water and fire.[25] According to Elder Doug Williams:

> When I was growing up, there was no such word as a medicine wheel—that came later, in the early 1970s, that's when I first heard it. Before that, the way the old people explained it was in terms of wind. Winds! When you talk about the four directions, they talked about the winds coming from that direction, *waabin*. *Waabun* is a spirit, that's the morning. *Waabinoog*, that's in that direction, *Waabinoog Noodin*, that's the east wind, then *Waabnoong noodin*. *Waabnoong* was also a spirit, they also had in addition to that a spirit called *Ziiqwan*. *Waabin, Ziiqwan*, to the south we had *Shawnoodin, neebin* for summer. To the west we had *Epingishmok* and *Nimkii-Bineshiinh*, the thunderbird, it's a little bit different there.

---

22 Basil Johnston, *Ojibway Heritage* (Lincoln: University of Nebraska Press, 1976), 53.
23 Lane et al., *The Sacred Tree*, 7.
24 Ibid., 32.
25 Ibid., 11.

Up north we had **beboon** and **mukqua** and **Giiwedinoong**, the direction. You know that's the whole idea of viewing the world was presented to me as a kid. There are certain things in the east and so on, so that's a form of medicine wheel but it wasn't called medicine wheel by the Anishinaabe. It was called—or say the four directions, alright a little different.[26]

This spiritual ecology manifests in the physical and spiritual realms, transcending the connection to the land. This includes stewardship of the land which encompasses the mysticism of the great mystery with the Original Instructions. Herb Nabigon refers to the Medicine Wheel path as "the spiritual interpretation of the Native world view [that] is divided into the Four Sacred Directions"[27] (Figure 2).

Many Indigenous authors and scholars such as Marie Battiste, Mark Dockstator, Brian Rice, and Herb Nabigon,[28] have guided users through the dynamics of learning about the Sacred Medicine Wheel. Most important is the message that everything is interconnected, equal, cyclical and never-ending. Standing on the shoulders of these Indigenous scholars, a description of the Medicine Wheel follows.

Visually, the Medicine Wheel is a circle reflecting the natural progression of life that has "... no beginning and no end."[29]

26 Personal communication with Doug Williams, July 11, 2012.
27 Herb Nabigon, *The Hollow Tree: Fighting Addiction With Traditional Native Healing* (Montreal: McGill-Queen's University Press, 2006), 58.
28 See Marie Battiste Battiste, *Reclaiming Indigenous Voice and Vision* (Vancouver: UBC Press, 2000) and *First Nations Education in Canada: The Circle Unfolds* (Vancouver: UBC Press, 1995); Mark Dockstator. "Toward an Understanding of Aboriginal Self-government: A Proposed Theoretical Model and Illustrative Factual Analysis," PhD diss., (York University, 1993); Brian Rice, *Seeing the World With Aboriginal Eyes* (Winnipeg: Aboriginal Issues Press, 2005); and Herb Nabigon, *The Hollow Tree*.
29 Ann Bird as quoted in Jane Ross and Jack Ross, "Keep the Circle Strong: Native Health Promotion," *Journal of Speech Language Pathology and Audiology*, vol. 16 no. 3 (1992): 291, (personal communication with Bird, 1990).

"The circle is at the root to true humility where each is seen as important to the whole and none is more important than any other."[30] As Sharilyn Calliou says, "The circle symbolizes the continuity and connectedness of events with the added dynamism of movement."[31] "In Aboriginal philosophy, existence consists of energy. All things are animate, imbued with spirit, and in constant motion. In this realm of energy and spirit, interrelationships between all entities are of paramount importance . . ." (Little Bear 2000, p. 77).

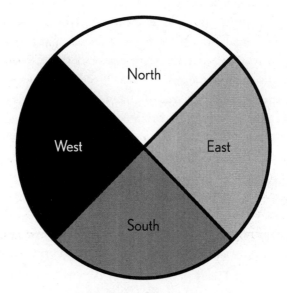

Figure 2. *Medicine Wheel Directions*

Please note that the colours that make up the Medicine Wheel are a crucial part of its extended meaning. The versions used in this text use the following colour formation: the North quadrant is white, the Eastern quadrant is yellow, the Southern quadrant is red, and the Western quadrant is black. The Medicine Wheels presented in this book have been approved by the Elders consulted for this work.

30 Scott Lee and Carol Washburn, *The Circle is Sacred: Stalking the Spirit-Powered Life* (San Francisco: Council Oak Books, 2003), 17.
31 Sharilyn Calliou, "Peacekeeping Actions at Home: A Medicine Wheel Model for a Peacekeeping Pedagogy," *First Nations Educaction in Canada: The Circle Unfolds*, ed Marie Battiste, Jean Barman (Vancouver: UBC Press, 1995), 51.

Within this circle, which is in constant motion, are the four directions: east, south, west and north (see Figure 1). Each direction has teachings and understandings that are important to learn. Some of the teachings for each direction follow.

From the Eastern Door

The eastern door is "a place of beginnings and enlightenment.[32]" This is the time (based on Anishinaabe teachings) of Creation and the Original Instructions. The Creation Story is the bones of Anishinaabe education and the foundation of internal governance. The Creation Story relays the telling about the formation of Turtle Island and shows the beginning of the relationships with Mother Earth and the reciprocal relationships formed with all of nature. Inherent within this relationship is a responsibility and accountability required of human beings. As her children, it is our responsibility to care and love our Mother. She in turn, takes care of us. The Original Instructions and the Seven Grandfather Teachings hold the values and morals of our people and are conveyed to us through our oral tradition and storytelling. These teachings remind us of our responsibility to understand and live by these values in order to seek and maintain harmony and balance. They are embedded within the social and political structures as Natural Law or *Anishinaabe-naakgonigewin*.

From the Anishinaabe perspective, the natural way of learning is from parents, grandparents, aunties and uncles, and Elders who offer the Traditional Teachings and role model these inherent values and behaviours. As Jon Reyhner and Jeanne Eder contend:

> Knowledge of tribal traditions was another component of children's education. Through ceremonies, storytelling, and apprenticeship, children learned the culture of their

---

32 Ibid., 67.

parents. Play was yet another means to educate Indian children. Some games called "the little brother of war" taught boys the skills necessary to handle weapons and developed physical endurance... Children learned by observing and then mimicking their parents.[33]

Respect for self, others and the environment is paramount to Anishinaabe education. Values, morals, and lifeways were integral to respectful relationships. The interconnectedness of all meant that we are all related and the hurt of one is the hurt of all. The connection was maintained to the land, cosmos, animals, spirit, as a whole and human beings were expected to pass these teachings and expectations onto their children as "principles of living in harmony with [the] natural world."[34]

From the Southern Door

In the South, it is a time of growing and changing and it is also an unsettling time for the youth. The youth are coming to know and this is a major time of learning for them, not only learning from the Elders through stories and storytelling, and from teachers but also from Creation. Through stories, Angela Cavender Wilson says:

> Stories in the oral tradition have served some important functions for Native people: [t]he historical and mythological stories provide moral guidelines by which one should live. They teach the young and remind the old what behavior is appropriate and inappropriate in our cultures; they provide a sense of identity and belonging, situating community members within their lineage and establishing their

---

[33] Jon Reyhner and Jeanne Eder, *American Indian Education: A History* (Norman: University of Oklahoma Press, 2004), 14-15.
[34] Benton-Banai, *The Mishomis Book: The Voice of the Ojibway*, 2.

relationship to the rest of the natural world. They are a source of entertainment and of intimacy between the storyteller and the audience.[35]

The stories handed down from grandmother to granddaughter are rooted in a deep sense of kinship responsibility, a responsibility that relays a culture, an identity, and a sense of belonging essential to ... life ... but also as an essential component in the survival of culture.[36]

Stories are enriched as they are told and retold again and again. "They are, more importantly, transmissions of culture upon which our survival as a people depends. When our stories die, so will we."[37] Louise Profit-LeBlanc, who was interviewed by Archibald, Friesen, and Smith explains:

> Since she could remember the young girl had been filled with many stories from her grandmother. Stories of the ancient past. Stories from another time, another world of existence. Stories of great courage, of transformation and trickery. Stories of great tragedies and struggles. Stories of grief and loss and resilience of a people who survived one of the most difficult environments for existence. Tales of wit or humour. She watched now as her grandmother took another sip of tea and lay back against the grub box. The spirit was charged and there was

---

35 Angela Cavender Wilson, "American Indian History or Non-Indian Perceptions of American Indian History?" in *Natives and Academics: Researching and Writing About American Indians*, ed. Devon A. Mihesuah (Lincoln: University of Nebraska Press, 1998), 24.

36 Angela Cavender Wilson, "Grandmother to Granddaughter: Generations of Oral History in a Dakota Family," in *Natives and Academics: Researching and Writing About American Indians*, ed. Devon A. Mihesuah (Lincoln: University of Nebraska Press, 1998), 27.

37 Ibid., 35.

that familiar anticipation of another of these recollections. She leaned forward to listen ever more intently ... She was being prepared for the future. Her mind was being taught to think on all levels and trained to understand things mentally but also emotionally and spiritually. Each concept of the stories was being heard by her heart.

You got three ears you know. Two on the side of your head and one in your heart. Make sure you always use that one too.[38]

Elders are said to be the keepers of these stories and oral traditions and feel more comfortable telling them in the "language," *Anishinaabemowin* (Ojibway). Elder Shirley Williams is an *Anishinaabe-kwe* fluent speaker and translator. She reminds us, "In Canada there are 11 Aboriginal language families, 53 languages, and over 200 dialects."[39] In *Anishinaabemowin*, "Many words describe feelings, and *Anishinaabemowin* is known as a 'feeling language'... when we speak it, we feel it ... As we watch, we feel the other person's spirit."[40]

One of the teachings youth learn from Creation is honesty. The trees fulfill their Original Instructions in growing straight and tall. We are expected to do the same and reflect honesty. We also learn a great teaching from the sun. The sun rises in the east, sits in the south all day and sets in the west. The sun teaches us patience.

This is also the time where we learn about creating a firm spiritual foundation. Young boys at this stage in their lives go out on a vision quest and young girls are taught about their moon-time and respect for their bodies. The Elders guide the young ones and teach them about balance and since the youth are no longer children, they

---

38 Jo-Ann Archibald, Val Friesen, Jeff Smith, eds. *Courageous Spirits: Aboriginal Heroes of Our Children* (Penticton: Theytus Books, Ltd., 1993), 27-28.
39 Shirley Williams, "The Development of Ojibway Language Materials," *Canadian Journal of Native Education* 27, vol 1 (2003), 80.
40 Ibid., 81.

must begin to develop accountability and responsibility and learn to listen to that spirit that teaches them about safety and intuition.

From the Western Door

In the west, it is a time of maturity and reflection. It is a time of looking at things twice and it is also a time for settling. We develop introspection and must learn how to transfer knowledge. The growth of the summer has come to ripen.

This is the time of being an adult, getting married and raising children. It is a time of responsibility, reasoning and respect. Creation has many teachings for us in this emotional, developmental stage. The first teaching is water. Water is a great healer. "When we cry, water carries our hurt away, washes it away and that water has a lot of responsibility."[41] The second teaching is the grasses, the great grasses of the plain. The grasses teach us to be kind and to walk kindly and softly on Mother Earth. The animals that reside in the grasses like the sparrow teach us to look at things differently, begin to develop an understanding of ourselves as "it's the beginning of the process of becoming an elder in another twenty years or so preparing knowledge."[42] The third concerns the teaching of the strawberry. The strawberry teaching refers to the story of two brothers. One brother accidently kills the other brother and is rife with guilt. After he buries his deceased brother, a strawberry plant grows from his grave. The strawberry teaching is about forgiving the brother who was the perpetrator, which is "one of the reasons the strawberry is for forgiveness"[43] and is known as the heart berry, but it goes beyond that and teaches us compassion even when someone is being very mean to us. The lesson is that we cannot judge their life path because we don't know what that life path has been. We must forgive them. This

---

41   Elder Doug Williams, personal communication, December 14, 2012.
42   Ibid..
43   Ibid..

teaching reminds us of "the responsibility to nurture our hearts, so we may be in balance...[which] teaches us forgiveness and peace."[44]

From the Northern Door

From the North we learn the "ways of doing" in practicing ethical principles and traditional values through endurance and wisdom.[45] We seek wisdom from the Creator and our Elders as spiritual teachers. The Elders remind us that all true knowledge is personal and experiential. There is no spirit in the teachings without Elders. "Elders are the keepers of culture and history; they are traditional teachers."[46] Elders embody stories and "lead by example, by living a balanced life."[47]

Elders are the heart of Anishinaabe communities. They listen and speak from their hearts and keep us rooted in our history, traditions, culture, stories, and ceremonies. They are charged with the responsibility for keeping the oral histories and passing the information on to future generations. They are a rich library of knowledge and must always be respected. They are my first destination (before written words), when I want to know and understand something important. This is our way and the way I have been taught.

Elders also possess deeper virtues as they are trusting, accepting, honest and kind individuals who love people and radiate that love. They are healthy, selflessly devoted to the betterment of others, and lead a spiritually based lifestyle in that "they teach it, and talk it and

44 Lillian Pitawanakwat, *Ojibwe/Powawatomi (Anishinabe) Teaching*, (2006). Retrieved from http://www.fourdirectionsteachings.com/transcripts/ojibwe.pdf.
45 Brian Rice, *Seeing the World With Aboriginal Eyes: A Four Directional Perspective on Human and Non-human Values, Cultures and Relationships on Turtle Island* (Winnipeg: Aboriginal Issues Press, 2005), 67.
46 Yvonne McLeod, "Change Makers: Empowering Ourselves Thro' the Education and Culture of Aboriginal Languages: A Collaborative Team Effort," *Canadian Journal of Native Education* 27, vol. 1 (2003): 110.
47 Herb Nabigon, *The Hollow Tree: Fighting Addiction with Traditional Native Healing*, 68.

live it."[48] Elders fiercely protect Indigenous knowledge. They determine what should become public knowledge and what remains sacred. Knowledge that is given is not given freely. The Elder expects to know why the person is asking for the knowledge and what they intend to do with it. The Elder then assesses the situation before offering the knowledge and also considers whom they are giving it to. We have a relationship with knowledge and a variety of ways of gathering it.

There are several concepts for consideration in this chapter. Our Anishinaabe paradigm emphasizes the good of all, the good mind, the hurt of one is the hurt of all—the collective consciousness. This is a means to honour our Anishinaabe ancestors and sutures the heart of our people. This philosophy offers insight into the natural development of Anishinaabe people. Our life force energy or *mnidoo bemaasing bemaadiziwin* is fed from the nutrients—the language, teachings, and ceremonies and their families.

Next, I will discuss the disruption to our life force energy through colonization and the doctrine of discovery.

---

48 Jonathan Ellerby, *Working With Indigenous Elders*, 10.

CHAPTER 2

The Work Process:
Relationship and Knowledge "*Nokiiwin e-zhimaajiihkag: Wiijikiiwendiwin miininwaa kendaaswin*"

> "Indigenous people have cellular memory embedded in their molecular structure and that this [sic] knowledge is what guides our people today."[1]
>
> —PATRICIA STEINHAUER

As previously stated, at the core of the Anishinaabe worldview and embedded in the Creation Story, are the bones and the bedrock or **kanan miinwaa nbagani-aasmaabkong**. I identified the bedrock as relationship and the bones as Indigenous knowledge which we acknowledge as gifts from the ancestors. This section speaks to the Anishinaabe relationship to acquiring knowledge; the sacredness of the relationship I developed with a group of residential school survivors and, the process we undertook for this journey.

Relationship and Knowledge

Embedded within the Medicine Wheel is relationship which has four layers: knowledge, ideas, self, and community (see Figure 3).

---

1   Patricia Steinhauer, "Situating Myself in Research," *Canadian Journal of Native Education* 25, no. 2 (2001): 184.

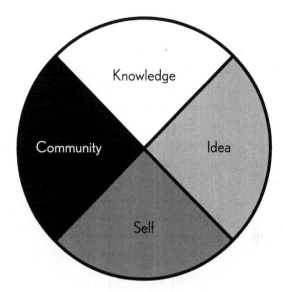

Figure 3. Relationship and Knowledge

Please note that the colours that make up the Medicine Wheel are a crucial part of its extended meaning. The versions used in this text use the following colour formation: the North quadrant is white, the Eastern quadrant is yellow, the Southern quadrant is red, and the Western quadrant is black. The Medicine Wheels presented in this book have been approved by the Elders consulted for this work.

In addition to our relationship through ancestral knowledge, Marlene Brant Castellano contends there are various sources of knowledge and several characteristics of Indigenous knowledge. She states that "knowledge valued in Aboriginal societies derives from multiple sources, principally tradition, observation, and revelation ... Traditional knowledge has been handed down" generationally through Creation stories, historical events, technology, behaviours (role models) and traditions.[2] Empirical knowledge is recorded from bearing witness and by watching and understanding processes and patterns. Revealed knowledge comes to individuals through

---

2   Marlene Brant Castellano, "Updating Aboriginal Traditions of Knowledge," *Indigenous Knowledges in Global Contexts: Multiple Readings of Our World*, George J. Sefa Dei et al., eds. (Toronto: University of Toronto Press, 2000), 23.

reflexive states of being in dreaming, vision quests and inward telling and knowing (intuition and cellular memory). Castellano notes that Indigenous knowledge is "personal, oral, experiential, holistic, and conveyed in narrative or metaphorical language"[3] and "validated through collective analysis and consensus building. Collective wisdom is arrived at by a process of 'putting our minds together'."[4] Personal knowledge is derived from the reliability of trust and integrity entrusted within the perspective of the individual. Oral transmission is the passing on of knowledge through storytelling and listening to the morals or values imparted in the personal stories.

Experiential knowledge is formed from participating in cultural practices such as harvesting medicines in the bush with an Elder. Holistic knowledge is captured in the Medicine Wheel teachings that teach us that everything has a spirit and as individuals we seek to be balanced within Creation. Narrative and metaphorical knowledge teach us how to be good role models and may be of a trickster nature. Knowledge "[is] a living fire, rekindled from surviving embers and fuelled with the materials of the twenty-first century."[5] As Anishinaabe knowledge holders, we must feel confident and have faith that the ancestors have placed the answers to our questions as fruit for us to feast from. Patricia Steinhauer describes the wisdom of the Elders as represented by a tree:

> The tree represented the key. Trees have roots that are firmly rooted in the ground. Their creation and growth involves a long nurturing process. When I think about this natural process and of how the tree evolves, it becomes easier to articulate the notion of inherent wisdom. I think of how solidly the roots are rooted in the ground and how they provide the life food, the knowledge, for the rest of the tree.

3   Ibid., 25.
4   Ibid., 26.
5   Ibid., 34.

I see these roots as representing our ancestors. Our ancestors play that role of rooting us to our place and keeping wisdom strong and alive. The whole metaphor came to life. Our ancestors bear this knowledge and continue to feed this knowledge upward. The trunk represents the community; the way knowledge is passed on in this upward spiral. The branches represent the families of the community. The leaves represent our young people. With the metaphor it all made perfect sense to me.[6]

Once the Anishinaabe knowledge holder has fostered confidence and faith in knowledge, they must form a relationship with an idea. This is the second layer of the relationship. "Ideas, in general, according to Native American studies disciplinary definitions, are to be generated from the inside of culture, not from the outside looking in."[7] Shawn Wilson explains that we must "form a respectful relationship with the ideas we are studying."[8] For example, spirituality is a key component of Indigenous peoples' healing. Wilson questions why Western society has distanced itself from anything spiritual.

The third layer of relationship embraces the notion of self and self-in-relation. Manu Aluli Meyer contends:

> The very notion of self is critical. Self is not autonomous self. It never is in Hawaii. Self is self and other . . . Self is self with other . . . Self is connected other, and this is an epistemological point. Based on ontology—ontology is the philosophy of essence—who are you, who are your people,

---

[6] Steinhauer, "Situating Myself in Research," 186-187.

[7] Elizabeth Cook-Lynn, "American Indian Intellectualism and the New Indian Story," in *Natives and Academics: Researching and Writing About American Indians*, ed. Devon Abbott Mihesuah (Lincoln: University of Nebraska, 1998), 129.

[8] Shawn Wilson, *Research is Ceremony: Indigenous Research Methods* (Halifax: Fernwood Publishing, 2008), 29.

where are you from, what difference does that make for you? That's ontology.⁹

Margaret Kovach, a Cree scholar, states that "the term epistemology most closely approximates the self-in-relation aspect inherent to Indigenous knowledge"¹⁰ which speaks to intuition (cellular memory), responsibility, and our ways of introduction to the community. Self is derived from our Indigenous identity with a true sense of belonging in community. According to Dr. Fyre Jean Graveline, a Métis (Cree) author:

> Fundamental to Anishinaabe worldview is the link between individual responsibility and community well-being. One must be responsible for their own actions in relation to their community and ultimately the world.¹¹

Before we take on the responsibility of knowledge, we must prepare ourselves. One must "go to the centre of yourself to find your own belonging."¹² Anishinaabe people must first put down tobacco and ask for the knowledge. When they seek knowledge from the Anishinaabe Elders, they must first present them with a gift of tobacco.

The fourth layer of relationship denotes community relations with respect to protocol, dialogue, ethics, respect, trust, voice, control, relational accountability, and the benefit to the community. Meyer summarizes her understanding of community:

> Hawaiian epistemology is founded in relationship—relationships with people, relationships with relatives alive and past,

---

9   Manu Aluli Meyer "Acultural Assumptions of Empiricism: A Native Hawaiian Critique," *Canadian Journal of Native Education* 25, no. 2 (2001): 8.
10 Margaret Kovach, *Indigenous Methodologies: Characteristics, Conversations and Contexts*, (Toronto: University of Toronto Press, Inc. 2009), 21.
11 Fyre Jean Graveline, *Circle Works: Transforming Eurocentric Consciousness*, (Halifax: Fernwood Publishing, 1998), 57.
12 Kovach, *Indigenous Methodologies*, 49.

relationships with an idea, or relationships with our environment ... The living relationships we have with our natural world are a fact that mediates how I see, how I experience, and how I understand ... We are all parts of a whole. This doesn't mean that collaboration is made easier; it's more a statement of connectability. So the idea of relationship is key in knowledge ... Call it negative psychology, but I call it community.[13]

Community means family,[14] connections,[15] networking,[16] relationality,[17] relational accountability,[18] and pre-existing and ongoing relationships.[19] Since Indigenous communities are now taking on the responsibility of conducting their own projects, as Anishinaabe people, we may be asked to participate within a project in our own communities. We must meet face to face with community members and dialogue.[20] We may already be in pre-existing and/or ongoing relationship(s) with members of the community and this is an important accepted characteristic of doing community work.[21] Confidentiality and trust become issues. Kathy Absolon shared her insider research experience:

> ... tact, awareness and diplomacy become important skills. Confidentiality is imperative and not divulging confidential information means that, you safeguard your knowledge

13 Meyer, "Acultural Assumptions of Empiricism," 8.
14 Cora Weber-Pillwax, "Coming to an Understanding: A Panel Presentation: What is Indigenous Research?" *Canadian Journal of Native Education* 26, no. 2 (2001): 166-174.
15 See Linda Tuhiwai Smith, *Decolonizing Methodologies: Research and Indigenous Peoples*, (New York: Zed Books Ltd., 1999); Wilson, 2008; Steinhauer, 2001.
16 Weber-Pillwax, 2001.
17 Wilson, *Research is Ceremony*.
18 Ibid.
19 Weber-Pillwax; Wilson, *Research is Ceremony*; Kovach.
20 See Greg Cajete, *Look to the Mountain: An Ecology of Indigenous Education*, (Skyland: Kivaki Press, 1994); Lewis Cardinal, "What is an Indigenous Perspective?" *The Canadian Journal of Native Education* 25, no. 2,1 (2001): 80-183.
21 See Kovach; Wilson, *Research is Ceremony*.

without others knowing, wishing you did not know what you did or wanting to say something but knowing you cannot ... and having respect for those relationships.[22]

Anishinaabe people may ask for assistance, a contact or liaison person to help introduce them to the community if the knowledge seeker is a stranger/outsider to the community. For example, an experienced community member stepped forward as my liaison for my community-based work. Effective communication is crucial. It is incumbent on the outsider knowledge seeker to introduce themselves to the community in a good way, in telling one's First Nation location and family name so that connections can be made and relations established.

Colin Gallagher's experience speaks to the importance of community relations whereby an Elder of the community led the way for him. The Elder went around to the fishers and asked if Gallagher could observe them in their work. He reminded us that "trust and respect from the community is paramount for the success of the project, but it does not come automatically; it has to be earned."[23] "The ability to be teased and joke around is crucial. Anishinaabe [people] love to tease and persons who may not like being teased and take things too seriously will not last long on a boat."[24] Respect is key and the giving of tobacco may be warranted; this practice will depend on the community custom.

For Anishinaabe people there is relational accountability.[25] "There is some form of community accountability."[26] The work

22 Kathy Absolon, "Navigating the Landscape of Practice: Dbaagmowin of a Helper," in *Wicihitowin: Aboriginal Social Work in Canada*, Raven Sinclair et al., eds. (Winnipeg: Fernwood Publishing), 188.
23 Collin Gallagher, "Quit Thinking Like a Scientist," in *Native Voices in Research*, Jill Oakes et al., eds., (Winnipeg: Aboriginal Issues Press), 184.
24 Ibid., 186.
25 Wilson, *Research is Ceremony*.
26 Kovach, 48.

"... that we do as Indigenous people is a ceremony that allows us a raised level of consciousness and insight into our own world."[27] This is a huge responsibility. "Relational accountability requires me to form reciprocal and respectful relationships within the communities..."[28], which means that proper protocol must be adhered to plus there are a number of additional factors that come into play such as sharing,[29] benefit to the community,[30] control,[31] guidelines (parameters)[32] and boundaries.[33] Sharing speaks to the "responsibility of ... demystifying knowledge and information and speaking in plain terms to the community... Oral presentations conform to cultural protocols and expectations."[34] "Sharing contains views about knowledge being a collective benefit and knowledge being a form of resistance."[35]

Benefit to the community and control are key factors in allowing work to be conducted in and on Indigenous territories. Ethics and boundaries come into play because researchers receive privileged information that may do harm. Some Anishinaabe people may feel a dual obligation, first to the community and second, to the work. "Communities are the ones who know the answers to their own problems."[36] Ideally "[t]he community itself invites the project in and sets out its parameters"[37] and decides if it will benefit from the work being done. As a relationship deepens, there comes a sense of loyalty and caring which may eventually lead to the knowledge seeker becoming family within a community. My experience of working with

27 Wilson, *Research is Ceremony*, 11.
28 Ibid., 40
29 Smith, *Decolonizing Methodologies*.
30 Weber-Pillwax.
31 Smith, *Decolonizing Methodologies*.
32 Smith, *Decolonizing Methodologies*.
33 Steinhauer.
34 Smith, *Decolonizing Methodologies*, 161.
35 Ibid., 160.
36 Ibid., 159.
37 Ibid., 147.

Indigenous organizations like the Children of Shingwauk Alumni Association (CSAA) is that they believe control and vision are major issues for them especially where archival and property ownership is concerned.[38] As Anishinaabe people we want to fulfill the obligations to our own people while doing the work, which can be a balancing act.

Anishinaabe knowledge seekers must collaborate with the community and the methods must mesh with the community and serve and benefit the community. Linda Smith surmises that establishing trust with Elders will be a major obstacle to obtaining consent as "the dynamics of relationships are by nature hugely complicated."[39] "Consent is not so much given for a project or specific set of questions, but for a person, for credibility."[40] We must treat participants as part of the family and honour them as such.

Anishinaabe people own their own data, cultural and intellectual property and negotiate agreements through protocol. There are a significant increase of Indigenous graduate students and their deep 'interpersonal' responsibility and obligation to their people through Indigenous methodologies such as storytelling is paramount.

The Process

While reading Margaret Kovach's (2009) book *Indigenous Methodologies: Characteristics, Conversations, and Contexts*," I felt a spark of recognition for organizing this process. Building on my teachings and the previous discussion of the Medicine Wheel, the four directions were used to describe this process (see Figure 4). We begin at the eastern door with a history of the relationship with the survivors and the evolution of this partnership in completing this journey. I proceed to

---

38 For example, the CSAA has worked closely with Algoma University to develop protocols through negotiated agreements whereby the CSAA is acknowledged as a stakeholder in the Shingwauk Archives.
39 Smith, *Decolonizing Methodologies*, 137.
40 Ibid., 136.

the southern door to discuss the necessary preparations, including preparing myself for this work. I continue in the west and listen to each former student's voice about their understanding of what resilience means to them. From my Traditional Teachings, the literature and journaling and through revealed knowledge I make meaning of resilience. Finally, in the north, I gift to the former students and their community by giving back their voices in the final narrative and the great respect they afforded me.

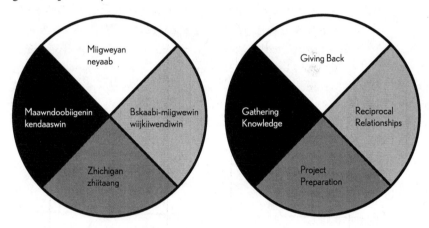

Figure 4. The Process. This Medicine Wheel was developed in consultation with Elder Shirley Ida Williams.

Please note that the colours that make up the Medicine Wheel are a crucial part of its extended meaning. The versions used in this text use the following colour formation: the North quadrant is white, the Eastern quadrant is yellow, the Southern quadrant is red, and the Western quadrant is black. The Medicine Wheels presented in this book have been approved by the Elders consulted for this work.

Reciprocal Relationships
"Bskaabi-miigwewin wiijkiiwendiwin"

The relationship with the Walpole Indian Residential School Survivors Group (WIRSSG) is fostered in the same spirit as our relationship with Mother Earth in that it is a reciprocal relationship, developed and formed from the original relationship I developed with the CSAA. There were many challenges and changes within this relationship as I had started out as a volunteer and eventually became a member of the family, the "Shingwauk Family."[41] Central to my journey, at the heart of the work, is the twenty plus year relationship that I nurtured and fostered with this group of residential school survivors. For me, the relationship has encompassed profound respect imbued with a deep commitment made in 1993 to continue to assist the survivors with their healing. Although this work is partnered with the WIRSSG, it is no different as this group is also part of the Shingwauk Family.

As explained earlier, my relationship with the survivor group grew out of a volunteer position back in 1991. My first initiation was being asked to volunteer as the registrar during the second Shingwauk Reunion and it was through this task that I learned the names and faces of my new family. Slowly I began to understand the history of residential schools and the egregious impacts suffered from this education system. I was taken by their courage, bravery and unseen bitterness displayed by the former students and was astounded by their strength and willingness to give. They taught me how to be a helper, how to show respect and learn about specific ceremonies such as the smudging ceremony and sweat lodge ceremony. They also taught me about caring, sharing and their strength of life or *zongwaadiziwin*. Most important was learning the Traditional Teachings and ceremonies practiced during a three-day healing circle, a talking circle, and the healing relationship. I quickly understood what was important to the former students. Knowing how the former students wanted to be treated, and acknowledging that each survivor's experience is unique but also knowing that as a collective, their experiences were the same emotionally, enhanced my own understanding of my tasks.

---

41 This is a particular discourse used by the survivors about their shared experiences at Shingwauk.

This reciprocal relationship developed with every activity. I was hired as the Office Administrator/Healing Coordinator for the CSAA in 1999. For the next four years, my relationship deepened with the executive council members and the reunion committee members while maintaining the day-to-day office tasks and facilitating two Shingwauk Reunions. As our relationship deepened so did my level of caring for this special group of people. As my children became exposed to this group, they also began to care for the members.

As the years passed, I met several Shingwauk Family members and listened to their stories. Being involved first as a volunteer offered a unique perspective as an observer with minimal responsibilities. The closeness and loyalty comes later as you begin to care about the survivors and their families. I earned trust from the survivors and treated them respectfully. This is the hallmark of our relationship. It was that special moment in 1993, when listening to the pain voiced by a survivor, that bonded me with all the survivors. I became one of their witnesses, and transformed, forever changed and charged with a personal responsibility. I had received the knowledge and was responsible for the awareness.

Because of my previous work, I was asked to become a part of the WIRSSG's work. Being invited into a community to work as a partner is phenomenal. Indigenous people are developing their own guidelines and protocols for work within the community.[42] For example, Walpole Island First Nation (WIFN) (Bkejwanong Territory) has built in safeguards for the community as protection for individuals and the land.

As previously mentioned, relationships for me are fundamental to doing any work. I could not proceed without an established relationship with the survivors. At the same time, the survivors would

---

42　For example see *Negotiating Research Relationships with Inuit Communities: A Guide for Researchers* prepared by Inuit Tapiriit Kanatami and Nunavut Research Institute (2007).

not speak openly to me about this topic and their experiences without a relationship. This is the reciprocal relationship that is central to this work. In the same spirit of the Original Instructions and Seven Grandfather Teachings, I experience a responsibility through my relationship with the CSAA and subsequently with the WIRSSG.

My role as a community partner was to listen to a group of survivors and document their life experiences in order to understand their resiliency. My responsibility was to provide a safe environment, listen in a sensitive and caring manner, and to do no harm. As an *Anishinaabe-kwe* insider for this work, I have fostered relationships with the survivors. As an outsider, I am not a member of the WIFN community nor am I a residential school survivor. Another responsibility was to take care and write in every day language so as to give voice to the survivors which is crucial. Further, it includes giving consideration to other particular sensitivities as they emerge.

Work Preparation *"Nokiiwin zhiitaang."*

This work uses an Anishinaabe way that is personal, experiential and community-based in that I deeply listened to the 13 survivor voices about their life experiences. This is a respectful way of working with First Nations communities and emphasizes relational accountability.[43] First, in 2008, I attended the CSAA annual meeting and requested their blessing to bond and work with their affiliate, an offspring, the WIRSSG. I would have been remiss not to include them as family members. In this partnership with the WIRSSG, they listened to the plan.

Second, I worked with the WIRSSG who obtained a letter of support from the Walpole Island First Nation Chief and Council. Third, an Advisory Group consisting of five individuals from the WIRSSG was established with Susie Jones as the liaison. The purpose of the advisory group was to provide assistance with the work process

---

43 Wilson, *Research Is Ceremony.*

and logistics (e.g., interview schedule, support mechanisms, gatherings); to comment on criteria for participants and interview questions; and comment on the final narrative. Members of this group received a small gift once the work was done.

I was officially introduced to WIRSSG at a commemoration of the Memorial Wall August 15, 2008 after attending the annual CSAA meeting in Sault Ste. Marie, Ontario, June 15-16, 2008. This trip proved to be an excellent opportunity to re-connect with the WIRSSG and deepen our relationships. Both of these meetings proved beneficial to the unfolding of this partnership. A formal preparatory event for the survivors occurred November 15, 2009. The purpose of this event was to officially acknowledge the partnership for this work and celebrate the establishment of the national "Truth and Reconciliation" process with two of the Truth and Reconciliation Commissioners.[44] This was also a time for another commemoration of the Memorial Wall erected at Walpole Island.

Gathering Knowledge
"Maawndoobiigegin kendaaswin"

Six methods were selected to understand how the WIRSSG understood their resiliency: listening to survivors, having conversations, understanding Anishinaabe Traditional Teachings, experiencing

---

44 The Truth and Reconciliation Commission (TRC) established in 2008 contends that "There is an emerging and compelling desire to put the events of the past behind us so that we can work towards a stronger and healthier future. The truth telling and reconciliation process as part of an overall holistic and comprehensive response to the Indian Residential School legacy is a sincere indication and acknowledgement of the injustices and harms experienced by Aboriginal people and the need for continued healing. This is a profound commitment to establishing new relationships embedded in mutual recognition and respect that will forge a brighter future. The truth of our common experiences will help set our spirits free and pave the way to reconciliation." Retrieved August 22, 2011 from http://www.trc.ca/websites/trcinstitution/index.php?p=7#Principles.

revealed knowledge, discussing what has been written about resiliency and journaling. These methods were synergistic with my twenty plus years of Indigenous knowledge and experience with the survivors enabling a rich contextual understanding of resiliency. I discuss each in turn.

Listening to Survivors

Deep listening to survivors is important as they view it as an opportunity to have their voice heard, and hearing from the survivors is taken very seriously in Anishinaabe country. For me, listening to the survivors whereby one goes to the very people affected, and asks questions, was a natural process for gathering information. In order to achieve the most effectiveness of listening, the survivor has to experience a level of comfort with me and the environment. Throughout my years, I have come to understand the limits and strengths of listening. There are factors occurring in the background involving residential school issues and impacts. I listened to 13 individuals of the 150 survivors living on Walpole Island as they came forward (volunteered) to tell about their life experiences. Most of the survivors were listened to in the comfort of their own home.

The survivors all lived at Walpole Island except for two. The survivors had attended Shingwauk (Anglican), Mount Elgin (Methodist) or the Mohawk Institute (Anglican). All of the survivors knew the language, **Anishinaabemowin**, prior to being sent to residential school. Of the 13 survivors, only two were fluent in their language after leaving residential school. Four of the survivors were five years old or under when entering residential school. Eight of the 13 survivors attended residential school for six or more years. Of the 13 survivors, at least 50 percent are second and third generation, as either mother, father or both, or a grandparent went to residential school.

Special considerations were taken concerning this process. The first concern was to make sure that the participants were taken care of as the information I sought was of a sensitive nature. I take very seriously this responsibility to do no harm, and understand that it is my responsibility to take care of the survivors. Susie Jones and I discussed this responsibility in advance and we decided to offer the services of a trained health support person (living in the community) once they told their life story. Fortunately, their services were not needed. In addition, we arranged a two-day gathering and offered a community feast after completion of the work. This was intended to lessen any difficult effects arising from the work. Further, the survivors were reminded that the WIRSSG peer social support network was available to them and to anyone who required their assistance. There was no waiting.

My approach was very much a family approach. When I went to listen to a survivor, I brought a teapot (as a gift) with several different kinds of tea so that they could make a selection. I also brought a box of tissues (just in case). Before we started, I asked them about their family, grandchildren and inquired about their definition of resiliency.[45] If they were not too sure I read them two definitions; two survivors requested the definition of resiliency.

As this work is intended to give voice to the 13 survivors and my understanding of their resiliency, there are specific protocols that must be followed. First, as I have learned from the survivors, my paramount responsibility is to remain respectful and keep the survivors safe. In doing this, I recognized that the boundaries included not to do harm by asking probing questions. I also must be observant in understanding and knowing what information can be shared and what can be put in writing.

In December 2010, I returned to Walpole Island and met with each survivor so that they could re-check his/her transcript to verify their words. Although all the survivors consented to using their

---

45 Each survivor read the consent form and was given the opportunity to ask questions before they signed the consent form.

full name, I decided that I would use only their first names to distinguish them from other survivors I had conversations with; they are: Eric, Geraldine, Gladys, Leonard, Louis, Mary, Patrick, Ronald, Susie, Sylvia, Una, Vernon and William. I had conversations with other survivors about their residential school and life experiences prior to and while doing this work. Their voices are also included.[46] Those survivors include: Garnet Angeconeb, Mike Cachagee, the late Dorothy Cunningham, Geronimo Henry, Shirley Horn, the late Ron Howard, Sr., and especially the late Susie Jones who drew me into in-depth discussions and ongoing guidance until she passed into the spirit world. I will forever be eternally grateful for her trust in me and my work.

Traditional Teachings

For me, gathering knowledge is personal and experiential and a lifelong process. For example, my introduction to medicinal plants began as a teenager when my Mother pointed at a yellow plant and explained its use. At the time, I was uninterested in obtaining the plant knowledge. The second experience was with an Elder who showed me a tree and shared the tree's medicinal purpose. The third experience that changed my life was meeting a medicine person. It was his knowledge that gave birth to me becoming an Anishinaabe sponge. Assisting this medicine person during community visits increased my hunger for Indigenous Knowledge.

The next layer of Indigenous Knowledge was meeting the residential school survivors. Following the introduction in 1991, my learnings from them included more ceremonies and the Seven Grandfather Teachings. This relationship deepened and is steeped in respect. Mutual respect was earned and fostered throughout a twenty plus year relationship. With this understanding and learning of respect for

---

46 The information was re-checked by phone, and they provided informed consent to be identified by their first and last name.

the survivors came the teachings of the roles and responsibilities of our place in Creation. I was taught that the role Elders play is a prominent place in our communities. They are the knowledge keepers of the old ways, values and morals, and are the role models, and leaders and advisors in their communities. I learned that to approach Anishinaabe Elders with tobacco and ask for assistance was a natural process.

Another Elder, Doug Williams continues to guide me on my life path. The conversations and learnings that I have had and gotten from Doug have been instrumental to my lifelong process. Another Elder I met was Shirley Williams. Knowing Shirley and listening to the many stories she shared with me gave me an innermost view of the deep emotional hurts felt by the children at residential school. Her memories are most telling and I will never forget them.

As mentioned, the Anishinaabe protocol in approaching an Elder to request assistance is to offer a tobacco[47] tie. First, one must give the specific topic much thought beforehand as this demonstrates respect for the Elder. At the outset, it is important to establish the goals and objectives and develop a set of questions. The Elder will know how serious you are by the energy associated with the gift. Second, one must obtain permission from the local authority. Third, one must be prepared to listen and rely on the Elder to know what type of information could be shared and what information should not be shared.

I know that through my own maturation process, the Creator has put many knowledgeable Elders in my path. Because of my passion to gain the knowledge of my Anishinaabe being, I have sought out the different avenues to learn our ways and the teachings. Many

---

47 According to our traditions, Anishinaabeg believed that Gchi-Manitou (the Creator) was always present. The Creator was present in particular places such as: at the top of a mountain, in a whirlpool, in a cave, on a small island, or in a cavern in the rocks at the water's edge—the Anishinabeg would offer tobacco to the mysteries who abided there. The offering was given partially to appease, and partially to acknowledge a presence. For whatever reason the act was performed, it was always done with reverence and holiness. (Johnston, *Indian School Days*, 33)

Elders and traditionalists have provided a path of truth. For example, Elder Doug Williams has been a pillar of knowledge throughout this learning journey. At different times in my life, teachers would just show up to help, guide, and strengthen me on my journey. Most important has been the teachings of etiquette, protocol and respect. For example, had I not been taught about giving back to the community I would not have taken on the responsibility of being the registrar at the reunion and would have missed meeting the CSAA along with the wonderful opportunity to serve the survivors. These teachings continue to serve me well in my life as do the Seven Grandfather Teachings—I never want my learning to cease.

Revealed Knowledge

Revealed knowledge surfaces from dreams and comes to me particularly when I am quiet, and getting ready to go to sleep. The ancestors send me information when I deeply listen. For example, in starting this work I observed something different, an energy that sprang from the survivors. Marlene Brant Castellano wrote that *"revealed knowledge* is acquired through dreams, visions, and intuitions that are understood to be spiritual in origin."[48] Lionel Kinunwa described this knowledge as cellular memory[49] which I refer to as the bones and the bedrock or **kanan miinwaa nbagani-aasmaabkong**. This ancestral knowledge is waiting for me and surfaces when I remain open-minded to receive the message. This deep listening could also be what Vine Deloria Jr. calls suspended judgment when he says that:

> Indians use a peculiar way of maintaining a metaphysical stance that can best be termed as "suspended judgment." People do not feel it obligatory that they reach a logical

---

[48] Brant Castellano, "Updating Aboriginal Traditions of Knowledge," 24. Author's emphasis.
[49] Steinhauer, 184.

conclusion or that they could summarize the world of experience in a few words or sentences... The hallmark of the true Indian philosopher was the ability to hold in suspended judgment the experiences he or she had enjoyed or was told, and to file away that bit of knowledge until the time when more data of closely related content came his or her way.[50]

Revealed knowledge is the process I used in coming to understand Anishinaabe life force energy or *mnidoo bemaasing bemaadiziwin*. I trusted my own observations, feelings and instincts.

Journaling

For me, journaling has always been an important part of my educational process, in school and during my professional years. Journaling has been a great source of review and reflection while creating, generating and developing reports, papers or feelings about different situations and times in my life. This resource helps me to relive joyful past meetings, recalling important voices long since passed into the spirit world, and holding the memory. I have come to rely on my journals throughout the years beginning in 1995 with my periods of employment. Furthermore, when I attended important functions such as the June 11, 2008 apology in Ottawa, I wrote several pages of observations and later produced a report.

During the time that I was employed by the CSAA, I maintained journals and reports about their developments and events. They rely on this information today to fill gaps in their evolution as an organization and/or with funding proposals. These journals have

---

50 Vine Deloria Jr, "American Indian Metaphysics," in *Power and Place: Indian Education in America*, Vine Deloria Jr. and Daniel Wildcat eds., (Golden: American Indian Graduate Center and Fulcrum Publishing, 2001), 6.

also enabled me to recall events and context, memories of experiences, and identify themes.

Discussion on Resiliency

The discussion comprised two areas: an overview of resiliency and an overview of studies about Indigenous peoples and resiliency. There were also studies from researchers who interviewed survivors although those studies did not concern resiliency. The approach and results of this search are discussed in Chapter Four. I have included the voices of other survivors from these studies within the work to add depth to the experiences.

Giving Back *"Miigweyan neyaab"*

Through my teachings as an **Anishinaabe-kwe**, I understand that when I go to visit people I bring a gift. As previously mentioned, I gifted the survivors with a teapot and tea. Great care was taken to transcribe every word I heard to reflect the survivors' exact words. When the was work was completed, the audiotapes and a manuscript were given to the respective survivor. The written data with no identifiers are stored in the Shingwauk Project Archives at Algoma University in Sault Ste. Marie, Ontario.[51]

In keeping with the Seven Grandfather Teachings a feast took place October 25, 2012 at Walpole Island which was a great way to practice reciprocity and to share the sincere thanks I owe to my family and community! During the feast, I provided the survivors an information summary.

---

51 The Shingwauk Project Archives is a digitized collection of photographs, documents, paintings and other items that have been collected since 1979 concerning the history of residential schools in Canada. For more information see http://www.algomau.ca/about-algoma-u/shingwauk-project.

This may be a good time to remember the following, I am *Anishinaabe-kwe* which to me means that I predominantly learn through personal and experiential encounters. My knowledge is through experiential learning in hearing the voices of the Elders and truth from the 13 survivors, including teachings and learnings as first-hand knowledge in my lived experiences. Throughout this narrative not only do I use my own words which are a manifestation of my twenty plus years of learning from many residential school survivors, including their teachings about role modeling, but also personal communications with Elders and survivors all of whom have been reviewed and approved by the source.

While deeply listening to their life experiences and through revealed knowledge, I found that there is a positive energy, an endearing and enduring legacy that springs from within the survivors—their life force energy or ***mnidoo bemaasing bemaadiziwin***. This life force energy is innate, holistic and within each of us. It manifests itself through all of our relations; land, animals, plants, ancestors and other people. The life force energy cannot be extinguished but can be severely dampened. The residential school system was an attempt to severely dampen the students' life force energy. The nutrients that feed and ignite the life force energy may be different for each person. For example, some nutrients may be language, ceremonies, and place.

At the heart of this work is the relationship fostered with a group of residential school survivors that has encompassed profound respect imbued with a deep commitment. Prior to and during this work, I regularly offered tobacco, according to the teachings of the Tobacco Ceremony, and asked for guidance in completing the work in a good way. The offering of tobacco is very close to my heart as I routinely offer tobacco to Mother Earth's lifeblood—the water. Putting down tobacco may help the survivors find their story in this work. I offer this with respect and humility. The survivors have much to tell us and they do so of their own volition.

Now that I have set out the foundation of this Anishinaabe work process with my way of acquiring knowledge, it may be useful to understand some of our past on Turtle Island. These episodes and events influenced the Anishinaabe and interfered with the Anishinaabe lifeways. This next chapter will briefly explain the policy and legislation that shaped the events that continue to impact an entire Indigenous population including subsequent generations on Turtle Island.

CHAPTER 3

Our Past Matters
"Gaa-bi-zhewebak gchi-zhaazhe gchi-piitendaagwaad"

> When colonization and colonial policy threatened our Indigenous ways of being, our peoples resisted, organized, and mobilized at every point in history—we were not passive victims of colonialism.
>
> —LEANNE BETASAMOSAKE SIMPSON[1]

Elders have taught me that we need to understand the past before we can understand the present and the future, and in order to do this we need to look at some of the literature. In this chapter, I give an overview of the policies and legislation that resulted in residential schools in Canada. I discuss the reclamation process featuring some of the key works concerning the legacy of residential schools in North America, and I provide an overview concerning the Shingwauk Indian Residential School and the development of its alumni affiliates, the Children of Shingwauk Alumni Association and the Walpole Island Residential School Survivors Group.

---

1   Leanne Betasamosake Simpson, *Lighting the Eighth Fire: The Liberation, Resurgence, and Protection of Indigenous Nations*, (Winnipeg: Arbeiter Ring Publishing Ltd., 2008), 13.

The Policies and Legislation

Indigenous peoples of Turtle Island experienced sustained contact with Europeans in the seventeenth century. As early as 1620, missionaries were sent as representatives of their respective churches to Turtle Island in order to find converts, and to teach the beliefs of their specific faith. The settlers initially relied on Indigenous peoples to physically and economically survive.[2] Later, the 1763 Royal Proclamation and the 1764 Treaty of Niagara would encapsulate an understanding of mutual sovereignty, alliance, and free trade.[3] The sharing of the land and the resources would be acknowledged with the giving of gifts and it was agreed that land would not be given without consent.[4] Indigenous peoples and Europeans would live in peace, friendship, and respect side by side.[5] Later, the settlers relied on different approaches to rationalize the theft of land and resources.[6] I remember Mike Cachagee, a member of Chapleau Cree First Nation (Fox Lake Reserve), and a survivor of three residential schools saying:

> I was telling you about Russell Means when he said that when the settlers arrived, the Europeans arrived over here, he called them the 'invaders,' and in that whole concept of

2   Mark Dockstator, "Toward an Understanding of Aboriginal Self-Government: A Proposed Theoretical Model and Illustrative Factual Analysis," Phd unpublished diss., (York University, 1993).
3   John Borrows, "Wampum at Niagara: The Royal Proclamation, Canadian Legal History, and Self-Government," in *Aboriginal and Treaty Rights in Canada: Essays on Law, Equity, and Respect and Difference*, ed. Michael Asch (Vancouver: UBC Press, 1997), 170.
4   Ibid., 171.
5   Ibid.
6   For more information see Robert J. Miller's *Native America, Discovered and Conquered: Thomas Jefferson, Lewis and Clark, and Manifest Destiny* (Lincoln: University of Nebraska Press, 2008), and Boyce Richardson's *People of Terra Nullius: The Trail and Rebirth in Aboriginal Canada* (Seattle: University of Washington Press, 1993).

God being white and creating, and changing—making Jesus a white person and then how they destroyed and rationalized destruction and killing other people, they de-spiritualized them. In what he said, "our people had no spirit." If they had a spirit in not being Christian well then they were well within their right to kill it or destroy it.

I sit here and I look out and see all the trees, you know they've got spirits, everything's got a spirit out here and even in the winter time, all these things are all sleeping under this big white blanket and in the spring, they all wake up. But all their spirits are still out there. Did you ever see a wisp of snow? You know those wisps of snow I don't know what you call it; they have a name for them. But our people would always say that, I remember my great, great uncle I guess, telling me when I was a little boy in Moose Factory, told me that was **Wasakajec (Wesakejig)**, the trickster running around or **Nanaboozhoo**, the Anishinaabe would call him. This stuff was all based upon our interpretation of spirits and these white people all think spirits are confined in the church and if you don't belong to that church then those spirits are of no significance and like I say I think that's how they started the Indian Residential schools. It was all based upon them looking at our people and saying "they're pagans" so if they are pagans, then they have no spirit. They had to restructure our spirits so that they can connect with their definition of spirit, their white spirit. People won't admit that. That's how it happened.[7]

One approach was to assume the land was empty with the absence of formal sovereignty and thus theirs for the taking. Terra nullius has been used frequently to describe this approach although

---

7   Mike Cachagee, personal communication, January 15, 2012.

the term itself was not applied until much later.[8] What is important to acknowledge is that the relationship changed from one of usefulness to one of domination intended to enslave, assimilate or "kill the Indian in him, and save the man."[9]

Subsequent signed treaties between the settlers and Indigenous nations were to guarantee that the settlers would share and "take care of the land."[10] Anishinaabe oral tradition indicates that the settlers were expected to carry on this sacred trust of the land much like the Indigenous peoples who fostered a sacred reciprocal relationship with their "Mother" who is Mother Earth. She takes care of her children as her children take care of her—taking only what is needed from the plants and animals and leaving enough to regenerate.[11] Further, John Borrows, an Anishinaabe legal scholar, affirms that according to Elders in Saskatchewan, the negotiated treaties "flowed from a

8 Terra Nullius is one concept emerging out of the "doctrine of discovery." Recent discussion suggests that this term has been used without an understanding of its origins. For more information see Andrew Fitzmaurice's "The genealogy of Terra Nullius," *Australian Historical Studies* 38, no. 129 (2007): 1-15.
9 See Richard Henry Pratt, "The Advantages of Mingling Indians with Whites," in *Americanizing the American Indians: Writings by the "Friends of the Indian" 1880–1900*, ed. Francis Paul Prucha (Cambridge: Harvard University Press, 1973), 261; and John S. Milloy, *A National Crime: The Canadian Government and the Residential School System, 1879 to 1986* (Winnipeg: University of Manitoba Press, 1999), 27.
10 Robart A. Williams Jr., *Linking Arms Together: American Indian Treaty Visions of Law and Peace, 1600-1800* (New York: Oxford University Press, 1997), 46-47; and Leilani Holmes, "Heart Knowledge, Blood Memory, and the Voice of the Land: Implications of Research among Hawaiian Elders," in *Indigenous Knowledges in Global Contexts: Multiple Readings of Our World*, edited by George J. Sefa Dei et al., (Toronto: University of Toronto Press, 2000) 44. Also see Canada, Royal Commission on Aboriginal Peoples, *Report of the Royal Commission on Aboriginal Peoples Volume 2: Restructuring the Relationship* (Ottawa, ON: Canada Communication Group, Part One Section One, 1996).
11 Simpson, *Dancing On Our Turtle's Back*, 109; Menno Boldt, *Surviving as Indians: The Challenge of Self-Government* (Toronto: University of Toronto Press, 1993), 40-41; and Gret Cajete, *Native Science: Natural Laws of Interdependence* (Santa Fe: Clear Light Publishers, 2000), 158.

sacred source ... [and were] legally binding promises ... made with the Creator as well as the Crown ... [and that] one law was given, Indian and white" as both needed to respect the treaty as mutual beneficiaries.[12] According to Elder Doug Williams, this sacred relationship is referred to as the "Original Instructions."[13] The settlers did not honour this agreement and severed this special relationship as they immersed themselves in individualism, capitalism, ownership and deconstruction of the land.[14]

Acting on the heels of the United States in promoting settlement and civilization through the Methodist religion, the Canadian government in 1830, officially adopted a similar policy of civilization and Christianization towards the Indigenous peoples.[15] Their primary goal was to move the populations to reserves and convert their monetary annuals to tools and other instruments to push them towards farming. The Indigenous people were forced to embrace Christianity and a new way of life.

Also by this time the tribal populations were no longer required as military allies. In 1842, Governor General Sir Charles Bagot established the Bagot Commission to thoroughly examine the operations of the Indian Department in Canada[16] and to identify recommendations. The recommendations filed in 1844 would become the foundation for the future legislated Indian Act. In 1845, the government tabled a report in the Upper Canada legislative assembly recommending that schools be set up to educate Indigenous children. By 1847, Dr. Egerton Ryerson was contacted as the area head of the Methodist education. He suggested partnering with the many Churches to deliver the education services. With the passing of the

12 John Borrows, *Canada's Indigenous Constitution* (Toronto: University of Toronto Press, 2010), 25-26.
13 Doug Williams, personal communication, September 23, 2007.
14 James Rodger Miller, *Skyscrapers Hide the Heavens: A History of Indian-White Relations in Canada* (Toronto: University of Toronto Press, 1989), 15.
15 Milloy, *A National Crime*.
16 Today this department is currently known as the Indigenous Affairs and Northern Affairs Canada.

British North America Act of 1867, the federal government retained the right to deliver education to the First Nations populations and First Nations day schools were built.[17]

In order to complete the plan of aggressive assimilation of the Indigenous population in the Province of Canada, the legislature in 1857 passed the Gradual Civilization Act. According to John Milloy:

> The Act was a straightforward solution to the developmental problem facing the Department in the mid-1850s. It circumvented the tribal position on reserve land and reformulated the civilizing system by providing a place for Aboriginal people within colonial society. Any male judged to be "sufficiently advanced in the elementary branches of education," to be of good character and free from debt could, on application, be awarded fifty acres of land "and the rights accompanying it." He would be enfranchised, relinquishing tribal affiliation and "any claim to any further share in the lands or moneys then belonging to or reserved for the use of his tribe and [would] cease to have a voice in the proceeding thereof."[18] He would be thereafter a full member of colonial society.[19]

With Confederation through the British North America Act in 1867, aggressive assimilation was stepped up. This Act fully entrenched that the federal government was solely responsible for "Indians and lands reserved for Indians."[20] In 1869 Parliament through the Enfranchisement Act continued previous provisions and "introduced stronger measures that would psychologically prepare Indians for the

---

17 Deborah Chansonneuve, *Reclaiming Connections: Understanding Residential School Trauma Among Aboriginal People* (Ottawa: Aboriginal Healing Foundation, 2005).
18 As cited in Milloy from the Statute of Canada 1857, 20, Vic., c.26 10 June.
19 Milloy, *A National Crime*, 18.
20 Boldt, *Surviving as Indians*, 113.

eventual replacement of their traditional cultures and their absorption into Canadian society."[21] Subsequently the Indian Act in 1876 would cement assimilation.[22] First Nations' peoples in Canada were pushed onto reserved lands and were held captive by this legislated government racist policy. This Act "controls almost every aspect of the life of a registered Indian person."[23] According to Peter Kulchyski:

> protection, by 1927, had come to justify control. instead [sic] of implying a policy of secure land ownership for native peoples, protection had come to mean, for the government, knowing more than native peoples about what was in their best interests. this [sic] in turn justified interference in many apects of native peoples' lives, including a curtailing of basic civil liberties.[24]

The federal government, in seeking a more economical way to provide educational services to Indigenous children, and following the United States' lead of aggressive civilization, commissioned Nicholas Flood Davin to go to the United States to investigate the Indian industrial school system and report back. Impressed by the highlights of the industrial schools, Flood, upon his return, highly recommended the system and wrote in his 1879 report, "if anything is to be done with the Indian, we must catch him very young."[25] For example, Captain Richard H. Pratt, founder of the Carlisle Industrial School in Pennsylvania, worked towards the ultimate goal for the

21 Canada. Royal Commission on Aboriginal Peoples *Report of the Royal Commission on Aboriginal Peoples Volume 1: Looking Forward, Looking Back* (1996), 252.
22 For more information see http://laws-lois.justice.gc.ca/eng/acts/I-5/.
23 Patricia Monture-Angus, *Thunder in My Soul: A Mohawk Woman Speaks* (Halifax: Fernwood Publishing, 1995), 155.
24 Peter Kulchyski, *The Red Indians*, (Winnipeg: Arbeiter Ring Publishing Ltd., 2007), 104.
25 Celia Haig-Brown, *Resistance and Renewal: Surviving the Indian Residential School* (Vancouver: Arsenal Pulp Press, 1988), 26.

students attending the schools as "into civilization and citizenship"[26] and explained that Indians were equal, deserving to take their place amongst the *zhaaganaash* or white population and not be held captive on reservations after they had proven their worth. He thought that this could be accomplished by attending off reservation industrial schools to learn a trade whereby students were farmed out as cheap labour for farmers.

The schools would be built away from the reserves with the primary goal to "be the culmination of an education deliberately designed to sever young Indians' connections with their ancestral culture."[27] Pratt had envisioned that if the children moved off the reservation and lived civilized lives in society that the parents would follow. Roland Chrisjohn, Sherri Young and Michael Maraun called this cultural genocide and gave an example of why the British adopted this policy of assimilation in trying to solve the Indian problem. Their example explained how the British cast their "imperial aspirations [against] . . . the descendants of the Indigenous Celtic tribes of the so-called British Isles: the Welsh, the Irish, and the Scots"[28] and therefore contend that the residential school policy was a well-tested practice and that the Canadian government of the day knew full well the implications of the boarding school system.

The schools were part of this assimilation policy that worked with the various religious institutions that hoped to envelop and "make whitemen" of all Indigenous peoples.[29] Viewed as primitive,

---

26 Richard Henry Pratt, *Battlefield and Classroom: Four Decades with the American Indian, 1867-1904* (Norman: University of Oklahoma Press, 2003), 294.
27 Brian Titley, *A Narrow Vision: Duncan Campbell Scott and the Administration of Indian Affairs in Canada* (Vancouver: UBC Press, 1986), 78.
28 Roland Chrisjohn et al., *The Circle Game: Shadows and Substance in the Indian Residential School Experience in Canada*. (Penticton: Theytus Books, Ltd., 2006), 82.
29 As cited in Milloy, 174.

inferior[30] and savage, the Indigenous people were forced to take on the lifestyle and imagination of the colonial, oppressive government of the day, and bow to their ways of justice, consumption, industry, health, education, and general state of being. The Indian agent was the primary conduit to ensure that very young students were sent to participate in the Indian Residential School experiment.

Children were forcibly taken from their homes. Some were loaded onto trucks like cattle every fall. "Most people now refer to this truck as the cattle truck, but at that time it was called the school truck."[31] Some would travel long distances by boat, car or train to reach the residential school. After 1945, to further oppress the First Nations peoples, the parents were told by the various agents of the government that if they did not allow their children to be taken it would "result in the immediate cancellation of the allowance"[32] and/or they were threatened that the Royal Canadian Mounted Police (RCMP) would be called and they would be arrested and/or imprisoned.

The legacy of Indian residential schools remains a black mark on the landscape of Canada. In keeping with the criteria outlined in the Residential School Settlement Agreement[33] which initially was launched as a lawsuit on behalf of the survivors, the Prime Minister of Canada, on June 11, 2008, issued a formal apology "to former students, their families, and communities for Canada's role in the operation of the residential schools"[34] Additional criteria of the settlement led

---

30 Vandana Shiva, "Foreword: Cultural Diversity and the Politics of Knowledge," in *Indigenous Knowledges in Global Contexts: Multiple Readings of Our World*, ed. George J. Sefa Dei et al. (Toronto: University of Toronto Press, 2000), vii; and David Maybury-Lewis *Indigenous Peoples, Ethnic Groups, and the State*. (Needham Heights: Allyn and Bacon, 1997).
31 Haig-Brown, *Resistance and Renewal*, 43.
32 James Rodger Miller, *Shingwauk's Vision: A History of Native Residential Schools* (Toronto: University of Toronto Press, 1996), 170.
33 For more information see http://www.residentialschoolsettlement.ca/english.html.
34 http://www.trc.ca/about-us.html.

to the establishment of the Truth and Reconciliation Commission (TRC) through which survivors offered testimony about their school experience so that the truth would be told. According to the TRC's 2012 Interim Report, "Generations of children were traumatized by the experience.[35] The TRC has now made 94 recommendations, or "calls to action" as part of its findings.[36] We may always be on the crest of knowing elusive information.

Reclamation of Spirit

The Royal Commission on Aboriginal Peoples was a way to renew the relationship between Indigenous peoples and the people of Canada. This 1996 report provided information and testimony from Indigenous peoples on all aspects of their lives and, in particular, offered a scathing picture of the residential school experience. The formation of the AHF would follow with several publications and healing initiatives. The AHF described their vision as:

> Our vision is of all who are affected by the legacy of physical, sexual, mental, cultural, and spiritual abuses in the Indian residential schools having addressed, in a comprehensive and meaningful way, unresolved trauma, putting to an end the intergenerational cycles of abuse, achieving reconciliation in the full range of relationships, and enhancing their capacity as individuals, families, communities, nations, and peoples to sustain their well being.[37]

---

35 Truth and Reconciliation Commission of Canada. *Truth and Reconciliation Commission of Canada: Interim report* (2012), 1. Accessed at http://www.trc.ca/websites/trcinstitution/index.php?p=580. For more information see http://www.residentialschoolsettlement.ca/english.html.
36 A document of the TRC's 94 calls to action can be found at http://trc.ca/assets/pdf/Calls_to_Action_English2.pdf.
37 Retrieved August 21, 2011 from http://www.ahf.ca/about-us/mission.

The work of the RCAP was in part the foundation for reclaiming our cultural practices, traditions, identity and our voices. As Jan Longboat, Mohawk, Turtle Clan of Six Nations of the Grand River, says:

> Culture is only three things: land-based, language-based, and a social structure and everything we do fits into one of these structures. If one of those is taken away, there is no culture. We must protect our land, language, and social structures; that's where our ceremonies come in, walking the good road. It is all part of reclaiming who we are as a people. It is a reclamation.[38]

During the RCAPs' proceedings an Elder was recorded as saying:

> One of the things that we found out ... as we talked with many different groups, is the common motif that occurs all over the place which makes reference to Turtle Island. Turtle Island encompasses the whole North American continent, Ellesmere Island in the north representing the head, Labrador representing one of the flippers, Florida another flipper, Mexico the tail, California another flipper, Alaska another flipper, and then the shell is divided into 13 areas. There is this custodian in each area—and we belong to one of them. In our language we use the word Shoo-pii to describe the Turtle, which means an area which is high. This area that you are in right now, what we have here is that the water flows off in all directions from this area, which represents the high spot. All these areas, as in the live turtle, are what represents our sacred constitution, the Constitution of Turtle Island ... This Constitution has been there for a long time. It still exists. We can still utilize it, which we do.

---

38 Jan Longboat, personal communication, February 10, 2012.

> It has its own legal system; it has its own economic system; it has its own education; it has its own philosophy; it has its own language; it has its own logic. We can utilize those things. We have been doing it for the last 500 years. It's nothing new. It is something that, if more people realized what it was and realized it's not a threat, it's who we are, it's what we are, it is something that is very real and we can use it. I use it every day.
>
> STAN KNOWLTON, SIK-OOH-KOTOKI FRIENDSHIP SOCIETY
> LETHBRIDGE, ALBERTA, 25 MAY 1993

Elder Stan Knowlton gives us direction to reaffirm the Constitution of Turtle Island. Duran and Duran posit that as Indigenous people we "must struggle to recapture our own mode of representation and go beyond Eurocentric stereotypes to invent a postcolonial identity imagining ourselves richly."[39] Will the return to our cultural identity be the key to restoration? Leanne Simpson would say yes, "Recovering and maintaining Indigenous world views and applying those teachings in a contemporary context represents a network of emancipatory strategies Indigenous Peoples can employ to disentangle themselves from the oppressive control of occupying state governments.[40] Simpson also acknowledges the words of Linda Tuhiwai Smith:

> Restoring is a project which is conceived as a holistic approach to problem solving. It is holistic in terms of the emotional, spiritual and physical nexus, and also in the terms of the individual and the collective, the political and the cultural ... The restoring of wellbeing spiritually, emotionally, physically and materially has involved social workers and

---

39 Eduardo Duran and Bonnie Duran, *Native American Postcolonial Psychology* (Albany: State University of New York Press, 1995), 136.
40 Simpson, *Lighting the Eighth Fire*, 15.

health workers in a range of initiatives ... Restorative programmes are based on a model of healing rather than of punishing ... Restorative justice in Canada, for example, applies concepts of the "healing circle" and victim restoration which are based on indigenous processes.[41]

Furthermore, Smith in discussing "reclaiming, reformulating and reconstituting indigenous cultures and languages" highlights several approaches, including claiming our histories, oral testimonies of our experiences, reclaiming our stories and revitalizing our ceremonies and languages.[42] For example, "Indigenous testimonies are a way of talking about an extremely painful event or series of events."[43] This reclaiming process reminds me of the healing/talking circles in which the survivors participate.

Reclamation means that the voices of the survivors which were absent and silenced for far too long needed to emerge. One example is the 1994 report of the Assembly of First Nations titled *"Breaking the Silence: An Interpretive Study of Residential School Impact and Healing as Illustrated by the Stories of First Nations Individuals."* The Report's purpose was "to understand the impact of residential schools on First Nation individuals, families, and communities, and to explore ways to heal the wounded First Nation people who live and work in their communities"[44] and it was based on an interpretive study of thirteen survivors. Although the report was considered ground-breaking at that time, it has since gone off into oblivion, hardly ever referenced.

41 Linda Tuhiwai Smith, *Decolonizing Methodologies: Research and Indigenous Peoples*. New York: Zed Books Ltd., 1999), 155.
42 Ibid., 142.
43 Ibid., 144.
44 Assembly of First Nations, *Breaking the Silence: An Interpretive Study of Residential School Impact and Healing as Illustrated by the Stories of First Nations Individuals* (Ottawa, ON: First Nations Health Commission), 1.

In addition to the above report, other publications followed that dealt with the legacy and documented survivor stories from an arms length perspective.[45] There are also other publications written by the residential school survivors. These works detail personal testimonies of being forced to leave their families and being separated from siblings while at school, blatant racism, acts of abuse and corporal punishment. As Mary Fortier says, "It was a decimation of my individuality."[46] As Robert Matthew says, "The real strength of the survivors of the residential schools can be found in their stories."[47] The voices of some of these survivors will resonate later.

---

45 See Miller, *Shingwauk's Vision*; Agnes Grant, *No End of Grief: Indian Residential Schools in Canada* (Winnipeg: Pemmican Publications, 1996); Milloy, *A National Crime*; Agnes Jack, *Behind Closed Doors: Stories from the Kamloops Indian Residential School* (Michigan: The University of Michigan; Secwepemc Cultural Education Society, 2006); Jan Kahehti:io Longboat *Idawadadi, December 1999 – March 2010: Coming Home, Stories of Residential School Survivors with Contributions by Aboriginal Women* (Ottawa: Aboriginal Healing Foundation, 2010); *Speaking My Truth: Reflections on Reconciliation and Residential School*, an AHF publication (2012); and Canada, *Aboriginal Peoples, and Residential Schools They Came for the Children*, and *Truth and Reconciliation Commission of Canada: Interim Report* both by the Truth and Reconciliation Commission of Canada (2012).

46 Mary Fortier, *A Survivor's Story of the Boarding School Syndrome* (Belleville: Epic Publishing, 2002), 178.

47 Cited in Jack, viii. Additional examples of this reclamation include Shirley Sterling's *My Name is Seepeetza*; Isabelle Knockwood, *Out of the Depths: The Experiences of Mi'kmaw Children at the Indian Residential School at Shubenacadie, Nova Scotia*; Basil Johnston, *Indian School Days*; Mary Fortier, *Behind Closed Doors: A Survivor's Story of the Boarding School Syndrome*; Enos Whiteye, *A Dark Legacy: A Primer on Indian Residential Schools in Canada*; Madeline Dion Stout and Gregory Kipling, *Aboriginal People, Resilience and the Residential School Legacy*; Tim Giago, *Children Left Behind: The Dark Legacy of Indian Mission Boarding Schools*; Roland Christjohn et al., *The Circle Game: Shadows and Substance in the Indian Residential School Experience in Canada*; Alice Blondin-Perrin, *My Heart Shook Like a Drum: What I Learned at the Indian Mission Schools, Northwest Territories*; and Cliff Standingready, Standing Buffalo Warrior's *Children of the Creator*.

There are also documentaries and films written or directed by descendants of survivors such as *Celebrating Survival: A Tribute to the Residential School Survivors of Walpole Island First Nation*, by the Wallaceburg District Secondary School Future Elders Program, 2009.[48] More recently another documentary, *Silent Thunder: The Search for Truth and Reconciliation* by Dave McGowan and produced by CHEX TV highlights interviews with three former students of Ontario's Residential Schools, as well as members of the Truth and Reconciliation Commission to discuss the impact the schools had on their lives.

Finally, two documents *Minishenhying Anishnaabe-aki: Walpole Island: The Soul of Indian Territory* (1987) and *Gaagnig Pane Chiyaayong: Forever We Will Remain: A Report on the Memorial Wall Project* (2002) provided me with two essential histories: the history of the territory and the history of my project partner, the Walpole Island Residential School Survivors Group. For me, there is no comparison to listening to the survivors speak about the history, their experiences and the legacy. The expression of emotion experienced by the survivor and the emotion experienced by me as the listener, can never be matched in reading accounts.

We now continue this journey to learn the essence of Chief Shingwauk's vision and the unfolding legacy of the Shingwauk Indian Residential School. We will begin by learning about the development of the Shingwauk Indian Residential School and the school's alumni, and the activities that led to their association and the development of their affiliate the WIRSSG.

---

48 See also *Muffins for Granny*, a film directed by Nadia McLaren (2008), and *Last Call Indian*, a documentary directed by Sonia Bonspille Boileau (2010). *Where the Spirit Lives* written by Keith Ross Leckie and directed by Bruce Pittman (1989) is another film, although it was not written or directed by descendants of survivors.

Shingwauk Indian Residential School and Survivors

Shingwauk Indian Residential School grew out of a special vision very different from other residential schools. Janet Chute documented that "Chief Shingwaukonce, also known as Shingwauk or 'Little Pine'" (1773-1854), was a wise and politically astute leader of Garden River First Nation which is located near Sault Ste. Marie, Ontario.[49] He prophesied the coming of settlers who would land on the shores of Turtle Island and settle in the Anishinaabek territory.[50] Having "... fought alongside Tecumseh and Brock against the Americans in the war of 1812-14,"[51] he knew in order to compete and communicate with the settlers, his people would have to learn to read and write. "After the peace, he developed a new strategy of Aboriginal rights and self-determination for his people."[52] His vision was a teaching wigwam, which he easily shared and communicated to his people.[53] "Through 'treaties' and 'teaching wigwams' he urged peaceful co-existence and partnership between Europeans and the Anishnabek."[54]

The first "teaching wigwam" was the Shingwauk Home for Boys founded in 1834. Little Pine eventually walked from Bawating (Sault Ste. Marie) to York (Toronto) to petition the then Lieutenant Governor Colborne for teachers to teach his people reading and writing while still retaining their own language and culture. Chief Shingwauk became a

---

49 Janet Chute, *The Legacy of Shingwaukonse: A Century of Native Leadership* (Toronto: University of Toronto Press, 1998), 3.
50 The Anishinaabek territory stretches from the southwest, Aamjiwnaang First Nation near Sarnia to the Northeast to Nipissing First Nation, further northeast to Pikwakanagan near Pembroke to northwest, Fort William First Nation near Thunder Bay. The area is represented by the Union of Ontario Indians political organization and encompasses 39 First Nations with a population size of 55,000 people (Union of the Ontario Indians, 2010).
51 Retrieved from http://www.shingwauk.auc.ca/shingwauktrust/shingwauktrust2.html.
52 *The Sault Star*, June 18, 1992.
53 Chute, *The Legacy of Shingwaukonse*.
54 *The Sault Star*, June 18, 1992.

devout Anglican, to ensure support, and bonded with the missionary Reverend Edward Wilson, who at first did not believe or agree with Shingwauk's vision.[55]

In 1873, Shingwauk's sons Chief Augustin Shingwauk and Chief Henry Buhkwuijene, along with Reverend Edward Wilson, built Shingwauk Home for Native Children at Garden River. The building burned down six days later.[56] Arson was rumoured by band members opposed to English schooling.[57] The following year Reverend Wilson purchased 90 acres of land within the limits of Sault Ste. Marie, Ontario and rebuilt the Shingwauk Home. In 1874, the second Shingwauk Home was completed and opened in August with fifty male students.

In 1877, another school was built for girls and named the Wawanosh Home. The girls from the Wawanosh Home were moved into an extension built onto Shingwauk Home in 1911. This brought the number of students to 75. Following a dispute with the Anglican Church, Wilson left the province and deeded the land to the Anglican Church under the explicit condition that the property was to be held in permanent trust for the education of Native youth.[58]

A day in the life of a Shingwauk student consisted of a half a day of academic studies and the other half learning trades (e.g., tailoring, carpentry, shoemaking, domestics). "These trades were considered quite important for the students to survive in the main-stream of Canadian society."[59]

In 1935, the existing brick building was constructed on the Shingwauk site to replace the original stone building. In 1956, the Anna McCrea Public School was built and opened on the Shingwauk

---

55 Chute, *The Legacy of Shingwaukonse*, 193.
56 Shingwauk Project, 1980, 3.
57 Jean Manore, "A Vision of Trust: The Legal, Moral, and Spiritual Foundations of Shingwauk Hall," *Native Studies Review* 9, no. 2 (1993-1994): 7.
58 Ibid., 2.
59 Retrieved from http://www.shingwauk.auc.ca/welcome_index.html.

site and a year later, the Sir James Dunn Secondary School was constructed and opened. In 1970, the Shingwauk Indian Residential School closed and Algoma University College moved into the main building appropriately titled Shingwauk Hall.

Shingwauk Reunion

In 1979, Elder Dan Pine Sr., a descendant of Chief Shingwauk and a former Chief of Garden River First Nation realized that there were changes that needed to be addressed at the former site of the Shingwauk Indian Residential School. Dan, along with then Garden River Chief Ron Boissoneau asked Don Jackson, a professor at Algoma University College, to help them realize Shingwauk's vision. In answer to the Elder's call, a former Shingwauk School student suggested that there be a reunion for the former Shingwauk Indian Residential School students. As a result, the Shingwauk Reunion was planned in 1981. Elder Pine's instructions were to "bring them together and they will know what to do . . . they have to put back what they have taken away."[60] The "they" Elder Pine referred to is the Anglican Church and the federal government and this has been the mindset of the former Shingwauk students as well.

Residential schools were likened to "total institutions,"[61] "forcing houses for changing persons"[62] with institutional tactics such as extreme power relations between inmates and supervisory staff. For many of the former students, the memory of their residential school experience was a horrible experience and the thought of returning to

---

60 Don Jackson, "The Shingwauk Project Archives: The Residential School Legacy and the Canadian Narrative," a talk prepared for the Archives Association of Ontario Annual Conference (Sault Ste. Marie, ON: Algoma University, 2005), 2.
61 Assembly of First Nations, *Breaking the Silence*, 164.
62 Erving Goffman, *Asylums: Essays on the Social Situation of Mental Patients and Other Inmates* (Garden City: Anchor Books, 1961), 12.

relive such a time was inconceivable. Some students were outraged but some were excited. When it was suggested that the Shingwauk students come together at a gathering, many of the former students gasped! Undeterred, the organizers, all Algoma University students and one faculty member, set about organizing the first Shingwauk Indian Residential School Reunion.[63]

After the 1981 Reunion, when the former students returned to their home communities, word spread quickly that the Shingwauk Reunion had been an excellent idea and enjoyable experience. Others were disappointed they had not taken the opportunity to attend. But, they admitted, no one knew what to expect, were leery and waited to hear from others about the reunion experience. "There is no doubt in my mind that I was reborn in 1981."[64] Agnes Grant acknowledges in her book, *No End of Grief: Indian Residential Schools in Canada* that "a camaraderie that goes deeper than mere friendship is evident among survivors of the schools. As students were cut off from their family, they turned to their peers for comfort; these ties have lasted a lifetime."[65] The late Susie Jones said that "it goes much deeper than camaraderie, we were Shingwauk brothers and sisters from our shared experience."[66]

Another call went out to gather for a second Shingwauk Reunion in 1991, but it was different this time. The former students had taken control of what needed to be done and formed a reunion committee to plan the events for their time back at their former home. When the scheduled agenda was printed up it included the opportunity for the students to share their feelings and give personal testimonies through healing circles during this three-day celebration. Children and grandchildren of the former students took the opportunity to go into the talking circle along with former staff of the Shingwauk School.

63 Don Jackson, personal communication, September 20, 1999.
64 Susie Jones, personal communication, April 26, 2000.
65 Grant, *No End of Grief*, 277.
66 Susie Jones, personal communication, September 21, 2002.

There were times when it was tense. For example, one survivor found himself in a talking circle with his abuser and he was angry. For some of the survivors this was the first time they were able to seek help for their grief and residual anger. The Anglican lay members voiced their concerns that they had nowhere to go to debrief and that not all Shingwauk staff should be blamed for all the injustices.

In 1993 the Shingwauk group turned their focus to healing and held the first of two Three Day Healing Circles. Students from other schools (Spanish, Brantford and Sioux Lookout) came, feasted and there was the offer of the sweat lodge. For me, I remember, this was an intense dark time and it was at this Circle that I made my commitment to this group. Hearing the stories of suffering touched me. Their courage touched my soul and motivated me to make sure that they were treated with the dignity and respect that they so richly deserved.

The Children of Shingwauk Alumni Association

Another reunion was held in 1996 and former students and families from other residential schools, including Chapleau, Moose Factory, and Fort George in Ontario began coming to the reunions. Different survivors on their healing journey would welcome newcomers at the reunions. On the last day of the 1996 reunion, the Children of Shingwauk Alumni Association (CSAA) was officially formed. This new association issued a declaration reiterating that they were the primary beneficiaries of the spirit of the Shingwauk site with a reaffirmation indicating that they were one of the major stakeholders on the site. Could this be the reawakening of Chief Shingwauk's vision?

At the same time during this reunion, a number of individuals came forward and formed the core executive council that was designated to speak on behalf of the new CSAA. The executive members would act as representatives of the group in communicating awareness of Indian Residential School issues, give interviews when requested, provide input to write proposals, and assume responsibility as volunteers to chart a future course for the Association. In attending reunions and reconnecting as the Shingwauk Alumni and Family, they had found a sense of belonging and developed a relationship of strength with core goals and objectives and a collective responsibility. Linda Smith acknowledges that:

> ... to be connected is to be whole ... connecting members of families with each other ... connecting people to their traditional lands through the restoration of specific rituals and practices ... is about establishing good relations ... is related to issues of identity and place, to spiritual relationships and community wellbeing.[67]

The Shingwauk Alumni have many dreams. Foremost in their collective minds was to see the CSAA continue as an organization functioning with an office and visitor center where alumni and their families can come and look at the photo albums, and hopefully make new happy memories. They may view other photo collections that have been preserved over the past forty years. They also want their important work to continue especially their healing initiatives that would see the continuation of the reunions and the development of curricula for Shingwauk University. They would like to establish a national centre to house the collections archived at Algoma University. And last, they would like to see the fulfillment of Chief Shingwauk's vision as this has been the main motivator for their work. This has always been a shared vision and goal of the Alumni and they have persevered and never wavered from this goal. The Shingwauk Alumni have asked that Algoma University change the university's name to Shingwauk University.

By returning to the site of the school, the survivors faced their fears and grieved and mourned their losses. As Mike Cachagee says, the survivors "saw that there was no boogeyman hiding underneath

---

67 Linda Tuhiwai Smith, *Decolonizing Methodologies*, 148-149.

the bed."[68] They celebrated their survival by returning and reconnecting with their Shingwauk Family members. They brought with them their own children and grandchildren so that they could meet and share the new more positive experiences plus gain knowledge and awareness of the bad experiences. They introduced a new generation to the truth but with a different sense of awareness. The survivors' children held their own anger and I had heard the same feelings over and over again how they felt the government should send each and every survivor a letter of apology. Many former students did not share their life experiences with their children, parents or relatives. Some of them buried their hurt deep inside and never recovered.

> Thinking of the experimental implanted surgery that was done to me while at Shingwauk for what reason—I don't know. Apparently, I am not resilient. What I accomplished in my life so far had nothing to do with recovering from the shock or permanent effects. I have never recovered. (William, October 5, 2010).

The three-day healing circles were conducted away from the original school site, one in the Garden River First Nation Community Centre in 1993 and the second one, in 2001, at the newly constructed Dan Pine Sr. Healing Lodge in Garden River. Sweat lodge ceremonies were included. Participants came from Shingwauk and other schools. Everyone was welcomed and treated well.

The Shingwauk Alumni found within themselves what they needed to do to reclaim what the church and the government had taken away: their language, their culture and their dignity. Most important was reclaiming their life force energy or ***mnidoo bemaasing bemaadiziwin*** and completing what the late Dan Pine Sr. said needed to be done.

---

68 Mike Cachagee, personal communication, July 2, 1991.

The Alumni[69] has always been inclusive rather than exclusive and they viewed all former students as brothers and sisters whether they went to Shingwauk or not, because of their shared experiences. They also felt an enormous responsibility to the former students as not all residential schools were organizing or holding reunions to facilitate healing. Not everyone was ready to begin the journey. Healing practices were offered and never pushed on anyone, as the responsibility to heal always lies with the individual. The Alumni acted as the conduit when they were called upon to help in whatever capacity they were needed. My paid employment ended with the CSAA in 2003 but not my relationship. Over the years, I have continued to provide information to them and have helped with funding proposals and they have asked me to write a book about the history and evolution of their organization.

Now that the development of the Shingwauk vision and the formation and mission of the CSAA have been summarized, we can focus our attention on the specific group of survivors, an offspring of the CSAA that formed as a result of the CSAA. The group that I am referring to are the Walpole Island Residential Schools Survivors Group (WIRSSG), a community group.

The Walpole Island Residential Schools Survivors Group

With funding from the AHF, a group of Indian residential school survivors facilitated an Indian Residential School Conference at WIFN, February 4-6, 2000. Walpole Island (Bkejwanong Territory) is situated 20 minutes south of Sarnia, Ontario (see Figure 5). Many of the group had attended the Shingwauk School reunions held in 1981, 1991, and 1996 at Sault Ste. Marie, Ontario. The conference entitled

---

69 Alumni means all the members of the CSAA unless otherwise indicated.

"Maam'pee Day'aaw'meh Kay'ah'beh," (We Are Still Here)[70] resulted in the formation of the "Walpole Island Residential Schools Survivors Group [which] . . . is composed of former students who attended various residential schools throughout Canada."[71] The lead person/spokesperson for this organization was Susie Jones.

Initially the group came together to talk and to share companionship.[72] The group decided to construct a memorial wall to recognize and remember the former students of the residential schools. The names of all the people from their community who attended residential schools would be inscribed on the wall. A proposal was developed and submitted to the AHF. There were five purposes for building the Memorial Wall. First, the group believed that the Wall would "continue to create awareness about Residential Schools."[73] Second, the Wall would continue to educate the citizens of [the] neighbouring communities who visit the Island to view historical monuments. Hopefully, this new 'wall' will always lead visitors to ask for more information on residential schools and the experiences of Aboriginal people who attended them. Third, the group hoped that the wall would help "build community capacities under [the] New Structure for Social Services using [the] current programs and resources"[74] because the effects and the legacy of residential schools are still felt in the community and will continue for several more generations. Fourth, the Memorial Wall would be an everlasting reminder of what Walpole Island residents have endured and fifth, would explain an often "misunderstood and forgotten chapter in Canadian and American history."[75]

---

70 Uriah Dodge, *Gaagnig Pane Chiyaayong: Forever We Will Remain. A Report on the Memorial Wall Project* (Walpole Island First Nation, 2002), 1.
71 Ibid., 1.
72 Ibid., 2.
73 Ibid., 1.
74 Dodge, *Gaagnig Pane Chiyaayong*, 1.
75 Ibid., 2.

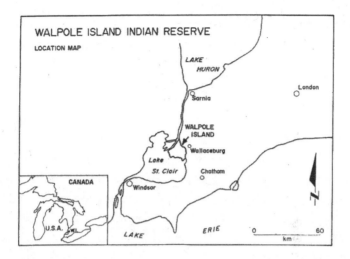

Figure 5. Walpole Island.[76]

Further, there are other memorials on Walpole Island, for example the Anishinaabe leader Tecumseh's bones are encased in a cairn on Walpole Island. The Report on the Memorial Wall Project notes that the residents at Walpole Island have a major connection with residential schools. Shingwauk School lists the first WIFN band member as a student as early as 1874. The Mohawk Institute Residential School at Brantford, Ontario lists two Walpole Island band members as early as 1833. This process continued well up into the 1960s.

Shingwauk Indian Residential School closed in 1969-70. The school had operated for almost one hundred years. Shingwauk School registered 370 students or 69% of Walpole Island's students.[77] In total 534 Walpole Island children passed through seven residential schools with many of the students attending more than one residential school.

---

76 This map appears courtesy of Dean Jacobs, Director and Consultation Manager of the Walpole Island First Nation Heritage Centre.
77 Ibid., 5.

In 2002, approximately "one hundred and fifty (150) [former students were] still alive."[78] These figures were compiled with the efforts of many people including volunteers, the former students and archival documents from the Shingwauk Project, the former Mohawk Institute, biographical information, and medical records.

The documentation of names was undertaken with great care. Some of the surviving former students did not want their names on the Memorial Wall and those wishes were respected. If need be, additional names can be added later. As more information continues to come forward from the Indian Affairs files, more names will be known. During the awareness conference in 2000, the organizers distributed surveys: 100 surveys were handed out with 66 completed. It was estimated that out of the 225 people who attended the conference, 50 were former students of residential schools. One of the questions in the survey asked about what direction the community should take in the creation of awareness of the legacy of residential schools. Most respondents replied that they would like to see a working group formed to promote awareness of residential schools.

Second, they wanted to see another awareness conference regarding residential schools, and third, they wanted to see a community healing circle.[79] Presently, the WIRSSG fulfills the first goal as representatives of the WIRSSG are invited to conferences and schools to speak about the legacy of residential schools. The group meets on a regular basis and is involved with students who attend Western University. I felt deeply blessed that they honour me in partnership in the completion of this journey.

As I previously mentioned this is a brief overview of the policies and legislation that led to residential schools. There is certainly much more to Anishinaabe history within Turtle Island although that is beyond the scope of this work. As we move forward, we will

78 Ibid.
79 Dodge, *Gaagnig Pane Chiyaayong*.

learn about resiliency, resilience and resiliency theory and begin to explore resiliency from the perspective of the survivors. Having said that, I am reminded of the words of the late Susie Jones, "I believe that historically we have been resilient just as a people."[80] This is a profound, true statement that has been proven for all Indigenous peoples globally, but I believe especially the Anishinaabek[81] people living on Turtle Island.

---

80 Susie Jones, personal conversation, October 2, 2010.
81 Anishinaabek is spelled differently throughout this document depending on who is speaking. When I use the word which is the plural of Anishinaabe, I spell it Anishinaabek.

CHAPTER 4

Understanding Life Force Energy

"Nsastamowin mnidoo bemaasing bemaadiziwin"

> "There is much to learn but even more to understand."
> —DR. THERESA TURMEL

I remember Susie Jones telling me that in her travels and work concerning residential school groups and events, she kept hearing the word 'resiliency.' It was the new buzzword to describe the survivors of the residential school system. In this chapter, I explore resiliency and resilience, resiliency theory, and discuss its relevance to Anishinaabe peoples. This exploration uses three approaches. The first method employed a search of the literature on: resiliency, resilience, resiliency theory in Canada and the United States. This strategy included searches in Google Scholar, ProQuest Theses and Dissertations, and Scholars' Portal with a date restriction of 1998-2011 and a language restriction of English. The second method explored views by Indigenous residential school survivors in print and video in North America, and in particular the publications of the RCAP and the AHF. Additional sources were also identified via citations offered in reference sections of documents as well as sources identified in conversation with survivors and colleagues. Most important were the interviews with the WIRSSG residential school survivors that form the heart of this work.

After I completed my search and findings I defined my learnings and and juxtaposed it to the energy I observed when I worked with the survivors. I begin with a wonderful story from Elder Shirley Williams, a Survivor of St. Joseph's Residential School who described a quilt piece she created.

> This is my story of how I maintained my resilience while I was at St. Joseph's Residential School in Spanish, Ontario. My father used to give me two dollars at the beginning of September and that two dollars used to keep me in money until April, then I would say that I was broke. At the school we had store hours once a month if we all behaved. The store had candies, chocolate bars, and jelly beans. Jelly beans were the cheapest to buy because one could buy five jelly beans for a penny! So, I would get jelly beans for my comfort food. Whenever my true friends or I got sick or lonely or if we got a scolding or strapping for speaking our language, one of the things that I did was get my bag of jelly beans. I would get my true friends together and we would gather outside somewhere and then we would circle around each other and share one jelly bean. This jelly bean had to be eaten and bitten equally by us! None would bite more than the other but shared equally to wipe away our hurts.
>
> After sharing our jelly bean then we could wipe our hurts or loneliness and we would become strong again and able to laugh and to go on functioning in the school. We would tell ourselves that this is just for a time till we would be 16 years old and we would be free to leave here! I used embroidery work to sew my piece (see Figure 6). There are three girls that I remember that I was close with, Mary Ann, Mary Elizabeth and Louise from Gchi-minising. One of the girls has tears dripping from her face. The dresses we wore were grey or sometimes blue. The bag that I am holding is

full of jelly beans and like I said if one of my friends got hurt or lonely, we would get together to share this candy. The lines represent the sharing of hurt, the strength we had, and how we helped to nurture one another. From the sharing, we were able to survive and give caring to each other. The fence represents how we were locked up and the broken green line represents the lack of kindness, love and emotional support that we needed in order to grow mentally well. The yellow lines also represent the spiritual growth we got from each other in order to go on within the institution.

Figure 6. Elder Shirley Williams's quilt piece.[1]

When I first heard Elder Shirley Williams tell this story and show me the quilt piece she had fashioned based on her painful experiences at residential school, I had mixed feelings. The simple act of sharing a jelly bean having the power to lift Shirley and her true friends from a place of darkness to a place of light, made me smile. At the same time, I was also reminded of the intense stories told by survivors of the loneliness they endured during their time at residential school. This jelly bean ritual was repeatedly practiced by Shirley and her

---

1   Retrieved from http://quiltinggallery.com/2009/01/22/anishinaabe-kwes-resilience/.

fellow inmates[2] and kept their hope alive with the knowledge that they could leave St. Joseph's Residential School at age sixteen. At the same time, my memories were evoked of similar stories from other survivors of the residential school.

As set out in the beginning, the goal of this work was to listen to 13 residential school survivors from Walpole Island First Nation tell their life experiences in order to understand their resiliency. Perhaps it is best to start by explaining resiliency. Initially, I was amazed by the survivors' strengths and gifts. After having learned about the life experiences and treatment that the residential school students had endured, one would expect their behaviour might be laden with bitterness, sadness, regret and anger. The people I met in July 1991 had spoken about problematic episodes in their lives, but those events did not control their lives. For me, I found the survivors enthusiastic, engaging, happy individuals ready to take on challenges with rigor and cooperation together. So, why resiliency? Upon remembering what Susie Jones had said and understanding my feelings and observations about the survivors, I knew that there was something different, an energy that sprang from the survivors. It was only later revealed to me as Anishinaabe life force energy or ***mnidoo bemaasing bemaadiziwin***. I decided that based on their staying power and ability to spring back from the adversity brought on by their residential school experiences, that understanding resiliency might be the place to start.

---

2   According to Susie Jones "some of the survivors refer to themselves as inmates" (personal communication, April 13, 2012). In addition, Titley writes in *A Narrow Vision: Duncan Campbell Scott and the Administration of Indian Affairs in Canada* that then Inspector W. M. Graham referred to the students as inmates (Titley, *A Narrow Vision*, 82).

Resiliency and Resiliency Theory

Resiliency is complex. I offer one definition of resiliency and two definitions of resilience. Glenn Richardson, a professor with the Department of Health Promotion and Education at the University of Utah, and author of "Metatheory of Resilience and Resiliency" defines resiliency "as the process of coping with diversity, change, or opportunity in a manner that results in the identification, fortification, and enrichment of resilient qualities or protective factors."[3]

According to a former Ajunnginiq Centre policy analyst, the late Marja Korhonen, resilience "means the ability to move through difficulties and maintain hope, mental wellness and positive coping methods".[4] Boris Cyrulnik, a leading proponent of the theory of resilience theory, uses sociologist and demographer Stefan Vanistendael's work to define resilience as "the ability to succeed, live and to develop in a positive and socially acceptable way, despite the stress or adversity that would normally involve a real possibility of a negative outcome."[5] Cyrulnik states "resilience is knitted. Resilience is not just something we find inside ourselves or in our environment. It is something we find midway between the two, because our individual development is always linked to our social development."[6] This resiliency is tapped whenever we experience an adversity, trauma or significant wound. Survival of the adversity, trauma or wound can turn weaknesses into strengths,[7] and more importantly, we learn to live beyond the problematic episode or event. "When we have survived the ordeal,

---

3   Glenn E. Richardson, 2002. "The metatheory of resilience and resiliency," *Journal of Clinical Psychology*, 58 no.3 (2002): 308.
4   Marja Korhonen, *Resilience: Overcoming Challenges and Moving on Positively* (Ottawa: National Aboriginal Health Organization (NAHO), Ajunnginiq Centre, 2007), ii.
5   Boris Cyrulnik, *Resilience: How Your Inner Strength Can Set You Free From the Past* (Toronto: Penguin Books, 2009), 5.
6   Ibid., 284.
7   Ibid., 283.

life tastes different ... an invisible spring allows us to bounce back from the ordeal by turning the obstacle into a trampoline, fragility into wealth, weakness into strength, and impossibilities into a set of possibilities."[8]

> The pearl inside the oyster might be the emblem of resilience. When a grain of sand gets into an oyster and is so irritating that, in order to defend itself, the oyster has to secrete a nacreous substance, the defensive reaction produces a material that is hard, shiny and precious.[9]

Cyrulnik also suggests that there is a price to be paid with resiliency. For example, when he speaks about youth in German prison camps, he states: "Their depression forced them to look for happiness. This oxymoron really is the price we have to pay for resilience"[10] and suggests that genetics has a role to play.

Richardson would likely agree with Cyrulnik that resiliency is innate and has a genetic component. He contends "ecological sources provide or trigger resilience in people. The energy or force that drives a person from survival to self-actualization maybe called quanta, chi, spirit, god, or resilience."[11] He concludes that resilience and resilient reintegration means "growth or adaptation through disruptions rather than just recover or bounce back."[12] In essence there is an "increased energy to grow, and the source of the energy, according to resiliency theory, is a spiritual source or innate resilience."[13] Based on his meta analysis, he indicates there are many theories of resiliency.

The information concerning resiliency is predominately written by non-Indigenous researchers and scholars. The emphasis is on resilience

---

8   Ibid., 286.
9   Ibid., 286.
10 Ibid., 21.
11 Richardson, "The Metatheory of Resilience and Resiliency," 315.
12 Ibid., 315.
13 Ibid., 315.

rather than resiliency although the terms are often used interchangeably. Adrian Van Breda through his work with the Military Psychological Institute, Social Work Research and Development, conducted an extensive review of the evolution of resiliency theory, including its definitions. He indicates that the field is approximately 70-80 years old. His investigation suggests that resiliency research began with "individual" resiliency with an emphasis on children, and moves toward family and subsequently, community-based resiliency.[14]

Dennis Saleebey, Professor Emeritus with the University of Kansas, builds on the work of Garmezy and defines individual resiliency as ". . . the skills, abilities, knowledge, and insight that accumulate over time as people struggle to surmount adversity and meet challenges. It is an ongoing and developing fund of energy and skill that can be used in current struggles."[15] Resiliency theory, in this context, consists of defining protective factors in families, schools, and communities that are present in the lives of successful human beings. The protective factors are juxtaposed against risk factors and compared with groups of troubled individuals. The idea is to identify ways by which individuals resist life stress. Richardson describes these protective and risk factors.

In the original form, researchers assigned protective factors (e.g., employment, hardiness, excellent fitness both physically and emotionally, positive relationships, optimism, and autonomy) and risk factors (e.g., poverty, parental discord, low socio-economic status, malnutrition, life stress, anti-social behaviour, and poor health), to a group and drew inferences from those factors for outcomes. According to Van Breda, "an individual's resilience at any moment is calculated by the ratio between the presence of protective factors and the presence of hazardous circumstances."[16]

14 Adrian Van Breda, *Resilience Theory: A Literature Review* (2001). Accessed at http://vanbreda.org/adrian/resilience/resilience2.pdf.
15 Dennis Saleebey, "The Strengths Perspectives in Social Work Practice: Extensions and Cautions," *Social Work* 41, no.3 (2003): 298.
16 Van Breda, *Resilience Theory*, 5.

For example, both Van Breda and Richardson discuss the research conducted approximately 70-80 years ago by Emmy Werner and associates. This longitudinal study followed a group of 698 biracial babies born on the Hawaiian island of Kauai, "the westernmost county of the United States."[17] The researchers initially "examin[ed] the children's vulnerability . . . their susceptibility to negative development outcomes after exposure to serious risk factors, such as perinatal stress, poverty, parental psychopathology, and disruptions of their family unit."[18] As the study continued the researchers "looked at roots of resiliency in those children who successfully coped with such biological and psychosocial risk factors and at protective factors that aided in the recovery of troubled children and youths as they made the transition into adulthood."[19]

The babies were observed during certain stages of development: age one, age two, age 10, age 18 (graduating from high school) and mid-30s. Based on the aforementioned risk factors, one third of the sample population was identified as high-risk. While two out of three of these children (n = 72) later developed serious learning problems and subsequent mental health problems, the remaining one-third became "competent, confident, and caring young adults. None [of these children] developed serious learning or behavior problems in childhood or adolescence."[20] In fact, these children were not only doing well, they had "developed a positive self-concept and an internal locus of control."[21] As a result, the researchers contended that resiliency emerges regardless of existing risk factors. Their method of assigning protective factors (strengths) and risk factors (negatives) including behaviours associated with those risk factors and comparing those with factors for success in adults became the method of choice.

17 Emmy Werner, "Risk, Resilience, and Recovery: Perspectives From the Kauai Longitudinal Study," *Development and Psychopathy*, 5 (1993): 503.
18 Emmy Werner and Ruth S. Smith in Werner, 1993, 503.
19 Ibid., 503-504.
20 Ibid., 204.
21 Ibid.

Bonnie Benard in working with youth, brought the concept of resilience to national and international audiences, and considers resilience "a universal capacity."[22] She says:

> The development of human resiliency is none other than the process of healthy human development... Distinctions between resiliency and concepts like "thriving" fail to recognize that resilience is itself normative... an innate capacity bolstered by environmental protective factors.[23]

Further, she identifies four categories of personal strengths: "social competence," "problem solving," "autonomy," and "sense of purpose."[24] Social competence, for Benard, "includes the characteristics, skills, and attitudes essential to forming relationships and positive attachments to others."[25] Similar attributes such as insightfulness and critical thinking encompass problem solving. Autonomy as defined by Benard is "the development of one's sense of self, of identity, and of power [and]... involves an ability to act independently and to feel a sense of control over one's environment."[26] Finally, a sense of purpose proposes that one's life has meaning, being alive. Benard contends that in order for youth to realize their own resilience, caregivers should explore, acknowledge and model for youth their own innate resilience. This enables them to transform risk into resilience.

Van Breda notes that the medical sociologist Aaron Antonovsky, in taking a different approach, challenged the problem-oriented or pathogenic model to health. Rather than asking "why do people get ill?" he offered a different approach, instead asking "why, when people are exposed to the same stress which causes some to become ill,

---

22 Bonnie Benard, *Resiliency: What We Have Learned* (San Francisco: WestEd, 2004), 7.
23 Ibid., 9.
24 Ibid., 13.
25 Ibid., 14.
26 Ibid., 24.

do some remain healthy?"[27] He termed this approach "salutogenesis,"[28] meaning the origin of health. Antonovsky wrote:

> ... my goal here to propose such a foundation, in terms of what I call the salutogenic model. It is, however, not a theory which focuses on "keeping people 'well'"[sic]. Rather, in that it derives from studying the strengths and the weaknesses of promotive, preventive, curative and rehabilitative ideas and practices, it is a theory of the health of that complex system, the human being.[29]

His work was a major contribution to looking at health promotion from a positive perspective.

Van Breda also indicates that researchers placed the spotlight on individual factors such as "sense of coherence, hardiness, learned resourcefulness, self-efficacy, locus of control, potency, stamina and personal causation."[30] Furthermore, he indicates the evolution to exploring the role of family as central to individual resilience was not without difficulty. For example, McCubbin and McCubbin define family resiliency:

> ... as the positive behavioral patterns and functional competence individuals and the family unit demonstrate under stressful or adverse circumstances, which determine the family's ability to recover by maintaining its integrity as a unit while ensuring, and where necessary restoring, the well-being of family members and the family unit as a whole.[31]

27 Van Breda, *Resilience Theory*, 14.
28 Ibid., 12.
29 Aaron Antonovsky, "The Salutogenic Model as a Theory to Guide Health Promotion," *Health Promotion International*, 11 no. 1 (1996): 13.
30 Van Breda, *Resilience Theory*, 54-55.
31 Marilyn A McCubbin and Hamilton I. McCubbin, "Resiliency in Families: A Conceptual Model of Family Adjustment and Adaptation in Response to Stress and Crises," in *Family Assessment: Resiliency, Coping and Adaptation: Inventories for Research and Practice*, edited by Hamilton I. McCubbin, Anne I. Thompson, and Marilyn A. McCubbin, (Madison: University of Wisconsin, 1996), 5.

Hawley and DeHann offer a similar definition and discuss family resiliency in two contexts: first, as a risk factor and second, as a protective factor. According to Charles Barnard protective factors include:

> ... a good fit between parent and child, maintenance of family rituals, proactive confrontation of problems, minimal conflict in the home during infancy, the absence of divorce during adolescence, and a productive relationship between a child and his or her mother.[32]

Van Breda explores a number of models (e.g., Hill's ABCX Model, Family Strengths, McCubbin's Resilience Model) concerning family. For example, McCubbin and McCubbin investigate family stress research and contend that there are "ten fundamental assumptions about the ecological nature of family life and intervention in family systems."[33] Those assumptions are:

- Families face hardships and changes as a natural and predictable aspect of family life over the life cycle.
- Families develop basic strengths and capabilities designed to foster the growth and development of family members and the family unit and to protect the family from major disruptions in the face of family transitions and changes.
- Families also face crises that force the family unit to change its traditional mode of functioning and adapt to the situation.
- Families develop basic and unique strengths and capabilities designed to protect the family from unexpected or nonnormative

---

32 Charles Barnard, "Resiliency: A Shift in Perception," *American Journal of Family Therapy* 22, no.2, (1994): 140-141.
33 McCubbin, Marilyn A., and Hamilton I. McCubbin. 1992. "Research utilization in social work practice of family treatment." In *Research utilization in the social sciences: Innovations for practice and administration*, edited by Anthony J. Grasso, and Irwin Epstein, 149-192. New York City: Haworth Press Inc.

stressors and strains and to foster the family's adaptation following a family crisis or major transition and change.
- Families benefit from and contribute to the network of relationships and resources in the community, particularly during periods of family stress and crisis.
- Family functioning is often characterized as predictable with shaped patterns of interpersonal behavior, which in turn are molded and maintained by intergenerational factors, situational pressures that have evolved over time, the personalities of the family members, and the normative and nonnormative events that punctuate family life throughout the life cycle.
- Family interventions can be enhanced and families supported by both a diagnostic and an evaluation process which takes the strengths, resources and capabilities in the family system as well as the deficiencies of the family system into consideration.
- Family functioning can be enhanced by interventions that target both the vulnerabilities and dysfunctional patterns of the family unit.
- Family functioning can be enhanced by interventions that target both the family's interpersonal capabilities and strengths which, if addressed, can serve as a catalyst for other family-system, wellness-promoting properties.
- Families develop and maintain internal resistance and adaptive resources, which vary in their strength and resiliency over the family life cycle but which can be influenced and enhanced to function more effectively. These resources can play a critical role in fostering successful family adjustments and adaptations even after the family unit has deteriorated to the point of exhibiting major difficulties and symptoms of dysfunction.[34]

---

34 Ibid., 155-156.

Van Breda reveals that family resiliency research addressed some of the criticisms concerning individual resiliency. Models of resiliency began to consider interpersonal and intrafamilial factors and offered the opportunity for clinical intervention. For example, "it is more possible, for instance, to develop a family's support systems, patterns of communication and cohesion, than to develop an individual's sense of coherence, hardiness or sense of self-efficacy."[35] However, while resolving some of the criticisms, the underlying assumptions were reflective of individual resiliency.

Van Breda posits that community resiliency is relatively new. According to Laurence J. Kirmayer, Megha Sehdev, Rob Whitley, Stéphane F. Dandeneau, and Colette Isaac, "Community resilience is the capacity of a community or similar group to withstand, recover from, and respond positively to a collective crisis or adversity."[36] They highlight three types of resiliency factors for communities or groups: resistance, recovery, and/or creativity.[37] This means the community or group may resist change, return to their previous state after the prolonged disruption and/or find new ways of adaptation. Although these researchers acknowledge that resiliency for Indigenous peoples can be found in community, Van Breda's observation remains true that the emphasis continues to be on identifying a number of protective factors including "extended family, religious communities, the local community, [and] the work."[38] Also included are a number of stressors including "poverty, crime, political instability, discrimination and lack of community resources."[39] This raises the concern that community resiliency models continue to revert to individual attributes and that the area remains underdeveloped. Van Breda

---

35 Van Breda, *Resilience Theory*, 139-140.
36 Laurence Kirmayer, et al., "Community Resilience: Models, Metaphors and Measures." *Journal of Aboriginal Health* 5, no.1, (2009): 72.
37 Ibid.
38 Van Breda, *Resilience Theory*, 141.
39 Ibid.

highlights that the challenge is for researchers to move beyond the "... individual aggregates as the conception of community resilience ... in order to move truly to the collective level."[40]

Finally, Van Breda briefly explores cross-cultural resilience and indicates the research is minimal. He does indicate that some of the research suggests "that there are various unique strengths and resiliencies in African families, many of which grew out of decades and centuries of oppression."[41]

According to Richardson, the next stage of evolution concerned an exploration of the resiliency process. Researchers made assumptions about dysfunctional processes for individuals—identified those who fit those assumptions, and assessed how those individuals overcame the obstacles. For example, as discussed by Cyrulnik:

> According to resilience theory, the damage is done by external rather than internal factors, but the ego that experiences it must still be in control of the emotional upheaval it causes. When the organism suffers emotional damage as a result of social violence or the mental violence inflicted by other people, stress is part of the shock. The stress is usually chronic, and its insidious effect damages both the organism and the psyche, which do not understand what is happening.[42]

The third evolution of resiliency inquiry examines the motivational forces within individuals and groups that are innate and the experiences that drive the individuals to tap into those forces to overcome disruptions. Richardson suggests that spiritual measures such as "purpose of life, locus of control, religiousness/beliefs in a higher power, creativity, humor, and affect"[43] are as important as environmental, social and developmental factors.

40 Ibid., 162.
41 Ibid., 215.
42 Cyrulnik, *Resilience*, 285.
43 Ibid., 313.

Work continues in the area of resilience. Gunderson and Holling offer an interdisciplinary (sociological, economic, and ecological) approach to researching the topic, and have established a Resiliency Network. Within this network, Brian Harrison Walker and David Andrew Salt define resilience as the "capacity of a system to absorb disturbance and still retain its basic function and structure".[44] These researchers believe that working across cultures and disciplines offers new insights into the nature of resilience. The authors suggest that there are both large and small factors which are fast or slow that influence systems. Their hope is to identify these factors more precisely with further research.

Work Involving Indigenous Peoples

There has been some work done concerning Indigenous peoples and resiliency.[45] As previously discussed, the first was the Kauai Longitudinal Study conducted by Werner and associates and is the foundation for resiliency research. John Wilshere, in his master's thesis, documents the thoughts of seven alumni who attended Shingwauk Residential School as children from 1929 to 1964. The data from this study centred around three themes: journeys, losses and needs. The definition of "substitute family" listed in the cultural losses section interested me. Three of the informants spoke about their Shingwauk Family. One male responded that this peer family was the "only family I've known."[46] Another male respondent said that his peer family had replaced his natural family. A female

---

44. Brian Harrison Walker and David Andrew Salt, Resilience Thinking: Sustaining Ecosystems and People in a Changing World (Washington: Island Press, 2006), xiii
45. The participants in this project were not participants in the studies about to be discussed.
46. Donald John Wilshere, *The Experiences of Seven Alumni Who Attended Shingwauk Residential School as Children 1929-1964.* Unpublished MA Thesis. Lakehead University.

respondent spoke quite fondly about her experiences at Shingwauk with her substitute family. She remembered that for the ten years she was there that her friends "took the place of her biological family"[47] like sisters whom she still associates with today. Is this a creation of the Shingwauk Family or an aspect of resiliency and/or an example of Anishinaabe life force energy or *mnidoo bemaasing bemaadiziwin?*

For her master's thesis, Rosemary Nichol interviewed four women and two men who attended residential school between 1939 and 1966 in Canada. Her interviews compared residential school survivors' protective and risk factors with those found in the literature. She suggests that while there are similarities with the existing information, there is an important difference, that being that the interventions should include authentic Indigenous history and spirituality as a means to improve self-esteem.

Brent Debassige's master's thesis titled, *Navigating the Rapids and Stumbling Through the Bush: A Study in Understanding Resiliency Through the Lens of Anishnaabe* investigates "resiliency (educational and cultural) amongst Anishnaabe secondary students."[48] Debassige argues that outcomes are a measurement of resiliency. Using the work of Marshall and Tryon, Debassige measures a variety of constructs, such as self-esteem, academic performance, physical health, coping and adaptation, and the absence of psychopathology or delinquent behaviours.[49] He subsequently interviewed two Anishinaabe students who graduated from secondary educational institutions and two students who did not graduate.

His data showed that "a moderate Anishinaabe cultural connection amongst the participants during elementary school and a limited

---

47 Ibid., 25.
48 Brent Debassige, *Navigating the Rapids and Stumbling Through the Bush: A Study in Understanding Resiliency Through the Lens of Anishnaabe*. Unpublished MA thesis. (Queen's University, 2002), i.
49 Ibid., i.

cultural connection during each participant's high school experience"[50] did not translate into a stronger cultural relationship upon graduation from secondary school. Furthermore, the non-completers of secondary school went on to strengthen their cultural connections. Debassige suggests that the more students resist Eurocentric education, the stronger their cultural connection. He calls this "resistant resiliency" defined as "the notion of overcoming adverse circumstance by limiting the acculturation of an individual."[51]

Another publication authored by Madeleine Dion Stout (a survivor) and Gregory Kipling presented research concerning resilience and the residential school legacy. They report that "in many cases, children found themselves in situations where they could continue to assimilate a positive outlook and values. Most notably, this is seen in the development of social support networks in which students sought to protect one another, teach useful skills, share stories or simply offer a sympathetic ear."[52] They also reported that protective factors included: pre-school supports from parents and families, positive relationships they developed with other students, prayer, optimism, competitive sports, religious beliefs, and reunions with their families.

Christopher Lalonde, a professor of psychology at the University of British Columbia, engaged in a study in which 600 teenagers were interviewed over 14 years in First Nations communities within British Columbia. His research concerned identity formation and cultural resilience. He states that a "higher burden of risk is borne by the Aboriginal population"[53] and he draws "parallels between the continuity

---

50   Ibid., i.
51   Ibid., 64.
52   Ibid., 38.
53   Christopher Lalonde, "Identity Formation and Cultural Resilience in Aboriginal Communities." In *Promoting Resilience in Child Welfare*, 52-71 (Victoria, British Columbia: University of Victoria, 2004), 7.

of person and the continuity of cultures."[54] Lalonde asserts that the promotion of culture in the community functions as a protection against adversity. He infers a strong link between collective cultural identity and self-government including related service, with the reduction of the youth suicide rate. Lalonde, however, cautions against using resiliency theory as a blanket resolution for all Indigenous peoples' suicide crises. He indicates that:

> The most pointed dangers—but also the most promising benefits—will come from applying the lessons of research on resilience in children to intervention efforts meant to minimize the effect of risk factors and maximize the effect of protective factors for whole cultural groups. In the current case, our work has identified a set of cultural or community practices and forms of indigenous knowledge that are associated with "better" youth outcomes. These findings threaten to set in motion a well-intentioned, but potentially disastrous, application of the standard "knowledge transfer" model. What I have in mind here is a variation on the "trait trap" that would see these findings taken as license to begin a strip-mining operation bent on extracting some set of cultural "best practices" from beneath the feet of "resilient" communities for processing at some central plant and eventual export to those poor "non-resilient" communities. Though that may seem harsh characterization, in the context of research and policy as it has been applied "to" indigenous communities in Canada and elsewhere, it is a well-founded fear.[55]

In 2007, the Ajunnginiq Centre published a report by the late Marja Korhonen titled *Resilience: Overcoming Challenges and Moving on Positively*. The report used Western concepts of resilience along

54 Ibid., 8.
55 Ibid., 7.

with transcripts provided by focus groups conducted with Inuit[56] Elders for a 2004–2005 project concerning suicide prevention. The report summarized factors and guidelines that support resilience, specifically cultural resiliency. Korhonen contends that one Elder from Tuktoyaktuk (Ajunnginiq Centre, 2007) pointed out:

> We cannot be surprised when hard times come to us. We have to know how to face problems and get through them. We can't lose our way when we have worries; we have to keep ourselves calm and steady. We can't let ourselves get scared or down. We need our energy to solve the problems, not to get too down about them.[57]

Celia Haig-Brown (1988), in her Master thesis titled *Resistance and Renewal: Surviving the Indian Residential School* chronicles her interviews with 13 former students of the Kamloops Indian Residential School. She describes how the students resisted the institutional physical abuse in that they stole food to survive; "In my time," she says, "we were always hungry"[58] Being able to barter with food gave the students a "sense of power and control."[59] There was a great sense of camaraderie in creating cleaning teams and stealing food; a group effort as someone had to act as the lookout. Acts of resistance included female students wearing makeup and curling their hair, as well as students running away and opposing rules and regulations. "In retrospect, these actions can be viewed as the actions of strong

---

56 The term "Inuit" refers to the peoples who according to the Inuit Tapiriit Kanatami "have occupied the Arctic land and waters from the Mackenzie Delta in the west, to the Labrador coast in the east and from the Hudson's Bay Coast, to the islands of the High Arctic" (Inuit Tapiriit Kanatami n.d. https://www.itk.ca/about-inuit) The focus groups were conducted in the Inuvialuit Region, Nunavut, Nunavik and Labrador.
57 Celia Haig-Brown, Resistance and Renewal: Surviving the Indian Residential School (Vancouver: Arsenal Pulp Press, 1988), 99.
58 Ibid., 99.
59 Ibid., 100.

people against a system which degraded and dehumanized" them.[60] Haig-Brown presented this commentary in the Epilogue:

> In innumerable ways, they fought for some control in an impersonalized system: for decent daily lives without cold and hunger, and for the means to survive the oppression around them while maintaining a sense of self and family.[61]

Imbued with cultural practices, resiliency becomes cultural resilience through resistance knowledge. In *"Navigating the Landscape of Practice: Dbaagmowin of a Helper,"* Kathy Absolon, an **Anishinaabe-kwe** from Flying Post First Nation equates circle work (connectedness) with resistance knowledge to stories of resiliency to empower the person telling the story:

> I currently prefer holistic circle work as a primary methodology in practice. It facilitates connectedness, which counters colonial alienation. For Indigenous people it fosters a group memory, power, togetherness and hope ... Resistance knowledge provided an approach to reframing experiences of trauma pain and despair into stories of resistance and empowerment. It moved us from victim to survivor living.[62]

She states, "Those who attend a circle are the strength and the resource."[63] "Beginning with community strengths and resiliencies is imperative to working through traumatic community crisis back toward that place of resilience again."[64] She further notes "resistance knowledge" is "an approach to reframing experiences of trauma,

60 Ibid., 114.
61 Ibid., 126.
62 Kathy Absolon, "Navigating the Landscape of Practice: Dbaagmowin of a Helper," In Raven Sinclair, Michael Anthony Hart, and Gord Bruyere (Eds.) *Wicihitowin: Aboriginal Social Work in Canada*, (Winnipeg: Fernwood Publishing, 2009), 176-177.
63 Ibid., 179.
64 Ibid., 190.

pain and despair into stories of resistance and empowerment."⁶⁵ I call it to "re-story." Abosolon also contends that:

> Resistance knowledge tends to focus on how people have used their strengths and resources to resist oppression, racism, colonization and other attacks on their life. It strives to identify what strengths and resources they draw upon in their resistance. This theory states that people will resist being harmed and hurt because of our human instinct to survive. It works on the premise that humans have the capacity to survive. It works on the premise that humans have the capacity to resist being empowered or oppressed. Focusing on and highlighting when resistance occurs can turn many stories of oppression, despair and suffering into stories of resilience, strength and resistance. I really find resistance knowledge useful in turning stories of despair into stories of power and strength.⁶⁶

The Survivors Speak About Resilience

As previously stated, when the Truth and Reconciliation Commission launched its unaugural event in Winnipeg, the word resiliency had become a buzz word. As I listened to the following five survivors define resiliency, my sense was that they thought of the experience as normal, not extraordinary. For example:

> Some days with resilience up there, just to survive, you know—because we were fighting for food—maybe stealing it off your plate or trying to get it off your plate, I guess that made me meaner other than that I guess that old saying rolling with the punch too. (Patrick, October 2, 2010)

65 Ibid., 176.
66 Ibid., 198.

Resiliency means a lot of things happen in your life, hurting, joy, whatever it is. I learned early on as one of eight kids you win some and you lose some . . . to roll with the punches. Here it's an island so we did a lot of swimming and sometimes you're treading water and to me that's kind of how the Mushole[67] was. You went in, and you didn't know what was happening. I was nine years old when I went. I feel that I was socialized by that time and knew how to get along with others. Eight of my mother's ten children survived to adulthood and I actually have an older brother and he was my dad's son by a lady before he married my mother so I knew how to get along with others. My parents taught us to help, and I learned how to take orders from my older sister and give them to the next ones coming up. When I got to Mohawk Institute and it was a hard change but I learned the lay of the land, and how to cope—there is a resiliency. You can either lie down and cry forever or get back up and do what you can. (Sylvia, October 3, 2010)

I believe it's my own make-up, each even—we all have our own make-up no matter what. We're given that when we're born and from that experience I had at the school, I don't know how to place it but we learned how to like defend ourselves. I guess a lot of stuff for—look at a lot of people taking a beating from the staff and we could you know see it but instead of breaking down ourselves we just kind of look at it and watch with a straight face and not say nothing cause it didn't really mean nothing to the staff if we did say anything. (Ronald, October 3, 2010)

To me, I guess being—understanding life after a rough life that you have to come through and held on to what you

---

67 Mushole refers to the Mohawk Institute Residential School located in Brantford, Ontario.

have been proving it. Be better than what you came through. Prove that the stuff way back wasn't that bad and they could overcome that—that's what I gathered from that. (Eric, October 7, 2010)

I just accepted it and that a lot of times you know— I lived in loneliness and just being—not being able to be with your family and your people you know, although there was all Native kids there and, a lot of them. I felt a little bit better because they were from Walpole that I had gone to school with so I felt like I wasn't the only one from Walpole. (Gladys, October 9, 2010)

As you read these quotes from the survivors, pictures form of children having a difficult time and we learn that many of them lived with the loss of their family and extreme loneliness. These young ones were having a tough time. There is a sense of fighting the good fight—fighting for food and fighting not to cry. Family, survival and how they adapted to the challenges of their early lives echo with these reminiscences. These children likely had to dig deep to retain the language, for if they were caught, they would receive the strap or some other form of punishment.

Before continuing it is useful to highlight how this work fits with the larger context of work concerning residential schools, and also to highlight what it does not do. First, this work builds on recent initiatives such as the work of the TRC wherein Indigenous peoples are deciding the nature of the project, how and the way my work proceeds, who facilitates the work, and how the work benefits Indigenous peoples in a practical way. It is within this context of an *Anishinaabe-kwe* being invited into a community by Anishinaabe survivors, using an Anishinaabe approach whereby life force energy or *mnidoo bemaasing bemaadiziwin* is revealed. While there is some discussion about life force energy within the Indigenous information, the non-Indigenous information does not explore the essence of this energy. Second, this work also builds on the Assembly of First Nations (1994) *Breaking the Silence: An Interpretative Study of Residential School Impact and Healing as Illustrated by the Stories of First Nations Individuals*. We should be mindful that the term life force energy may not be used by all Indigenous peoples and may not be experienced in the same way.

Learnings

There are two aspects of resiliency of young people that Benard brings forward that I do agree with: critical consciousness and insight. She quotes Paulo Freire and bell hooks indicating young ones have the capacity to develop critical consciousness and an understanding of oppression and develop strategies to move beyond victimhood. In my opinion, this is part of what happened to the survivors.

As I read the information, I found myself reflecting on my experiences with survivors through my *Anishnaabe-kwe* lens. I found in first working with survivors, that they were amazing because although I knew nothing about them, they were jolly, hard-working, and quick to laugh. I would not have known they had survived such an experience. They were being blessed, watched over and endowed with strength. They survived to tell their story.

Rather than extraordinary, the survivors I listened to believed that this resiliency is an ordinary process for them. As I have stated earlier, I found the resiliency information did not resonate with my experiences with the survivors. There was no understanding of the holistic, spiritual nature and interconnectedness of relationships. Having said this, there are some relevant points worth commenting on.

First, I concur with Cyrulnik who suggests that resilience is a natural process.[68] Resiliency comes through "when it is important

---

68 Cyrulnik, *Resilience*, 13.

to survive."[69] Resiliency seems to have an elasticity that we bend and shape for our purposes. However, I suspect there is something deeper to probe. I wonder whether this innate resilience is related to Anishinaabe life force energy or **mnidoo bemaasing bemaadiziwin**? I believe this life force energy is innate, holistic and within each of us. It manifests through all of our relations: land, animals, plants, ancestors and other people. The life force energy cannot be extinguished but can be severely dampened. The residential school system was an attempt to severely dampen the student's life force energy or **mnidoo bemaasing bemaadiziwin**.

I have been moved spiritually many times during my life. One time I stood looking out over the Bay of Fundy. I had never experienced such a peaceful feeling of contentment which I suspect is deeply steeped in my Anishinaabeness. The feeling is hard to describe; it is not tangible but rather intangible. For me the energy can be described as the following. One day I was standing in my living room folding clothes. I looked out the window and saw the wind pick up a discarded plastic bag. The winds brought the bag up, floating in front of the house across the street then gently back to the ground. The wind tossed the bag over and over again, as it skipped along the ground and it took it back behind the house where I no longer could see it from my living room window. The energy I speak of is like this wind. One cannot see it with the human eye but one can witness the outcome of what it does. A second time I was moved was when I accompanied an Elder into the bush to harvest medicines. I could feel the spirituality of the harvest within my psyche. For me it still resonates as a beautiful remembrance of my time at school.

Second, I believe that the residential school survivors would likely relate to Debassige who speaks about bicultural resiliency as "the ability to maintain a cultural identity while adopting traits of a new culture."[70]

---

69 Elder Shirley Williams, personal communication, October 11, 2011.
70 Debassige, *Navigating the Rapids and Stumbling Through the Bush*, 65.

For example, a residential school survivor can work for a government agency and yet retain their native language or can practice an organized religion and not have it negate their innate Anishinaabe spirituality. As Susie Jones philosophizes, "even though I never lived in a wigwam... I was still Indian."[71]

Third, I agree with Lalonde who cautions that researchers should never attempt to paint all Indigenous peoples with the same brush. I would also caution against the use of non-Indigenous positive and negative factors being relevant to Indigenous peoples. For example, Werner and Smith define poverty as an at-risk factor, and yet many Indigenous peoples live at the poverty level and are resilient as "one who keeps his soul centred, allowing that person to overcome, regardless of the onslaught."[72]

Fourth, while more recent efforts concerning resiliency thinking extend across disciplines and involve partnering with Indigenous traditionalists, there still seems to be the same mindset for stacking variables. There is a sense that variables can be isolated, managed or controlled in nature. While there may be value to investigating those definitive factors, I believe it misses the holistic essence of our being.

Fifth, the studies do not sufficiently address an Anishinaabe worldview, which holds the bones and the bedrock or **kanan miinwaa nbagani-aasmaabkong** at its centre. For example, there appears to be a strong kinship amongst the alumni of CSAA that formed when they were children which continues with the WIRSSG and is extended to other residential school survivors which in my estimation is a comfortable sense of belonging. This raises the question of whether relationships were integral to survival and maintaining their life force energy or **mnidoo bemaasing bemaadiziwin**. All the researchers and practitioners who developed the concept are now looking at how resilience itself develops.

71 Suzie Jones, personal communication, January 14, 2012.
72 Susie Jones, personal communication, November 5, 2008.

While there is documentation of residential school experiences, particularly with the TRC's work, there remains very little published work given to the survivors' voices especially around resiliency. This work highlights survivors' voices from an Anishinaabe perspective using an Anishinaabe approach.

Sixth and most important, I believe Richardson was on to something when he spoke about an innate resilience, a person's capacity for extraordinary strength. He describes an energy or force from within that enables resiliency. Willie Ermine, a Cree member of Sturgeon Lake First Nation, describes an "energy [that] manifests itself in all existence because all is connected, and all of life is primarily connected and accessed through the life force."[73] I sense the survivors have tapped into this inner energy that comes from a much deeper place. "In their quest to find meaning in the outer space, Aboriginal people turned to the inner space. This inner space is that universe of being within each person that is synonymous with the soul, the spirit, the self, or the being."[74] Building on Richardson's explanation, I asked Elder Doug Williams about this energy or force within and he said:

> The life force, I don't know anything about resilience but the life force within—Anishinaabe always believed that there are spirits within each of us. There's actually, it could be maybe perhaps said that we can't separate that from you as an individual because your spirit never leaves you. It comes—it was there before you were born. It was there at the process of birth. It's now here with you and it will stay with you after your body leaves the earth. What is that then? Alright, what it is I think to me and I've thought about this over time, that it's the center of your—it's really used in the language in a

---

73 Willie Ermine, "Aboriginal Epistemology," in *First Nations Education in Canada: The Circle Unfolds*, edited by Marie Battiste and Jean Barman, 101-112. Vancouver: UBC Press, 1995), 104.

74 Ibid., 103.

number of ways or it appears in the language in a number of ways. One of them—they use the word *Odeh*, your heart, your heartbeat, there's a physical heartbeat then there's that heartbeat, or fire within you, which is centred in you and it's around the middle of your chest and the middle of your belly and that energy is a combination of you as a physical being and as a spiritual being having come together. In fact they talk about it sometimes as you having two faces. That those two faces don't come together until you know your truth somewhere down—as you walk through life. That when you begin that path there is no—you really don't know who you are in that respect. You mature, play with your child then you go out and you wander. You're youthful. You look for a partner and so on until after that then you begin to know your truth and those two faces come together.[75]

Finally, much of the information remains at the surface and does not get at the root of what I have experienced as revealed knowledge, the energy that springs from the survivors. After reading and exploring the different types of resiliency, resiliency theory and those factors and definitions elaborated on by the resiliency theorists, I still did not feel the connection between what I read and the energy I observed and felt emitted from the survivors. There were only surface explanations. What I was hoping to do was draw an inference from my search to my 20-plus year lived experience with the survivors. For me nothing resonated or described that something different, the energy that sprung from the survivors. At this point, I looked to the survivors to provide me with the answer of what this energy is and what feeds the energy. From my Traditional Teachings I recognize that what is being shown to me is not resilience but something different, Anishinaabe life force energy or ***mnidoo bemaasing bemaadiziwin***.

[75] Doug Williams, personal communication, July 11, 2012.

As previously mentioned, the survivors I listened to were over 68 years of age and were asked to reflect upon their experiences at residential school and what contributed to their own resiliency from childhood to Elderhood. In the next four chapters I use the Medicine Wheel to depict the traditional Anishinaabe stages of life versus the real-life experiences of the survivors. Each quadrant is discussed in turn. Each chapter opens with the voice of a survivor which is unencumbered to ensure the honesty and integrity of what is being said. This is my obligation and responsibility that has been set out before me and is in keeping with two of the Seven Grandfather Teachings—Truth and Respect.

CHAPTER 5

"The Taken"[1] Arrival and Life at the School

The journey starts in the eastern door with childhood, the "place of beginnings and enlightenment."[2]

This is the time (based on Anishinaabe teachings) of Creation and the Original Instructions. This chapter begins with a voice of a survivor who describes being taken from his family, then I briefly describe how babies are welcomed into the Anishinaabe family circle and clan, and provided with nutrients such as a Creation Story, Original Instructions, Seven Grandfather Teachings, **Anishinaabemowin**, and ceremonies to nurture their physical and spiritual being. I then detail how children were taken from their family environment off to residential schools which virtually cut off important rites of passage and essential nutrients of growth and development. Finally, in spite of efforts to diminish the Anishinaabe *mino-bimaadiziwin* (the way of a good life), I discuss how the children were able to endure the horrible experiences and seek ways to nourish the Anishinaabe life force energy or *mnidoo bemaasing bemaadiziwin* within them.

1   Title from Susie Jones, personal communication, October 2, 2010.
2   Sharilyn Calliou, "Peacekeeping Actions at Home: A Medicine Wheel Model for a Peacekeeping Pedagogy," in *First Nations Education in Canada: The Circle Unfolds*, eds. Marie Battiste and Jean Barman (Vancouver: UBC Press, 1995), 67.

Six years and the winter of '36, don't know what month, it was cold. We were sitting down at a supper meal, my brother, my grandmother, my mother. In walked the Mountie and the Indian agent and we didn't quite finish our supper cause all he did was point at me and, my brother and say, "You and you, come with us." I was scared. So was my brother. He cried all the way which was just a short distance from where we lived by the school and, to this day I don't know which roads we took—how we got there.

They took us upstairs in what you call the new dormitory. I got a picture of that school over there. My brother was about eight or nine beds from me and he was crying. Me, I didn't know what to do. I'm lying there. So there was another fellow, he was a neighbour of ours that was also in that school. So, he kind of calmed my brother down. So, next day, they gave us new uniforms like the black overalls, black smock, and three quarter type proper boots, and socks, course I had gloves. Next day in school—I think they stuck me in number, grade number two if I can remember right, and I remember this day somehow—this teacher her name was Miss B. or something like that and she got up before the class and she said, I remember this very well, "You people have no religion, you are like paganistic-type people." I'll never forget that part and my brother took a beating the first day—of strapping. He had to go to the bathroom and he didn't know where it was so he went behind some bushes and got caught. The second day of school he got the strap and you look at that, and not a thing you can do about it. (Ronald, October 3, 2010)

I consider myself an avid listener, a keen observer and experienced over the years, but when I heard the above words spill out of an 81-year-old survivor, I was shaken to my core. I felt an awkward sense of honour that I would be so blessed to know the shadows of the mind that had endured such trauma. I felt heartsick for both this survivor, and his brother for their losses of childhood joy. To be ripped from the love of a mother and grandmother is sad. It was like envisioning a soul wound carved so deep that one wonders how such explicit recall after 70 or so years can be nothing other than a testament to this survivor's strength. As Anishinaabe people, there is another way to experience and understand the natural Anishinaabe development and growth.

Anishinaabe Mino-bimaadiziwin (The Way of a Good Life)

I understand that when we are born we receive our Anishinaabe spirit name by age two. We come from the spirit world and that is where our life path and destiny is defined. Once born, we do not remember anything from our time in the spirit world. We receive an earth name to distinguish us as human beings rather than spirit beings. The Elder, in giving our spirit name, considers such things as the weather and what is happening at the time of our birth. If named for the weather—it distinguishes Anishinaabe babies as earth beings because there is no weather in the spirit world.[3] For example, my **Anishinaabe-kwe** name is **Biidaaban Ntam Bi Yaad**, meaning the first one out, the light before the dawn.

Because children are close to the spirit world they are able to see ghosts. I have been taught that everyone is born with this ability and often lose it with age. One of the survivors relayed to me that one day when she was driving in her van with her daughter and granddaughter, her granddaughter exclaimed, "Oh look at that lady flying" and she was referring to seeing a lady flying in the air with no skydiving equipment or plane. This survivor had found out later that the flying lady had indeed passed into the spirit world.

3 Elder Doug Williams, personal communication, September 14, 2011.

A baby is born into a clan or totem. The Anishinaabe Clan System is connected to our Creation Story and is "a framework of government to give them strength and order."[4] There were seven original clans. Each clan is represented by an animal with its attributes and responsibilities. For example, I am Eagle Clan and have "courage and preknowledge."[5] Children of a union were assigned "to the clan of their father."[6] Part of the beauty of the Clan System was the "built-in ability to quickly resolve differences of opinion."[7] Intermarriage within the same clan is not allowed for children born to these unions would suffer defects and abnormalities.[8]

Children hold a special place in our society. According to Benton-Banai, a special baby was chosen as a messenger by the spirit beings, the Seven Grandfathers, to receive sacred teachings to teach us about how to live in harmony with Creation. The boy on returning to earth shared these teachings of wisdom, love, respect, bravery, honesty, humility, and truth with the people. He cautioned that each teaching had its opposite and reminded the people that in order to be healthy they must seek development of and balance in both physical and spiritual realms. He offered the knowledge of the vision quest, fasting, dreaming, and mediation in order to develop this spiritual side. These teachings are the fundamental principles for living **Mino-bimaadiziwin** (A Way of a Good Life). Children learn these teachings early in life through storytelling by the Elders and extended family. As Elder Doug Williams explained:

> I think in the old days and I'll use myself as an example that was introduced to me when I was four or five years old.

---

4   Edward Benton-Banai, *The Mishomis Book: The Voice of the Ojibway* (Minneapolis: University of Minnesota Press, 1988), 74.
5   Basil Johnston, *Ojibway Heritage* (Lincoln: University of Nebraska Press, 1976), 53.
6   Benton-Banai, *The Mishomis Book: The Voice of the Ojibway*, 105.
7   Ibid., 105.
8   Ibid., 77.

It may be different now. I know me and using me as an example, it's four or five they were starting to talk about values. You know how come it's important to listen to your Elders that kind of stuff, that's part of the Grandfather Teachings then you get told the story of Elder Brother, the name that I can't mention now, but who didn't respect Elders and was therefore punished or an animal didn't respect Elders was therefore punished that kind of thing so I heard those so that started early but you begin to narrow these things particularly at the time once you get married and you're expected to know all that stuff.[9]

They learn the rules of behaviour without judgment or blame. As one survivor said,

I really loved my grandfather cause he always talked to us you know. He always talked to us and told us things we done wrong. He'd correct us but he done it in a way where he was showing love to us not just using his authority.[10] (Mary, October 4, 2010).

Many Elders have said that children are our future and are the leaders of the next generations. They are to be revered, loved and always included in all activities and futhermore, guided to accept their responsibility. We believe that everything is for the children.

The Taken

For most Anishinaabe children, arrival at a residential school was a memorable, devastating experience. What I consider to be important information that needs to be conveyed is that these young ones

---

9   Elder Doug Williams, personal communication, July 11, 2012.
10 Mary, October 4, 2010.

were taken from their homes, from their communities, for some, quite abruptly as indicated by the opening story. For this reason, I have titled this section, "The Taken" (see Figure 7). The children, some as young as four years old, were taken from loving homes and whisked off by air, train, boat or automobile to an unknown place hundreds of miles from their original home.

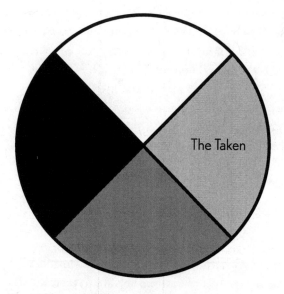

Figure 7. The Taken

Please note that the colours that make up the Medicine Wheel are a crucial part of its extended meaning. The versions used in this text use the following colour formation: the North quadrant is white, the Eastern quadrant is yellow, the Southern quadrant is red, and the Western quadrant is black. The Medicine Wheels presented in this book have been approved by the Elders consulted for this work.

In his autobiography, Basil Johnston, an Anishinaabe survivor of Spanish Residential School, retells his experience. He says that when the Indian agent came to the house, the agent had been instructed to retrieve two children to take to residential school and upon finding out that one was sick, the Indian agent turned to Basil's mother and grandmother:

"How about her?" he rasped, pointing at Marilyn, my four-year-old sister, who came running into the house to find out what was going on. "She can go; old enough ... and that'll make two!" Once more he demonstrated that he could count.

Mother and Grandmother were both appalled. "No! She's too young," they wailed. "She can't go to school yet, she's only four. No!" But the agent knew how to handle Indians, especially Indian women. "Well! If you don't want her to go, we'll take the whole family. Now! Get her ready. Hurry up!"

Mother and Grandmother whimpered as they washed and clothed my sister.[11]

As I listened to the survivors describe their experiences, I had the visual of very small children who were brought to residential school by strangers and as the children stood in front of the school viewing this overly large, ominous building, they would have had to experience the feeling of being powerless, and completely scared out of their wits. Then, they were greeted and met by these creatures, nothing that they had ever seen before—people clothed in strange materials with white faces; the fear must have been almost unbearable. The confusion and the fear must have raced in their minds as no explanation was given to them. The feelings felt by these children intensified as the staff only spoke English. Questions the children may have thought such as why did my parents send me here and why did my mother let them take me—could not and would not be answered. Furthermore, as they were ushered into the building, their peers immediately silenced them. They warned them not to speak their Indigenous language for swift punishment would follow. According to Elder Shirley Williams:

> When I saw [St. Joseph's] it was grey. A brick building when it rains is dark and grey, you know. It's an ugly day but the

[11] Basil Johnston, *Indian School Days* (Toronto: Key Porter, 1988), 20.

feeling was ... of ugliness. [T]he gate opened and the bus went in, and I think when the gate closed ... something happened to me, something locked, it is like my heart locked, because it could hear that [the clink of gates].[12]

Approximately 120 children attended Shingwauk Indian Residential School each year.[13] Siblings, brothers and sisters who arrived at the school together were immediately separated and rarely saw each other. Following their separation, their clothes and belongings were taken away and burned, and they were given a number and a uniform like a prisoner and directed to their bunk in a dormitory.

Depending on the number of children, it was not unusual for very small children to sleep two to a bed. The children were subsequently forced into a shower and deloused with kerosene (which burned their scalp) or had coal oil poured over their heads followed by a haircut. This haircut caused further confusion for the children as the cutting of hair could signify either punishment or a death in the family depending on their Indigenous affiliation. Others thought that they were being punished because that is what First Nations' members do to other members who have done something wrong. The haircut style was the same for each child. The girl's hairstyle was usually a Robin Hood style or pageboy cut. The boy's haircut was shorn very close to the scalp resembling a close crew cut.

However, one descendant of a survivor shared with me that when his light-skinned mother went to get her hair cut, she was treated differently. Her hair was not shorn completely. She was allowed to keep her bangs, but as she was walking down a school hallway afterwards, another female student attacked her. The other student was jealous because of the special treatment she received by the residential

---

12 Quoted from http://www.wherearethechildren.ca/en/blackboard/page-8.html.
13 The approximate number was calculated when another staff member and I sorted available attendance records and space available at the Shingwauk School.

school staff. Special treatment by the staff actually made the students targets of other students and this was not a good situation.[14] Susie Jones confirmed that because she was light-skinned, she didn't receive as much punishment as the other darker-skinned students.[15] Special treatment was also meted out to the students who joined the "Holy Order." According to one survivor, children were asked at the end of each term whether they wished to join the Order. Elder Shirley Williams said, "I did not know what holy orders meant."[16] If the student made a decision to join, the student was moved to separate quarters and given extra privileges, which further drove a wedge between this student and other students.

The children were indoctrinated into a regimental, institutional lifestyle. A bell rang several times each day to summon them to meals, classes, work and mass. Some children were assigned duties, tasks they needed to do every day. As the children grew older, they were assigned specific chores such as tending to the chickens, ploughing the fields, doing the laundry, washing the dishes, helping in the kitchen, and maintaining the furnace.

In the past, day schools that were constructed within the geographical area of First Nations children's homes were considered dismal failures as far as attendance. Authorities felt that the school aged children needed to be away from distractions of their own people and culture to complete their formal school education. It didn't matter that Indigenous people traditionally did not learn in a classroom; the environment was their school and their Elders and family members were their teachers. The environment, all of Creation including plants, and animals are considered to be "all our relations."

---

14 Dorothy Cunningham, personal communication, May 26, 2001.
15 Susie Jones, personal communication, October 2, 2010.
16 Elder Shirley Williams, personal communication, September 15, 2011.

Arrival at the school brought forth a range of feelings. Many speak of fear, abandonment, aloneness, confusion, heartsickness, feeling very small in a very large place with no one to talk to, and extreme loneliness. One survivor confided, "the first year I was there, I was so lonely, really lonely, heartbroken, and my mother couldn't read or write English so she couldn't write to me and so anyway I was really lonely." (Mary, October 4, 2010). Another survivor said:

> When you're little, I think you can get used to anything. You know when you're small, you can get used to anything. I think I just got used to it because I couldn't go nowhere. I had to be there. I knew I couldn't go anywhere. (Una, October 4, 2010)

Another survivor recalled:

> ... the memory that I have is in that the Second World War we used to have air raid practices in case the Germans came over and bombed the Sault Locks and being one of the smallest kids, I was right near the door of the dorm that held maybe 20, 25 kids, I can't remember. I usually say 25, maybe it wasn't that many but anyway, I was near the door of the dorm, and when the siren would sound, we were expected to get up, and put our shoes on and probably get dressed to a certain degree and go down to the basement of the building, and that's two floors, and we had to do that in the dark because the windows were covered with curtains because if the Germans saw the light, then they'd bomb the buildings. As a little child, I was very scared. Nobody explained anything to you. You just had to do what you were told and as an adult I look on all of those instances where I had to go through something, was not told how, why or when, and I had to learn to get through it somehow without too much emotion, and without too much of anything. You just got through it. (Susie, October 2, 2010)

In the dormitory at night, soft crying could be heard coming from the bunks. "My pillow was wet with tears, I was so sad."[17] Memories of helplessness and powerlessness were the uppermost emotions experienced by the former students. According to Basil Johnston:

> In the silence and the darkness it was time for remembrance and reflection. But thoughts of family and home did not yield much comfort and strength; instead such memories as one had served to inflame the feelings of alienation and abandonment and to fan the flames of resentment. Soon the silence was broken by the sobs and whimpers of boys who gave way to misery and sadness, dejection and melancholy, heartache and gloom.
>
> Besides the sobs and whimpers, which would come to an end by the finish of a boy's first week at the school, there were the muted fall of footsteps and the faint motion of a phantom form of the prefect as he patrolled the dormitory. "Shut up!"[18]
>
> The feeling of abandonment, never far from the surface, now swelled up and was intensified by each boy's inability to understand why his parents had given him up and turned him over to the priests. No one bothered to explain, "You're here because your parents are dead and we've been asked to look after you until . . . ;" or, "You were sent to us to look after because your father is dead and your mother cannot care for you;" or, "Your parents are no longer living together. We're going to look after you until they are reconciled." Even if such explanations had been given, it is doubtful that the hurts felt on Christmas would have been assuaged by one degree.[19]

---

17 Alice Blondin-Perrin, *My Heart Shook Like a Drum: What I Learned at the Indian Mission Schools, Northwest Territories* (Ottawa: Borealis Press, 2009), 19.
18 Basil Johnston, *Indian School Days*, 45.
19 Ibid., 80.

"Fear and loneliness often manifested in bed-wetting."[20] One of the former students told me about meeting a peer from residential school some fifty years later. This survivor came up to him and thanked him. He asked why he was thanking him, and the survivor replied that he had helped him dry his sheets in the morning so that the staff would not know that he wet the bed. The former student's kindness meant so much to this peer that he never forgot it. Students who wet the bed suffered tremendous humiliation.

> I remember these two friends of mine and what use to happen to them. They were brothers and they both had the problem of wetting the bed. In the morning when it was time to get up, the nun who was in charge of us would make her daily visit to their beds. When wet sheets were found, they would be paraded to the front of the dormitory dragging their wet sheets. They would have to stand at the front of the dormitory with their wet sheets draped around their bodies while the rest of us got ready for morning Mass. I guess the idea was that this type of humiliation would teach them to stop wetting their beds.[21]

As previously stated, other children at the school warned them not to speak their Indigenous language or they would suffer horrendous consequences. No reason was given. Yet there was no understanding why as many children arrived able to only speak their own specific language. "The first rule was not to speak the gobbleygook language."[22] If a student was caught speaking the language, they were immediately punished usually being strapped in front of other children to serve as an example to others. The humiliation and deep feelings of hurt and anguish were pushed off into the dark

---

20 Celia Haig-Brown, *Resistance and Renewal: Surviving the Indian Residential School* (Vancouver: Arsenal Pulp Press, 1988), 75.
21 G.J., Shingwauk Archives, Fonds No. 2010-082/001(002).
22 Elder Shirley Williams, personal communication, June 26, 2011.

depth of the young ones' minds to be compartmentalized for later until they peaked, and could no longer be kept hidden.

While I read pages and pages of transcripts, I cried knowing the experiences residential school students were forced to endure. What bothered me most was the fact that very young children were sent to residential school. Mike Cachagee, a survivor of three residential schools, remembers as a student seeing a baby, Billy Fletcher, sitting in a high chair at the end of the dinner table.[23] Older siblings, children themselves had to act as protector and nurturer at a young age. Christine Butterfly, age eight, had to be a mother to her younger sisters while at Shingwauk Residential School.[24] The first night at the school, her two-year old sister woke up in the middle of the night and while Christine was rocking her little sister, the matron came in and tore her sister from her and told her to get back to bed.

Brother and sister relationships were fractured because they could not communicate with one another unless they met in a family meeting room with staff nearby.

> They had a Tuesday or Wednesday night, I don't remember which night it was where you could go and visit your sister in the dining room after supper but it was pretty awkward, you didn't—there were so many people around you couldn't get back into being a family you know cause they were constantly watching you. You didn't know what to say to each other. (Louis, October 4, 2010)

The girls were segregated from the boys. At the Shingwauk School the boys were sequestered on the west side of the building and the girls were placed on the east side. Even during meal times the boys were on one side of the room and the girls were on the other side of the room so siblings remained separated at all times.

---

23 Mike Cachagee, personal communication, May 26, 2001.
24 C.W., Shingwauk Archives, Fonds No. 2010-047/001(010).

Spanish Residential School erected two schools, one for the girls and one for the boys. Susie Jones once told me that there were 25 girls in her Shingwauk School junior dorm and these young ones began to look to each other for comfort and established amongst each other a substitute family. This familial relationship was generated by the fact that they bonded as a group because of the loss of their own family relationship and felt that they had to nurture each other. They could not communicate with their own siblings even when they met during the "sibling meeting" night. Basil Johnston remembers during this time at Spanish Residential School:

> One Sunday afternoon, brothers and sisters met for their regular monthly visit of one hour in the recreation hall of the boys' school. Other than "Ahnee" ("Hi"), I had nothing to say to my sister Marilyn, and she nothing to me. It wasn't that I didn't try, but she was absolutely uninterested in my toilet-cleaning skills and in my pea-shelling exploits. If Sis and I said few words during that hour and subsequent rendezvous, and if we had little to discuss, the only explanation may be found in the barrier in communication that often exists between ten-year-old boys and four-year-old girls. For the first few moments, all Sis did was to look up at me, her eyes black and misty with sadness and bewilderment at being wrenched from her mother and sisters and transported to an alien place where "suffer the little children to come unto me" was largely forgotten by sisters and priests. After the greeting of "Ahnee," and some questioning glances between us, Sis snuggled up against my leg. An hour later we said "'Bye."[25]

Another former student commented that:

---

25 Basil Johnston, *Indian School Days*, 71-72.

My sister, on the other hand, she had nobody, so she went over into where the girls go, on the opposite side of the school, and we didn't—outside of the first month or so we gave up visiting on Wednesdays cause nothing come of it. You know, we didn't even know what to say, we didn't want to be there, might have been different if we could of just set us some place and left us alone you know so we could get used to being a family again but that didn't happen. (Louis, October 4, 2010)

There was no communication under this restriction. The staff at the residential school were cold much like the whole atmosphere at the school. These children had the same experience which further cemented their bond.

The children's lives were regimented in that a bell and the residential school staff monitored their schoolwork, play time, tasks, and daily activities. Throughout the years, students' birthdays were never acknowledged nor celebrated. During the school year, many of the students were physically, verbally, sexually, psychologically, and spiritually abused, and acceptance of the alien lifestyle did not come easy as these two survivors attest:

When I was there I kind of just felt like that's where I had to be. I mean there's nothing—no matter how I felt or what I did, I had to be there. I just accepted it and that a lot of times I—I lived in loneliness and you know just being—not being able to be with your family and your people—although there was all Native kids there but a lot of them. I felt a little bit better because they were from Walpole that I had gone to school with so I felt like I wasn't the only one from Walpole. (Gladys, October 9, 2010)

I think part of it—is when you needed help when you were a child, there was no one there. (Susie, October 2, 2010)

Integral to their survival were the relationships fostered and the development of their social skills as many students came to develop substitute families. Since the students shared an understanding of the residential school experience, they bonded as family members and today, some students call each other brother and sister because of residential school. In the words of one survivor, "It's the only family I've known."[26]

Summertime and holidays were precious to the children who got to go home. In essence they were able to continue their language and familial connections to their community. However, many students never went home, at least not until they left residential school at age 16, or fell ill, and were sent home and died. One of the students I listened to watched his older brother die. The school authorities made him watch as an example that this is what happens when you run away.

> My brother, yeah, I don't know how old he was when he died, probably about 15, 14, 15, and I was about eight, I think. He ran away from school. I don't know how long he was gone, maybe a week or so, then he got sick. He was in a bush, him and his buddy, he got sick and come to find out he had appendicitis I think. His buddy dragged him back to school or carried him, brought him back to school but they wouldn't take him to the hospital, you know, they just let the—the appendix broken and the poison spread and he died. They finally took him to the hospital so I imagine he died in the hospital. That's the way I get the story. I wasn't close to him but I cried a lot when he was gone. I must have cried a week straight and that's stopped so it really hurt. That was a big hurt in my life. (Leonard, June 9, 2008).

The children also suffered a significant loss of Anishinaabe spirituality. Unable to speak their respective language and practice their

---

26 M.C., Shingwauk Archives, Fonds No. 2010-047/001(008).

rituals and ceremonies dampened the children's life force energy or *mnidoo bemaasing bemaadiziwin*. One child describes his feelings of being cold:

> I'm always cold. I'm always cold and Shingwauk was always cold for me up there. It was those thin blankets we had, and like I said it was cold. I tried to get in bed with somebody to get warm and then the matron thought we were trying to get together like nasty boys but that was hard to take with that attitude. (Patrick, October 2, 2010)

As Herb Nabigon says, "The sacred fire represents the Creator who is inside every human being."[27] In contrast, another survivor, who went to residential school at age 10 and knew her language said:

> Every night we used to dream about home. I guess that's the last thing we used to think about and this one night something happened. I don't know I was upset and I was real lonesome and I wanted to go home. My mind was wishful thinking so I didn't know what was happening. I flew out of my body and I just saw myself my body lifting up. I saw myself lying down on the bed. Then I was in my parent's home. I could smell the wood smoke, the food. Then I'm visiting them and I was talking about all kinds of things what was happening at the school and then there used to be a nun who used to be checking the beds and that but I didn't hear her coming. You can always hear her footsteps cause I was always careful when to talk my language because I know she can be very tough and this time I didn't hear her footsteps until a little bit too late because it was just right near there but I couldn't bring myself back fast enough, back to my bed. I got caught and then all of sudden I felt her lifting the sheet

---

27 Herb Nabigon, *The Hollow Tree: Fighting Addiction with Traditional Native Healing* (Montreal: McGill-Queen's University Press, 2006), 87.

and she's standing right there, pretty equal with double beds and she said, "are you praying?" And I said, "yes Miss, oh yes!" That's how I brought myself back. I only understood that part when Tom Porter talked about soul travelling.[28]

Nurturing the Anishinaabe Life Force Energy "*mnidoo bemaasing bemaadiziwin*"

If you recall, these young ones found themselves in an alien place, impossible to escape. They experienced the suppression of their identity and being, felt powerless to change the circumstances or their environment, and ultimately accepted and resigned themselves to a regimental lifestyle where a bell told them what to do and when to do it. They all had the same hairstyle, uniform and received a number. They had to accept what was given to them all the while placating themselves with thoughts of freedom—relishing the time when they would attain the age of 16 and leave to make their own decisions.

As children they were expected to understand what they were being told and had to learn the English language. If they did not learn quickly, they were beaten and if they spoke their own Indigenous language they were beaten which forced them into silence. The children reached out to each other and bonded with each other much like prisoners and became a family; brother and sister. In these relational bonds manifested the flux of their Anisihnaabe life force energy or **mnidoo bemaasing bemaadiziwin.**

These children learned how to survive under formidable circumstances, and survival took many forms—physical, emotional, spiritual and mental. The older students often assumed the responsibility not only for their younger brothers and sisters but also for other students. Children under five years of age relied on the older ones to feed, protect and guide them.

---

28 Elder Shirley Williams, personal communication, May 13, 2011.

While all the former students I listened to for this work knew their language prior to being taken to residential school, only some would find ways to keep it. "I knew they could not knock the language out of me by using the strap."[29] Maintaining the language is an act of resistance. Keeping the language was a way of maintaining the connection to family and Mother Earth. The story of Elder Shirley Williams teaches me the strength of language and spirit as she had soul travelled at night to visit her family and thus experienced a sense of comfort being at home. Jean-Guy Goulet describes soul travelling as "experienced firsthand in dreams or in visions when the soul journeys away from the body. It is in the other land that one meets relatives who have passed away."[30] Mike Cachagee, a survivor of three residential schools fell off a roof at the age of 60 and subsequently went into a coma. He recounted to me his lived experience:

> When I went into a coma, when I first was going in and out of it, I guess they told my family that if he survived this in— three or four days, he may survive, he may not. If he does survive, he'll never walk again. When I came here, I was going in and out of consciousness at the hospital and then finally I went back into this coma for five days. While I was in there I guess, I was getting ready to die, my spirit was and I went down to—there was a big place, like I could remember down at M'Chigeeng in Manitoulin Island. I'd been there. I don't know how many years, four. There was a situation and there was a hill. Up on the hill, all the old people came out and my brother was there and they had long, long white robes on like buckskin robes. There was all in dark and the whole sight of them, I don't know how many were there and I was standing there looking at them and my brother Clarence

---

29 Elder Shirley Williams, personal communication, October 11, 2011.
30 Jean-Guy Goulet, *Ways of Knowing: Experience, Knowledge, and Power Among the Dene Tha* (Vancouver: UBC Press, 1998), xxvii.

the one that passed away there now, came out and looked at me and he waved, waved at me and all the old people behind him waved, then they turned around and went back in, into that mountain and then immediately after I had another one.

I was a little boy. I was running in the Prairie grass down by the water. The long grass that was there and I could feel the Prairie grass on my head. I was running and I went down and there was a clearing and in that clearing were all the grandmothers. There seven or eight grandmothers sitting there and then what's strange is that they told me that, all they were doing was talking Cree, and they told me that, "You got to stop, you got to watch what the whiteman's saying, be very careful, stop trying to be a whiteman" that's what they were saying in the language and so my granny, you know I never ever knew my great grandmother. I never knew her or my grandmother, either grandmother on my mother's side or father's side. They were there and they were all talking their language with me and then I was running back and forth in and out of the circle and they were just sitting there, and they all had long white hair very, very peaceful looking.

So they called me, and my granny called me and says, "Come on now," she says, "You go around and gives us all a hug," she told me in Cree, "it's time for you to go home now, you got to go back" and she said, "when you go back you got to take this medicine, it's the woman's medicine" she told me and that's when I woke up and I called Elaine then and I went and got a hold of Pat . . . Her dad was from Mobert and he's an Elder up there and I called Pat. I had to go get an Anishinaabe woman to go down and put my tobacco down at the water so I asked Pat.

She came in. She went down and put the tobacco down for me at the water cause I couldn't hardly move and then I called my daughter and then I told her "you got to go get me women's medicine and get a hold of Betty, she will know" so she went and got blueberries, strawberries, cranberries and then Betty came up and brought medicine up so that's what I was eating and it was in a big bowl. So, the nurses, for two days I ate like that, bring my food in and the nurses were like talking, "we don't know what he's eating, he's got that big bowl. He's got that big bowl of food there and that's what he's eating." I could hear them so I said, "there's nothing wrong with me, I broke my back," I said, "I didn't fall on my head!"[31]

Even though Mike Cachagee grew up in the residential school system, his life force energy or ***mnidoo bemaasing bemaadiziwin*** acted as insulation. A perfect example of his spirituality was his ability to soul travel and visit his late brother, and grandmothers that he had never met and while the intent of the institution was kept "to kill the Indian"[32] in the child, these Anishinaabe children were successful in keeping the fire within them alive. The Seven Grandfathers Teachings existed within their small bodies, as love, bravery, honesty, and truth were evidentiary in many aspects of residential school life. There are several examples that come to my mind: the sharing of food, the comforting of each other, being true to their language even though they were threatened with punishment, their strength of life and not forgetting their cultural identity. As one survivor indicated:

> When I got to Mohawk Institute and it was a hard change but I learned the lay of the land, and how to cope—there is a resiliency. You can either lie down and cry forever or get back up and do what you can. (Sylvia, October 3, 2010)

---

31 Mike Cachagee, personal communication, January 15, 2012.
32 Richard Henry Pratt, "The Advantages of Mingling Indians with Whites," in *Americanizing the American Indians: Writings by the "Friends of the Indian" 1880–1900*, ed. Francis Paul Prucha (Cambridge: Harvard University Press, 1973), 261.

Some resisted the institutionalized lifestyle imposed on them and found ways to maintain the essence of their beings. Many of the acts of resistance fed their Anishinaabe life force energy or *mnidoo bemaasing bemaadiziwin*. Speaking their language also peaked this soul-spirit[33] or life force energy. With the experience of residential school and what had to be done to survive at residential school, the children changed their behaviour to adapt to the life altering experience they were undergoing. Some of the children clung to their early life remembering the good in their lives and some remembered teachings and learnings they received from their relatives. However, the very young who were taken to residential school and had not experienced the bones and the bedrock or **kanan miinwaa nbagani-aasmaabkong** which was required to give them that firm foundation to know themselves in a foreign world, were most impacted and suffered greatly for it.

Once the children learned the regimental routine of the residential school, they constructed ways to survive the experience. Many developed coping survival skills and techniques imperative to keeping a low profile. These strategies included hiding from the big boys or going into the bush behind the school in the hope of staying out of sight of the predators who worked at the school. One survivor told me that he was raped by two of the other students at the residential school. Many learned fighting skills in order to defend themselves and/or protect their younger siblings.

In the next chapter, I discuss that in spite of missing Anishinaabe rites of passage, the children found the various ways to feed their life force energy or *mnidoo bemaasing bemaadiziwin*. I want to make it clear that their life force energy or *mnidoo bemaasing bemaadiziwin* was always present in these young ones, and as they grew older they found what they needed to do to survive including changing a behaviour.

---

33 Basil Johnston, *Indian School Days*, 12.

CHAPTER 6

"The Knowing" Youth and the Roots of Resistance

The journey continues in the southern door and this is a time of growing and changing and, for the youth, may be an unsettling time. The youth are coming to know and this is a major time of learning for them. This chapter opens with a voice of a survivor who describes his experience of running away, then I briefly describe some of the nutrients such as spirit naming, fasting, the "Walking Out" and "Full Moon Ceremonies," which the youth would have experienced from their family and community to nurture their physical and spiritual being. I then detail some of the experiences of the survivors and how they survived with little food and resisted the regimental routine, and managed the pain of being away from their families and community. Lastly, despite enormous, deleterious efforts to diminish the Anishinaabe *mino-bimaadiziwin* (the way of a good life), the youth found creative ways to nourish the Anishinaabe life force energy or *mnidoo bemaasing bemaadiziwin* within them. The following is a detailed example of one survivor's account of how a group of students escaped for a short period of time.

> Yeah I think there was six of us, or seven of us, and what happened, these guys worked in the cow barn, the dairy farm, that's where I got my head busted in there. They were off

done milking the cows, eight of them, then we had to feed them the hay after you know, water them, and the water trough that looked like a bell, oh maybe a foot opening on the top, maybe a foot deep and so we're standing there and we're done, three, four of us boys, standing there, get laughing about something, here comes this guy up the aisle and he swings this club at me, a cane, and that cane, he had a long strap on the end of it, he called it a cull strap, maybe he did, I don't know, but I caught my arms, and, but manger was only so deep about here on my legs but I tripped backwards, my head hit that bell shaped thing, the water trough where the cows drink out of, after I got caught, bust my head, knocked me out and these boys sort of pulled me out you know and they took me down underneath where they made churned the milk, you know, made cream out of it and all that sort of stuff, where the separators were and they sort of . . . this fellow sort of just sort of dunked my head, washed my head down, "There's no tell—there's nothing wrong with you."

But I was passing out so they walked me up to the boys' playroom to clean up for supper. One was on each side of me, walking me there. I was still in a daze, just poured water on me and I kind of come out of it. I went into the dining room and some how I just didn't feel like eating so they let me go up into the dormitory, blood all over the place you know, my shirt and everything and what was that guy's name? But anyways, that's as far as it went, I had no stitches and this was in June, maybe the early part of June.

I can't remember—Fraser—so anyhow they change around every six months. You work the cow barn, you work the chicken coop, you work in the pigpens, everywhere and we all had to learn how to milk those cows. It wasn't a bad job, somehow I got the job, Levis and I the ones who skipped a grade, got the job keeping furnaces going but anyway, we come from church, we get back there about one o'clock, and some of the guys say they are going to run away because they got beat up by the same guy. Beat them up with that stick he's carrying around and a whip. I think there was about three of them. Madder than hell, I says, "I'm going too." Couple of other guys, "We're going too." So we did. We changed our IDs a little bit, you know, from not from the black uniform we wore and I put on a big white sweater and we started walking down the railroad tracks from Muncey. They came to the courtyard, I guess there was a ferry at one time, took the train across—why we were coming this way, I don't know but we stopped the first night. We stopped at a farmer's house and right away they knew where we were from so they started chasing us. Somehow we were all pretty good runners from that school from running to the store all the time, everything we did was run. So, they couldn't catch us and they went up the other road thought they'd head us off. By that time they got the OPPs[1] or somebody out and here they come down the tracks not to far with flashlights. So I got another friend of mine, and I sort of lay on him, about that time of year in March, a little bit of snow, little piles here of white, this white flashlight, the light went over me and they thought I was just another piece of snow lying there so anyway, they left. So, we stayed there all night.

The next day, we went down the tracks again and we had a little bit of money and, in those days, they had little booths, no more than five foot by five foot along the tracks for the railroad people to stop, you know, buy little cigarettes and stuff, maybe a loaf of bread and that's what we ate. So that evening, the second evening, we stopped at a farmer's house and asked if we could sleep in his barn for the night.

---

1 OPP refers to the Ontario Provincial Police in the province of Ontario, Canada.

They knew where we were from. "Sure, sure." So we got up and he says, "I got some horse blankets for you—stay in the hayloft." Believe it or not hay is a lot warmer than straw. So we had a good night sleep, just dark, cause it was still getting dark. It still gets dark early March. So we gets up in the morning, we're used to getting up early. We cleaned his barn out, cleaned his horses, he had one or two cows to milk, so we asked the farmer when we were running up there, we woke him up, "Can we have a couple of pails to milk your cows?" "You guys can milk?" We said, "Sure we can, all of us." We even squared his manure pile, cleaned everything up so we milked the cows and he come in there and he saw, "oh my god," we cleaned the floor, everything and he said, "I've never seen this so clean since I built it." I'll never forget that.

So he says, "My wife is making breakfast for yous." He says, "I know where you're from, you ran away from that school." We said, "yep." "I'm not going to take yous back. What I'll do is I know how far you can walk during the day, I'll call all the farmers up, they'll call each other and let yous stay at their place for the night." That's what we did. We were gone for over a week. We ended up in—I forget that little town's name and on the main street there was this big hotel with a couple of stores, and we were in this place and it started to get cold, my brother Arnold says, "I'm cold." He wasn't the only one who was cold.

This was about five o'clock in the morning comes a man come walking down the street. Somehow he heard us in there. "Oh there you guys are, I heard about yous from some people. Come on in." He owned the hotel. So he got the cooks up and he says, "Feed these kids." They fed us you know and threw some mattresses on the floor in one of the rooms upstairs and we all slept. We said we'd clean this place up, sweep and everything; which we did. We were there two days and he says,

"They know I have you." The Mounties came. "I'll take yous back tonight, but they're going to promise me that they will not beat you." So he took us out, jumped all in the car, took us back after we ate supper.

So they must of been getting through the prayer meeting again, we were back up in our own bed. They took away all our clothing, everything, we had no nightgown, nothing. We were stark naked up there—kept us up there for a couple of weeks. It started getting warm, March, the end of March, and the principal made a promise to this fellow that they would not beat us, so when here they come up the steps. We knew what was going to happen, so they beat us on the rear end, give us the strap on our hand, god my hands, everybody's hands, you know, sometimes the strap would hit you up in there, and couldn't sit down or couldn't grab nothing. So we went back to school again. Everybody looked at us as heroes, but we weren't heroes, nobody really. (Ronald, October 3, 2011)

This survivor's experience is another example of the Seven Grandfather Teachings living within these young men. They were resisting regimented school life while protecting and nurturing each other. They were honest and had integrity with the farmers, never denying that they escaped from the residential school. In return for food and a bed, they worked hard on the farm, never expecting something for nothing. This is part of the Anishinaabe way of being and growing.

Anishinaabe Mino-bimaadiziwin (The Way of a Good Life)

As explained earlier, we are given an earth name when we are born and a spirit name by age two. The Elders watch us and assess when we are ready for the next rite of passage. Often this is in adolescence although some children as young as five years old, may be assessed as having the gift to carry the knowledge for transmission to future generations. As Elder Doug Williams says:

> This assessment is important, but they do that in cultural ways. They look at the boy, and that is again, one of the rites of passage. By the Elders looking at the men, looking at the boy that determines how much information that would be fed, or given, or told...[2]

When the child is ready, the Elder prepares him for the big fast.

> The big fast is one where you begin to know your spirit, the one that guides you. They could also change your name at that time so that initial fast, that very important fast where you get your spirit guide or your protector, and that's the one you don't let anyone know you're being protected by because if you do, you're weak. You have a weak point. You have to kind of crack that. Now, the only one that should know that is your Elder, your guide, so it's very important to pick that individual that you will be confiding in all your life...[3]

Your name may change as a result of this fast, and often the name references an animal. The spirits now recognize you by this name. For young men this is also the time when they are encouraged to live off the land and hunt on their own. The Elders remark, "You should have learned something by now so they're saying, "You go out there, you're on your own, whatever you kill, you bring here and we'll feast it."[4]

The young man, having learned the Seven Grandfather Teachings, puts into practice the protocols of respect, humility and sharing by

2 Elder Doug Williams, personal communication, September 14, 2011.
3 Ibid.
4 Ibid.

finding and bringing back his first moose, deer, or bear to the community to feast. Once the young man has completed his big fast, received his spirit name and provided for the feast, he may have another ceremony that prepares him for marriage. He learns how to treat women and how to be a partner which is an important learning experience to ensure a successful relationship required of a life partner.

Young girls have their own fast or "Walking Out Ceremony" and for women, the "Full Moon Ceremony" is taught in the language, *Anishinaabemowin* where they learn to respect themselves and others. They are given the teachings about their sexuality and moon-time. They learn how to take care of themselves including avoiding being around men and avoiding active participation in ceremonies during this special time. They also learn the difference between sexual desire and a relationship, and their responsibilities as a woman.

The rite of passage for both males and females integrate a sense of responsibility for all their respective actions. These children know themselves and have learned to respect themselves as well as others. Teachings and life experiences continue to reinforce the Seven Grandfather Teachings including dealing with disappointments. Elder Shirley Williams tells of an important experience in her life:

> I guess it's from the teachings of my own father because there was one time when I was nine years old, ten years old, he promised me that he would buy me a hatchet and rubber boots and rubber boots are very important in the spring and I wanted those and the hatchet was for peeling pulpwood because you helped to peel the pulpwood for your father. The better it is and be measured and you get paid lots, well lots, at that time for a young girl because I knew you had to work for it—to earn a living and you are part of the economics that you're contributing to the family so that he would provide for us so mine was helping out and trying to earn this hatchet and I was shown how to peel the

pulpwood and pile it but then what I forgot to do was when you pile wood this way, you put a stop there so these don't fall. I didn't do that. So I piled wood without something to stop it so what happened was when I put the log in there because they were very slippery, it slipped and all the poles also the wood moved and what happened was when they started to move—you had to get out of the way because all the rest are going to come down and I ran away as fast as I could and I hit a hole in the ground, that's where I stepped in and I fell in the ground and all the men, I mean there were lots of men who were doing the same thing, peeling piles and piles of wood and they knew, they saw and they heard. They all came running including my father and so when my father picked me up—I don't know how he got there so fast but I know enough to run away from this disaster that was occurring when it fell.

    I ran far enough so I wouldn't be hurt and he picked me up—well I was getting up anyway but he picked me up and said "let's just go home and have our lunch" because it was lunch time and he said, "we're going to have our tea" so he was holding hands with me and we were walking because I was crying I guess from fright. I wasn't hurt but it was from fright, being frightened and then my father said, "that's going to happen in your life, there will be times when there will be difficult times, maybe you are going to be working so hard, and so intense and something will happen and your work will be destroyed in one second, or lost or whatever. When that happens, well so it's nice to cry, have a good cry, brush yourself off and get to work again." I always remember that so when I went to residential school—yes there was always things that was beyond me that I couldn't do anything about—out of my control so our thing was to remember that this was only going to be happening for a time till you're 16, then you'll be out of there. "So whatever they did, do not forget your language, whatever they do to you in there—be strong, don't forget who you are and go learn about the Indian Act and come back and teach us."

So I never learned about the Indian Act, there's no way they would talk about Anishinaabe things or ways, or nothing—it was forbidden. Any time that we talked about it, it was witchcraft, that's what they said, so we didn't talk about it but it was there behind—when we'd go home or go for a walk but we never talked about it in front of the nuns.[5]

These experiences and teachings prepare young men and women for adulthood. The assumption is not about achieving perfection but rather being aware of and responsible for one's actions. We become unbalanced when we encounter difficult times in our lives. When this happens, we turn to the ceremonies to become balanced again. Fasting remains an important part of cleansing, healing and reaffirming the teachings throughout life. Elder Doug Williams relays the importance when saying,

> Anishinaabe have been dealing with the human condition of illness and health for a long, long time. It's just that we eschewed nowadays because we go to a doctor who is supposed to tell us what's wrong when we present a symptom. The old days they worked on it before you presented a symptom and one of the ways of doing that was to fast and you would clean yourself...[6]

Unfortunately, many of the younger children who went to residential school missed these rites of passage.

---

5 Elder Shirley Williams, personal communication, May 13, 2011.
6 Elder Doug Williams, personal communication, September 14, 2011.

The Knowing

The students learned both technical skills and defensive skills. The Canadian government residential school system forced the students to work half a day and attend class for the second half of the day.[7] The boys learned how to bale hay, farm and garden, and maintain the school's furnace. As one survivor said:

> Though we did get a good job like half a day, taking care of the furnace, keep it running you know and they got a stoker put in there. All we had to do was fill that hopper to keep that furnace going, after that it kept the whole building warm, that was a huge building. (Ronald, October 3, 2010)

The girls learned how to sew, cook and do laundry. By having the students perform these duties and jobs a financial saving was realized by the residential school.

The youth, feeling the loss of family and community led to strained relationships, and the students turned to each other for support. The understanding of relational responsibility inspired hope in many of the children and within this hope they wanted to recapture the immediate family they had lost so they turned to their peers and bonded with them as family members. This sense of camaraderie helped the students form a substitute family among their peers. As Haig-Brown comments in her study:

> The camaraderie which developed within the groups provided a welcome respite from the cultural attacks. As Native children working together, they could revert to traditional ways of dividing the labour in what may have approached the familial way: the older students acting in the role of parents

---

7 John S. Milloy, *A National Crime: The Canadian Government and the Residential School System 1879 to 1986* (Winnipeg: University of Manitoba Press, 1999).

expecting the younger ones to help as they could and gradually to become aware of the more complex tasks to be done.[8]

The older students at residential school recognized that the treatment of students by staff at the residential school was not right. Some of the students had come from very loving family environments and some had attended school in their home community.

> I knew going in, I was older, I was 11 when I went there and I knew that all that was happening there was wrong but yet I couldn't do anything about it. You had to just persevere through that experience but my prayer there every day, every night when I'd go to bed, I would pray that I would not wake up in the morning, that was my prayer but it never was answered so I had to deal with all that anger. (Geraldine, October 5, 2010)

As the survivors conveyed to me, they quickly learned to "play the game" (Susie, October 2, 2010) and "roll with the punches" (Patrick, October 2, 2010) and, as William states, "You go with the flow for survival" (October 5, 2010) (see Figure 8). Students learned survival skills and fighting skills to protect themselves and siblings:

> At Shingwauk, I don't know, I just—I just did what I did to survive I guess, and Arnold and I—there's nothing really extraordinary, I had to fight for him because like I said he was a little chubby guy and could never fight so well and I guess it was that protection but after a while it got to be that he didn't want to see us, he didn't want the others to see that at Shingwauk where I would fight for him cause it would be the bigger boys would step in again to agitate him and make us

---

8   Celia Haig-Brown, *Resistance and Renewal: Surviving the Indian Residential School* (Vancouver: Arsenal Pulp Press, 1988), 71.

fight but we survived that, that was the—we never got hurt. I got bounced around a lot. (Patrick, October 2, 2010)

You have to be strong to defend yourself. I used to get beaten up constantly the first few months I was there and sometimes several times a day—not just an isolated incident, it was constant so I was always having to watch my back. So you had to be strong, you just had to be otherwise you were a victim all the time. (Geraldine, October 5, 2010)

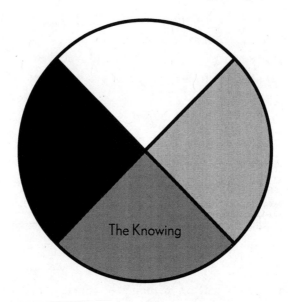

Figure 8. The Knowing

Please note that the colours that make up the Medicine Wheel are a crucial part of its extended meaning. The versions used in this text use the following colour formation: the North quadrant is white, the Eastern quadrant is yellow, the Southern quadrant is red, and the Western quadrant is black. The Medicine Wheels presented in this book have been approved by the Elders consulted for this work.

Paramount for the students was the protection of younger siblings and protection of others. Some of the older students took on the responsibility of taking care of their younger siblings. This responsibility instilled in the caretaker gave them a sense of purpose. One of the survivors described it this way:

> I had two sisters, but I was the oldest so it was my responsibility to look after them so I made it clear to others that they were to keep their hands off or they would have to deal with me and I think being the oldest gives you added responsibility and maybe that helps. That responsibility builds up the resiliency in yourself. (Geraldine, October 5, 2010)

Other students survived by putting other students first. Another student described how her protector looked out for her while she was at residential school.

> But my protector there—I had a girlfriend who was from Walpole, and she was a little, tiny thing. I mean I was small and skinny too but she was more petite. She was a little fighter. We had our own little cliques and nobody messed with her. I was kind of chicken at age nine. I was socialized and got along with people pretty well considering. (Sylvia, October 3, 2010)

Many of the students were motivated to look after the smaller ones while others made younger students fight each other for their own amusement:

> ... some of the older boys were good to us, you know they treated us like little brothers and stuff but then there were some are very mean, they beat us and everything else—the bigger kids. When you get in there, you know they'd grab your back of your neck and some other kid could be your best friend and make us fight and we didn't like that part so in the evening, what we'd do, after we ate supper, us little guys, we'd get up into this step, going up to these— these were steps on this side gone up to these dormitories.

We'd all get up in there and sit on the steps; it'd be dark in there. (Ronald, October 3, 2010)

I do not know how many survivors of the residential school were charged with the responsibility of younger siblings or how many brothers were charged with the protection of their sisters. I do know that for some it was a motivating factor to be strong and could also invoke feelings of guilt. Isabelle Knockwood, a survivor of Shubenacadie Residential School, says, "When they went to the Residential school, being unable to protect their younger brothers and sisters became a source of life-long pain."[9] Part of the residential school system was to break the bonds of family and destroy the children's spirit, and in some respects, these goals were accomplished for many.

We were punished if we told our parents about the ill treatment we received. One time the matron filled up the bathtub with scalding hot water. She picked up my brother by the ankles and dunked him in the water upside down. When our parents were leaving, the staff would stand behind the door and listen to us tell our parents about the bad treatment.[10]

Another survivor found ways to avoid predators altogether.

We had to learn to not—to stay away from predators and when I said that I spent most of my time in the bush, there were less predators in the bush then there were in the school ground. If you stayed in the school ground, you'd end up being bothered by all the supervisors whether—you know just doing what they think is right. They're trying to show

---

9 Isabelle Knockwood, *Out of the Depths: The Experiences of Mi'kmaw Children at the Indian Residential School at Shubenacadie, Nova Scotia* (Lockeport: Roseway Publishing, 1992), 16.
10 Mike Cachagee, personal communication, June 1, 1991.

you how to be something that you're not. They were trying to bring you into their fold in society so to speak they wanted to give up those old ways. (Louis, October, 2010)

The recognition of these circumstances fed the many acts of resistance such as running away from the school.

> Well I didn't really want to stay there. A guy and I, who was from Walpole Island, were going to run away and got certain pieces of equipment ready and stashed them and we were going to go on a real cold night and we were clothed well enough and he happened to mention it to somebody and that somebody squealed on us so him and I got into a lot of trouble over that. He got strapped and I got strapped in front of the whole school audience and the school audience was told what we were going to do. So after that a lot—kind of, a lot of privileges we had, were taken away, certain things that we had wanted to do and the rest of time, it was just miserable. (Vernon, October 2, 2010)

As Haig-Brown notes in her work of listening to survivors about running away, "From the time the school began, children recognized this option. For some it was a thrill and a temporary break from school; for others it was a graphic plea to those at home to save them from their misery."[11] When the students were caught and returned to the school, they were severely punished to make an example of them.

Summertime and school holidays were very traumatic for several Shingwauk Residential School students who never had the opportunity to go home. The students' family shouldered the responsibility to send fare (bus, train or taxi) for the residential school student to come home for special occasions. However, many students did not receive the fare to go home and or a taxi to pick them up. One

---

11   Celia Haig-Brown, *Resistance and Renewal*, 109.

former student shared that she felt no one at the school or in her family cared about her and felt she was abandoned (Susie, October 2, 2010). This situation created years of trauma for the students left behind at Christmas, Easter and during the summer.

The children began to change. The relational bonds with peers were also at risk, as personal safety became a constant issue. One Shingwauk student found safety within the seats of the chapel pews. Students were designated a place to sit in the chapel during services and this place became "their" place. Over the years students coveted this special place as their own and during reunions would return to this special seat in the chapel and reclaim it as their spot. Susie Jones remembers rebelling and sitting on the boys side in the chapel.[12]

Psychologically there was no trust and students spoke about being on their guard, watching their back and seeking revenge. "The school was a battleground for survival,"[13] and to me it sounded more like a war zone or prison. Two survivors told me that it was like a prison and one survivor explained:

> The thing about—the thing about the residential school is what it reminds me of in these times is a jail actually. You have almost the same rules that you have in a jail. You don't involve the police or the guards or anything like that so in residential school when you have troubles you never take it to the supervisors, those are the ones that are supposedly watching you. You don't never take it to them because they never understood anything. You could take them—somebody's doing something to me, you could take that, they would never understand it. They would never understand that it was like that because they thought—I don't know what they thought really but so you took care of things

---

12   Susie Jones, personal communication, October 13, 2012.
13   Linda Jaine, ed. *Residential Schools: The Stolen Years* (University of Saskatchewan: Extension Division Press, 1993), 79.

yourself. That's what you had to do if you got picked on by somebody. You waited until he wasn't ready then you got him back. (Louis, October 4, 2010)

Part of the change included what I call "compartmentalized pain"[14] which is the ability to section off one part of the brain that keeps the hurt inside. The hurt is stored in one part of the mind and protects the residential school students from certain situations. For example, as Patricia Baker (2008) writes in the April 26th issue of the Sault Star concerning her interview with Mike Cachagee:

> The older boys not only had to dig graves for those who'd died from tuberculosis, typhoid or starvation, they constructed pine boxes for burial. The dead were buried in unmarked graves, so there was no trace of their short lives.
> "There were maybe 40 kids in there," he said. "Their family would be out on the land perhaps, and the school authorities wouldn't be able to inform them of their children's death until they could be found." Plagued by these injustices, Cachagee suffers emotional pain to this day. He describes how the winter graves were shallower, as the earth was hard to dig into.
> Bears would come around in the spring, ravenous due to their long hibernation. They'd dig up some of the shallow graves and feed on the interred remains.

The residential school children became masters of hiding the pain. They accepted that there was nothing they could do as their siblings or fellow students were whipped, hit, slapped, had their ears tugged or were made examples of for running away. This was

---

14 Compartmentalized pain is the pain that survivors choose not to show. For example, if they witnessed another student being beaten or strapped they had to remain silent.

a quiet hurt on the outside but with a thunderous scream on the inside. Many students described being strapped and viewed many episodes of corporal punishment, enduring the pain with straight faces.

> I recall I used to count each strap that came down and it wasn't just a gentle strap like this. He would get right up on his tip toes and get his arm way back and come down with such force and there were many times I'd get ten on each hand and lots of times when I'd get 15 and I think 15 was the maximum I got on each hand so he went—was way beyond the norm for punishment of the day at that time and so I had to have been strong first of all to withstand all that. (Geraldine, October 5, 2010)

Others noted that the staff did not care about the student's reaction, so the students kept their pain and emotions to themselves. They would not give the residential school staff the satisfaction of hearing them cry out. One student found solace in the fact that she knew her time at residential school would end and that she could at some point return to her parents:

> I don't know, it seemed like I was just—I was just there and I had to do what they wanted me to do and I just thought about the time I could go back home—go back home to my parents, so that helped me cope, and it wasn't easy. (Mary, October 4, 2010)

Others found joy in working the farm and with animals or fishing. Since tasks were assigned intermittently, students were assigned one task one week then another the next week. Other students grew to love the animals especially the horses at Shingwauk School. Horses were used to plough the fields.

> I got on the good side of the farmer—the farm instructor and I showed him that I was willing to work and that my

brother, who wasn't supposed to be working on a farm because he was too young but, he used to come down there with me and it ended up being my job to feed the cows, the cattle, and take care of the bull and clean his bullpen out, take care of the horses, comb them and brush them down and feed them. I enjoyed it, that was one of the parts that I enjoyed was being able to do something and I wasn't afraid of horses or animals or anything because we used to have wild horses here on Walpole Island and they're magnificent animals. We had Clydesdales up there at Shingwauk to do the hard work, ploughing and stuff like that. (Vernon, October 2, 2010)

Others found ways to make a few dollars.

When it got warm, we'd be down in there swimming or fishing, and we'd catch fish and people from the Rez would buy fish off us. We'd sell it two, three cents cause the store was over here, a little over a mile about a mile and a quarter and so we got a few pennies and run to that store and get the marr balls they'd call them, black balls, you get three for a penny. (Ronald, October 3, 2010)

Many of the residential schools had gardens and raised chickens. In 1942, at the Mohawk Institute, every day 800 eggs were collected and sold to keep the costs of the schools down, although the students only got to eat one egg a week.[15]

Boyfriend/girlfriend relationships sprang up for the children at residential school. One female student conveyed to me that the young girls would stand at the Shingwauk Residential School second floor window and watch the new arrival of boys being unloaded from the cars. During this time, the girls would select their boyfriend from the lot.

15 Geronimo Henry, personal communication, October 13, 2001.

The girls would warn each other which boy belonged to which girl unbeknownst to the new boys.[16] The relationships that unfolded included notes being passed through the laundry and whatever other means they had at their disposal. I have observed former students when they arrive at residential school reunions who seek out their old boyfriends and girlfriends.

Since the budgets for the schools were tied to the school attendance, schools became overcrowded which resulted in several outbreaks of diseases such as tuberculosis. Many of the children were shipped out to sanatoriums to recover. As Haig-Brown notes in her work, "Children who became ill with scarlet fever . . . and other diseases were sent home or to hospitals. Many never returned to school."[17]

Food is always a worthy topic when discussing residential school; it usually consisted of two notes: that the food was bad, and that there was never enough to feed all the students. The ability to protect a younger sibling or a smaller student created a sensitive sensibility for some students. Extra food was scarce during this time and many older students when they had the opportunity, shared food with the younger students. "Other students stole food right off my plate during meals so I had to gobble it down as quickly as possible rather than lose it."[18] This sounds similar to Haig-Brown's study with 13 survivors:

> Stealing was common throughout the school. Because hunger was prevalent, food was the main target. It was stolen for immediate personal use, for sharing with smaller children, for barter, and to enhance the scanty meals of the dining room. Those who worked in the kitchen had easy access to food.[19]

16 Shirley Horn, personal communication, May 26, 2010.
17 Celia Haig-Brown, *Resistance and Renewal*, 115.
18 Michael Cachagee, personal communication, November 19, 2006.
19 Celia Haig-Brown, *Resistance and Renewal*, 98.

Some students stole food as a survival method and as most of the schools were farms, the students would steal chickens, kill them and roast them over a fire spit.

> Any time somebody gathered a bunch of food, they'd share it with everybody. A matter of fact the guys would eat half an apple and give it, share it with somebody else, "Here you want the core?" was a famous saying. "Give me the core, give me the core" and he'd eat half of it and share it that way so that's one of the things I guess that way we survived, but nobody got fat while there so that was one of the survival things we done. (Eric, October 4, 2010)

In contrast, when speaking about food, Haig-Brown reiterates that:

> Food in the school was rarely fit for swine, but the staff had their own cook and dining room and they ate like kings. . . The menus rarely changed, even after the federal government took over, and the kids were hungry most of the time.[20]

Many developed survival techniques which I like to call "collective resourcefulness"[21] that included stealing and bartering food. Some students bartered food for protection. As Phil Fontaine a former residential school survivor said, "you could buy protection with an apple."[22] Others would go to great lengths and sneak food after dark.

> And I think that's why they called it Mushole too so we got cornmeal, oatmeal, cornmeal, oatmeal, cornmeal, oatmeal every other day and we'd get two pieces of bread in the morning and one slice at lunch and that was why we'd call it mush. I guess that's where it got the name Mushole

---

20 Ibid., 18.
21 Collective resourcefulness is students working together to survive.
22 Phil Fontaine as cited in Linda Jaine, *Residential Schools: The Stolen Years* (University of Saskatchewan: Extension Division Press, 1993), 86.

> and at lunch time we got one piece of bread and I think we got one potato. It wasn't very much anyway. There's eight of us at the table and our plates were made out of granite like a pie plate, there's eight and one pitcher of skimmed milk on the table for us to share up, share that up. One pitcher I think it was only about maybe a quart, a litre is what you call—so surviving for food—we were always hungry, stealing. One incident there, we used to wear those bib coveralls and we went down and took the apples down in the storage bin and he went down there, the bib coveralls he put a whole bunch of apples in the top part you call a bib and he couldn't get through the window coming back out cause he had too big a load there and he got stuck there and we could see all this cause this was after we went to bed, we'd raid the place. (Eric, October 7, 2010)

Another survivor shared her story of how she was able to get food from the kitchen:

> I'd work in the dining room or kitchen. I'd steal food all the time. I stole prunes one time—wanted to cook them for the next day or somebody had them in a pot. Some of the girls were taking one or two, and me I got a little bag. The teacher asked, "Who took all those prunes?" They said, "Well, we took a little bit and Mary took a whole pack." She said, "What did you take all those prunes for like that?" I said, "I was hungry." I told her and she said, "Don't you know you could get sick?" By hook or by crook, I'm going to eat! (Mary, October 4, 2010)

Others (Shingwauk former students) would raid the garbage dump and search amongst the refuse for potential morsels.

> Another handy place we used to go to was the city dump. It was about two miles away—we had two paths leading to it.

We would go there looking for anything we could find to eat. You always had to have a stick with you because the rats were there looking for food also and they wouldn't back down easily. That was the reason for the sticks, to chase them away. Even when you found something that the rats had started eating, you'd just cut off that part and eat the rest. When you're hungry, you eat.[23]

I think the Great Spirit was looking out after me because the school or the city put that city dump right by the school and that's where I used to go for some food—cut off a half an orange or an apple, they weren't always rotten. They weren't all rotten through—running around, rummage through the garbage dump at the right time of the year like wintertime was a good time because food didn't spoil so fast. I remember going there a lot of times. (Leonard, June 9, 2008)

Other students would go to the store nearby and help themselves.

We would go to the grocery store over there and we'd swipe little cakes and stuff cause we were hungrier than hell and we would come back to Shingwauk and we got beat up. I guess that was part of building up a resilience. (Patrick, October 2, 2010)

Several of the students found ways to send letters home rather than giving them to the residential school staff. Letters home were censored by the staff, and much of what was written would be blacked out. One survivor spoke about sneaking to the store to mail a letter:

23 Donald Sands, *As Your God is My Witness: Rebuttal to Bernice Logan.* The Shingwauk Project Archives, 2010-004-006, (006), (Residential School Centre, Algoma University, 1996), 7.

That's how we'd used to sneak letters out too cause all the letters, we'd put on the blackboard. We just put it out or write it out and sign it. And in the other letter you'd have to go through here and they'd read it first, but we got smart and go to the store, send them out. But we never wrote much letters. (Ronald, October 3, 2010)

This example and all of the acts of resistance helped maintain their life force energy or ***mnidoo bemaasing bemaadiziwin.***

Nurturing the Anishinaabe Life Force Energy or *mnidoo bemaasing bemaadiziwin*

Most of the former students missed the ceremonies associated with this very important transformation in life from youth to adulthood because they were not with their family, clan, or community. They did not have the Elders watching over them and working with them to learn respect, or respect for themselves and others and cultural identity. They also did not have Elders watching to see if and when they needed ceremonies for rebalancing. As youth they were punished in a way that was not consistent with their traditional upbringing. Correction within traditional societies consisted of storytelling. A storyteller, without pointing fingers at anyone in particular, politely gives the understanding of what is acceptable behaviour.

As young Anishinaabe, we integrate our roles and responsibilities through our rites of passage. Being taken to residential schools interrupted this learning process for the students and interfered with their Anishinaabe responsibilities. No longer were these young women keeping the home fires burning nor were these men providing food for the family. They also were not participating in ceremonies or offering gratitude to the Creator. Yet, the youth found strength from their life force to survive. As one survivor said:

> I think primarily I used to try desperately to remember the good that I learned in my community to hold me together through those events at the school. I would remember my aunt who used to—who was a good homemaker, she did a lot of canning and helped in the community in ways that she could and I remember, tried to remember the loving, bonding that I had with my father and—my mother was the disciplinarian in our family so I felt closer to my father because he would never touch a hand on me and so those were the things that I would try to keep in mind to hold me together but then you also formed friendships there with peers that you can talk with and that's all we had, that's all we had. (Geraldine, October 5, 2010)

Although these young ones in adolescence were not in their traditional society, they were still able to endure because the Seven Grandfather Teachings were within them. For example, one survivor, through respect and wisdom, recognized the Great Spirit was looking after him, providing food and giving him the strength to go on (Leonard, June 9, 2008). Others drew on their innate strength. One survivor said:

> I think that strength was within me from probably in my genes from the time I was born you know. I think that's what has gotten me through because it was born within me and I had to find ways though to deal with that anger. You can't lash out, you can't, that's no way to live in this world. (Geraldine, October 5, 2010)

Other survivors were brave in running away from school, as was the case in the opening story. These boys, in their determination, never forgot the Seven Grandfather Teachings. They were honest, told the truth and maintained their integrity as they worked from farm to farm. The farmers acknowledged their gratitude for their work with food and shelter. Yet, when called heroes, they acted in humility by saying "We were not heroes." I remember Elder Shirley Williams once telling me that they did not celebrate the ones who ran away when the nuns were around. They went outside to the yard and waited until no adults were around; then they celebrated. In running away, and staying away for a week, those boys were seen as heroes and they fed everyone's life force energy or *mnidoo bemaasing bemaadiziwin* with this act of resistance. This act of resistance made the other students stronger which is important because the students found hope through the escapees' actions and these students' life force energy would surge with the knowledge that someone got away, successfully out on the lam. Strength and remaining strong became an important survival skill at residential school and building strength was a huge issue as it takes time; as Geraldine, a survivor states:

> ... but it takes time to build up your own strength to fight the toughest girl in there. I was such a skinny thing that you know if I weighed eighty pounds and that was the size of me and I was short. (Geraldine, October 5, 2010)

Many of the survivors found a collective resourcefulness, whether in work or in obtaining food. Haig-Brown describes a group of boys who developed a creative process to obtain cream for breakfast.

> At night, one of those that separated the milk . . . would come along and tap on that window from the outside . . . He'd have a beer bottle full of cream. I'd take it and put it down in that space in the chaff and leave it till morning . . . Then, after we clean the horses and feed them . . . I put that cream in my boot . . . And then, I'd take it into breakfast and we'd put that on our mush . . . I was the carrier. We done that and never got caught.[24]

Survivors I interviewed described other ways of being resourceful and passed on that information to others. For example:

---

24 Leo as cited in Celia Haig-Brown, *Resistance and Renewal*, 21.

"Where you guys going?" "We're going home" and he says, "You can't" I says, "yes, we are" and I said, "hey Norman, remember all that food I used to bring you? I'll show you the trick, how we did it." I have to get this big picture, show you. Pick it up, get in there, in that one window, open it up, there's a stick there, put it underneath there and this ladder, get it down in there, there's nothing but canned fruit that they buy from the farmers. We never got it, it's for the staff. He says, "That's how you did it?" and I said, "yep." (Ronald, October 3, 2010)

Another survivor described a cooperative provider:

There used to be a McCutheon's bread delivery there and he used to come right near the kitchen and the boy's washroom there and while he's in there, there'd be a guy throwing bread out of his truck down into the window, into the washroom, they weren't sliced then so that it'd hit the inside of—everybody was just grabbing, rip it up—got to be quick but anyways, managed to get about two or three loaves out of the window there but I think he knew—like the baker himself, the truck driver and he'd carry extra loaves just for us to eat because I think he kind of knew what was going on there, starving half the time—like I said we were hungry all the time. (Eric, October 7, 2010)

The survivors found ways to remain resourceful and continued to anticipate their freedom. Having said this, they had no idea what the future held. As Basil Johnston says, "Our knowledge about the world beyond our reserve communities or beyond the confines of Garnier[25] Residential School was equally scanty; we didn't know what to expect of that world or what it expected of us."[26] The next chapter tells the story of their transition.

25 Garnier School is another name for Spanish Residential School.
26 Basil Johnston, *Indian School Days*, 218.

CHAPTER 7

"The Transition" Young Adults Returning Home

The journey continues in the western door with the transition to adulthood (see Figure 9). In the west, this is a time for maturity and reflection. This chapter opens with a voice of a survivor as she transitions from the school to her outside life. I then briefly describe some of the nutrients such as the marriage ceremony, parenting teachings, and additional ceremonies that prepare adults for life. These nutrients nourish them with the knowledge and when to ask for the ceremonies, to remain in balance. I then offer some of the experiences of the survivors as they transitioned from the regimented school life and survived. Finally, despite efforts to diminish the Anishinaabe *mino-bimaadiziwin* (the way of a good life), I discuss how these individuals found creative ways to work, raise families and nourish the Anishinaabe life force energy or *mnidoo bemaasing bemaadiziwin* within them.

> Well I think at that time I was used to being on my own. When I left the school for the summertime, I actually took care of my older brother, fought for him, helped him get on the right bus, helped him get off. He eventually quit going to residential school before I did so he functioned just fine

without me but when we're together, I did the thinking and so I just kind of went on that way.

I remember the first time that I went to a home that I was an alien in and so I wanted to move out of there so the first summer I was out of the residential school and I made a decision to move out and I moved into the YWCA. Now, because I was only 16 I had to get permission from the Social Services of the State of Michigan to live on my own otherwise I'd be called a runaway so I went through all that and they gave me permission to stay at the YWCA and they put me in a room all by myself in a section of the building where there was nobody else. It was kind of like near the swimming pool and I felt so alone there and that was the first time that I was ever alone you could say and it made me stop and wonder whether I would survive in a world that I had never ever really lived in. I was used to so many kids in a room that we kind of nurtured one another. We didn't have an adult nurturing us but we had each other and so I really missed my family from school and I thought well I survived residential school, I'm going to survive this and the first night I had a lot of trouble sleeping but, after that, I didn't then so I'd been living, not living on my own cause two years later I was married and started having kids but, for those two years I lived on my own and it was very strange. (Susie, October 2, 2010)

As young adults the former students were now experiencing their first taste of freedom. While the freedom was sweet, very few survivors had a place to go, or a place to fit in. Imagine the loneliness of being at the Young Womens' Christian Association (YWCA) with no friends. This contrasts significantly to the Anishinaabe way of life of being welcomed into a family circle, a clan, a community and nation.

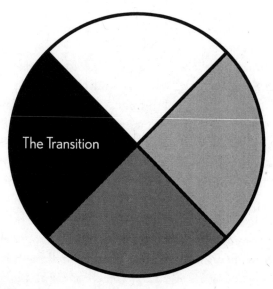

Figure 9. The Transition

Please note that the colours that make up the Medicine Wheel are a crucial part of its extended meaning. The versions used in this text use the following colour formation: the North quadrant is white, the Eastern quadrant is yellow, the Southern quadrant is red, and the Western quadrant is black. The Medicine Wheels presented in this book have been approved by the Elders consulted for this work.

Anishinaabe Mino-bimaadiziwin (The Way of a Good Life)

The next development of Anishinaabek maturation includes the teachings of the role of becoming both a marriage partner and a parent. We must participate in these ceremonies to make us aware of the responsibilities of what is required to be successful partners and caregivers. Elder Doug Williams describes the process of the marriage ceremony as follows:

> ... when the two partners have picked each other to marry, or the family have picked them for them. Just before that— they have a ceremony that we would call today a wedding

ceremony. In the old days it was called *wiijiiwaagan* that means that they are going to be joined. They are going to be joined with somebody they are going to be walking with. Now when that happens then for sure the men then get together with the young man who's going to get married. The women get together with the woman who is going to get married and the men go through the teachings about how to treat women and also the teachings of sexuality right so that's basically in a nutshell what happens.[1]

According to Basil Johnston, the marriage ceremony had a pre-marriage waltz. The first step is prudence, then acceptance, judgement, loyalty, kindness, and finally, the ceremony. The ceremony begins with the young man asking the woman's father for permission. Once accepted, the ceremony is performed by the grandparents. The young woman must be ready to marry and possess skills needed to maintain a home such as cooking and sewing. During the ceremony, the grandmother tells stories and the hems of their marriage coats are sewn. Ritual words are spoken followed by feasting and the playing of games.[2]

> The Anishnabeg word for the relationship between a man and a woman was *"weedjeewaugun"*[3] meaning companion—a term which referred equally to male or female. There was no distinction in sex: no notion of inferiority or superiority. More particularly, *"weedjeewaugun"* meant Companion on the Path of Life—"he who goes with" or "she who walks with." For both men and women, a companion was someone

---

1 Elder Doug Williams, personal communication, September 14, 2011.
2 Basil Johnston, *Ojibway Ceremonies* (Lincoln: University of Nebraska Press, 1982), 91-92.
3 As I have been taught by Elder Shirley Williams, the Anishinaabe word for marriage in her dialect is *"wiijiiwaagan."*

to walk with and be with through all aspects of life and living. Such was the notion of marriage: the taking of a companion. It is the strongest of bonds.

For the Anishinabeg, a woman's worth was not measured by a lithe body, an unblemished complexion, full breasts, or sensual lips. How well she cooked, how well she sewed—or even nature of her temper—were the things that counted in a woman. How many deer or fish he could find his family, and how frequently he could provide them, were the standards for a man.[4]

Part of what makes us Anishinaabek is the roles that we are assigned as human beings. As adults we are also assigned positions of authority, whether we agree or not. Learning the responsibility of a role is part of the maturation process. As Anishinaabek people it was our custom to obtain these responsibilities through rites of passage; for boys, it is the big fast. For the girls, it is the "Walking Out Ceremony," and for women, the "Full Moon Ceremony" among other important rituals. Since the children were taken off and put into residential school, these roles and responsibilities were never rooted in their psyche. This situation contributed to their roles being unfulfilled and further resulted in broken relationships.

The Transition

When the students left residential school some were still very young and continued on in school in their community. Others left at age sixteen and some eventually graduated and/or apprenticed at another institution. To be sure, many of the former students no longer had any conception of birth family or community (Susie, October 2, 2010), and Alice Blondin-Perrin, a survivor of St. Joseph's Roman

---

4   Basil Johnston, Ojibway Ceremonies, 79.

Catholic Mission School at Fort Resolution, Northwest Territories said "when I was in residential school, I did not even know what a family unit was.[5] When they returned home they felt like aliens in their own home (Susie, October 2, 2010) and community (Patrick, October 2, 2010).

There was a lot of residential school residue; the former students were angry about their traumatic experiences. They felt like no one cared about them. When they changed, so did their behaviour. They became guarded, untrusting, unable to count on anyone (Sylvia, October 3, 2010). They took these behaviours with them into their adult world. What emerged from the compartmentalizing of pain resulted in unacknowledged and unresolved anger. One survivor said that there were men survivors that were so mad at their family and the government that they never reconciled with anyone, but some men at the end of their life might reconcile with themselves (anonymous communication). Elder Shirley Williams commented, "a lot of survivors died due to unresolved anger."[6] Another survivor said:

> I say you should go to A.A., they'll tell you how to get rid of your garbage, said you'll have to take it all the way to the dump, you know, to get rid of it, you know, you don't have to carry it all your life. That's what I like about A.A. It's my lifesaver; it's my support group. It's been very good to me, showed me how to live a better life, a forgiving life, a peaceful life, serenity, peace, no more anger. It pops up, but I know how to get rid of it, anger, no more fear, you know, that's why that fear part, it used to scare me if anybody knew about my past, I would be afraid. I didn't want to dig into that but now the more I talk—I don't know how many people knew

---

5   Alice Blondin-Perrin, *My Heart Shook Like a Drum: What I Learned at the Indian Mission Schools, Northwest Territories* (Ottawa: Borealis Press, 2009), 27.
6   Elder Shirley Williams, personal communication, September 15, 2011.

about my sexual abuse. I carried that for 50 years I wouldn't let anyone know. (Leonard, June 9, 2008)

When I interviewed Leonard, it was important to him that his story needed to be told. He revealed to me that he was raped by two students at the Shingwauk residential school. He had also given his testominal before the Indian Residential School Independent Assessment Process because he felt it was important for the truth to come out. Leonard felt it was freeing that the truth be known and he made this decision so that it may be easier for other males to disclose.

Further, since the former students had never been taught to make decisions and were now free to do so, some lacked the confidence to believe in their ability to make choices, or feared doing so. Others, on the other hand, relished making their own decisions and felt empowered. Many of the former students feared authority and *zhaaganaash* people. As one survivor recalled her feelings as a student:

> I learned that white people were not all bad and out to harm me. In fact, they were very nice to me. This gave me the courage and my self-confidence grew. I didn't feel like such a wounded bird. (Geraldine, October 7, 2010)

Most of the residential school survivors I interviewed returned to families that were fractured or broken within their community. As one survivor said:

> I had to learn to cope then and I just wrote some thoughts a couple of weeks ago about the things that we felt as former students and one of the things that I wrote down was—when we came out of residential school and I'm sure that this is multiplied by thousands, we had no conception of our birth family and conception of community—the way it used to be. Now there were a lot of kids that went home to

happy families. Families that wanted them in the summertime and things like that, but there were also many families that were broken and I know from experience that families on reserves are fractured. They don't do the—they don't take up the responsibility of their position in other words, the mothers aren't mothering, the brothers aren't brothering, and aunties and uncles have bypassed their jobs too and of course the grandmas and grandpas they're around, they seem and try and nurture but there's a lot of them that don't either so I think that was hard for me—was not necessarily at the school and yet it was really a part of the school. (Susie, October 2, 2010)

Some former students who returned to their communities felt they no longer belonged to their home community or First Nation. "Yeah, we didn't fit in when we came back because we weren't part of a family. We were just two kids that were added to the community" (Patrick, October 2, 2010). Another survivor told me that when he left residential school, he went looking for his mother. When he found her, she didn't recognize him. This situation reminded me of the part in the movie, *It's a Wonderful Life* when George Bailey goes to his mother's house and he asks, "Mother don't you know me, it's George, I'm your son" and she responds, "I don't have a son." This same student, feeling rejected and abandoned by his mother again, ended up marrying a woman several years older than him because he was looking for a mother.[7]

Although some former students were able to maintain their language, others lost their language while in residential school. As one survivor said:

---

7   M.C., Shingwauk Archives, Fonds no. 2010-082/001(002)

> All the family in Detroit invited us over to visit them. They lived by Brigg's Stadium and we couldn't talk to them and they were mad at us probably thought we were standoffish. They didn't know that it got beaten out of us. It took a long time for us to discuss that—that's what really, really angered them. There was a nice clique of them in that area by Brigg's Stadium on Michigan Avenue. They were very disappointed in me and kind of—after that we didn't associate any more. (Patrick, October 2, 2010)

Many of the survivors did not return to Walpole Island or their home territory. This period is seen as a transition time when they had to make their own decisions rather than have residential school staff make decisions for them. Even this arrangement was problematic for the young adults. Many students only changed their regimented lifestyle from one institution to another. Three of the males I interviewed joined the military. One said enlisting in the military saved his life:

> After a while I got a notice—the F.B.I. came to my house one time. They wanted to know why I didn't register for the draft. I told them, "well I'm going back to Canada, and I'm going to Walpole tomorrow." They said, "Well before you go, go down to the register." Of course, when the F.B.I. comes to your door knocking, it scares the heck out of you, anybody would, so I was scared so I went and registered, signed. About six months later I got drafted cause I used to go back and forth from Walpole to Detroit you know. I'd stay over here a couple of weeks, couple there, couple of weeks, a week, a day, whatever, a month and I get this notice in the mail go down to the certain selected service board, and we want to talk to you and that was the end of that, then I was in the army.

That was a big turning point in my life I think, otherwise I would have made a criminal running the streets of Detroit. I would have wound up in Detroit. When I look back in hindsight that was really a good thing that happened that I got drafted in the army and taught me you know to obey and do things. I went to boot camp. I went to Texas for boot camp. I went to Germany for 18 months. All that was good in a round about way. Good came out of that for me. (Leonard, June 9, 2008)

One survivor joined the United States Marine Corps at 18 and later the United States Air Force. He served in Korea, did his basic training and eventually made sergeant. For him, the military allowed him to do a lot in his life. Once asked by an interviewer about his feelings about being at Shingwauk Indian Residential School, he contributed this:

A guy asked me to describe my feelings about Shingwauk and the best thing I could think of was—I was in the Vietnam War and I was in Vietnam three times. Once when I was a Marine and twice when I was in the Air Force and several times I come close to dying and that didn't seem to bother me too much. I did think about it. But I told this interviewer, I says, "I was in two wars in my life and I enjoyed Vietnam much more than I ever enjoyed the two years in Shingwauk." (Vernon, October 2, 2010)

As young adults, former students of the residential schools carried within them a different set of values and learned habits that they were forced to uphold as residual from that era. Unable to trust, many of them carried anger, which is understandable in this horrible situation. Many were loners, always on their guard, and ready to do battle. Many students had not learned their traditional ways of knowing or ways to deal with their unresolved anger through ceremony or other means to reconcile their feelings. It was pointed out to me by two survivors, that the earlier the child was taken to residential school, the more adversely affected their later adult life would be (Geraldine, October 7, 2010). Because the students did not experience any affection or emotional support from the staff, they would find parenting a challenge. This is a big issue and drawback for generations of children who were born to survivors.[8] One student remarked:

> My first baby died and, my second baby, he was born in 1953. My mother raised him because I didn't think anything about leaving, leaving my children because I was left, like when I was nine months old, my grandma told her to go work in Detroit and she left me. I didn't know I was abandoned. (Una, October 3, 2010)

Seeking Employment and a Sense of Place

Many of the former students were not only challenged to find a sense of place but also employment. Edmund J. Danziger, Jr. (1991), a professor of history at Bowling Green State University in the United States, describes the history of settlement in the Michigan area as robust because of the cession treaties.

> In the nineteenth century the expansion westward of many white farmers forced Indian cessions of vast land holdings. Ultimately they were confined to 226 reserves across Canada, where aggressive agents employed many of the same methods used by the BIA [Bureau of Indian Affairs] in Michigan to destroy traditional Indian cultures.[9]

---

8   Elder Shirley Williams, personal communication, September 15, 2011.
9   Edmund Jefferson Danziger, Jr., *Survival and Regeneration: Detroit's American Indian Community* (Detroit: Wayne State University Press, 1991), 18.

As a result, the ensuing consequence was that poverty and unemployment were rampant on the reserves and it was no different at Walpole Island. The people of this territory suffered the same fate of chronic unemployment and chronic poverty and resolved that there were no jobs on the reservation and the alternative was to starve.[10] By the 1970s, the unemployment rate was 60 percent prompting Walpole Islanders and former students of the residential school to migrate to where they could get a regular pay cheque. Since Walpole Island is located just across the water from Detroit, Michigan, this city proved to be a starting point for a number of the young adults who left residential school. Detroit had a large Indian population at the time and was a bustling metropolis. Jobs were a big draw, and many of the former students worked in Detroit. Some started working at a very early age as these two survivors illustrate:

> I lived in Detroit then, that's where I went after Shingwauk. My mother moved to Detroit during like wartime stuff. Plants were busy. My stepdad was making pretty good money—good money I think my sister said at that time, so that's where we went. We ended up in Detroit. (Leonard, June 9, 2008)
>
> I was 13 then she gives me a job where she worked. She was doing housework across the river and the guy phoned and said, "I'll give you work" so I was raking grass, cutting grass and all that, leaves, whatever. I even put up a garden for him but anyway that fall he took me down to Detroit and started working down there. He asked me, he says, "Come on down, I'll give you work" so anyway I went down there when I was thirteen and then started working for him. I stayed with him for about—probably about five years and he paid me cash cause he couldn't put me on payroll being underage and

10 Ibid.

from then I started working, never was without a job, never. (Eric, October 7, 2010)

Some survivors worked in the auto plants, one worked in a restaurant, another worked for the state, and one was a die and toolmaker. Other former students went into construction and one survivor reported that he was an ironworker. Edmund Jefferson Danziger, Jr. further writes that because of the bulging Native American population, services were stepped up to address the increasing needs:

> Innovative services also rested to a degree upon Detroit practices and institutions established before 1970: Indian personal networks of family and close friends, the bar culture, native neighborhoods, close reservation ties, and the venerable NAIA.[11] By the early 1980s, after a decade of heady revivalism, an extensive Indian social-cultural infrastructure had thus evolved.[12]

Love of family is an important factor in the survivors' lives. Many of the female former students got married, had children and were full-time caregivers and stay-at-home mothers. One survivor maintains that he has an enormous family because he wanted to be surrounded by love and lamented that:

> Yeah, well that was one of my things when I left school. I don't want to ever treat anybody the way I was treated. So that's where all the love came in for kids and family I guess, that's why we had a big family. (Eric, October 7, 2010)

Most of the survivors never spoke about their time at Shingwauk or any of the residential schools or about the trauma suffered while there. As a characteristic of Anishinaabek people, we think deeply

---

11   The North American Indian Association is a local Detroit Indian Group.
12   Edmund Jefferson Danziger, Jr., *Survival and Regeneration*, 164.

before we act by using our observational skills. The students by nature would remain silent as they were not allowed to speak their language and they did not know English. They would not talk about the experience of residential school because of the trauma. Some of the former students buried themselves in their work and one survivor admitted:

> I got a job at the Indian agency and I worked for the feds off and on and I got to be Band Administrator one time so it was a necessity for me to work because I couldn't just sit around and do nothing for a long time. It was tough trying to blend back with the Band. The people of the Band here—when we were up at Shingwauk, it was very difficult and still very difficult for me to have friends because I don't make friends very well without losing that friendship. (Patrick, October 2, 2010)

Other survivors became community leaders. For example as one survivor said:

> You can see it in a lot of them, for one thing a lot of residential school children ended up going back to their reservations and becoming leaders on those reservations. I noticed that when I came home from the military. I got a few calls from different places and these people were councillors, and chiefs and police officers, things like that ... But the ones, the ones that did make it became the leaders, they still had some problems about the school—I can't really put a thumb down on exactly what their problems were but you could tell that they did have problems. Sometimes in a group we would talk about it and there were a lot of tears that period of time and I was—I became emotional seeing people that I went to school with, with so many problems and I didn't know how I could show them or help them

deal with it. I think a lot of my anger was taken out of me because of the things that I did while I was in the military. (Vernon, October 2, 2010)

As adults, the survivors worked hard and in return their adult children, the second generation, became hard workers.

I once asked my daughter, "Why are you guys such hard workers?" All six of my children work very hard and they may have other bad qualities, but they are all very hard workers and when I asked that child, she said, "We saw you working mother, so we just thought that was the thing to do." Now my grandchildren don't have that but my children do and so I see that in all the other families whether it be just a homemaker or whatever it is. (Susie, October 2, 2010)

Nurturing the Anishinaabe Life Force Energy or *"mnidoo bemaasing bemaadiziwin"*

As Anishinaabek we are born into a set of relationships, a family, a clan, a community and nation. In this case, First Nations children were taken and placed in residential schools and while there they created substitute families. When they left residential school many found themselves alone; unable to return to their original family or original territory. Having never gained the Traditional Teachings from the Elders or the rites of passage, they lost their role and their identity in who they were supposed to be. Now they had to relearn to think, learn how to make decisions, relearn how to eat and how to live on their own. They needed to go forward without any guidance from anyone.

When you begin that path there is no—you really don't know who you are in that respect. You mature, play with your child then you go out and you wander. You're youthful.

You look for a partner and so on until after that then you begin to know your truth ... that energy is a combination of you as a physical being and as a spiritual being ... [13]

As previously stated, those two faces come together.

There is foreignness in being alone, as the essence of being Anishinaabek is through relationship. For these survivors, their art of strength, their Anishinaabe life force energy or *mnidoo bemaasing bemaadiziwin* was found in relationship: family, work, and/or military. Recall that a sense of belonging was key to feeding the survivors life force energy or *mnidoo bemaasing bemaadiziwin*. Other survivors I interviewed found family in work or military relationships. For example:

> He says "I can get you a job doing trade work on cars" so well same thing again I'd quit over here Friday. I worked over here, two years and two months I think in Algonac then I went to Detroit, same thing, I'd quit Friday and started working over there Monday. I kept working, work, work—like I said there was plenty of work and that was about 1952 I think but I met her [motioning to his wife] in '49. I think we went down—they could of had me for kidnapping cause I took her across the border, she was under age. We snuck away so anyway I was always working. There was a lot of work then I worked for that fellow for about 20, about 27 years altogether down Detroit off and on, like two years here, two years at Plymouth, about a year and a half in General Motors then he wrote me about three letters and the last letter he wrote me—"I guarantee you a lifetime job." Hey, that sounded good so I went and talked to him.
>
> Then I worked 23 years steady with him until the boys took over. He died—passed away so that broke that lifetime job.

---

13   Elder Doug Williams, personal communication, July 11, 2012.

What his sons figured—I guess and after he died, the way he used to run business was the bigger contractors they'd subcontract, subcontract maybe they ended up about three, four subcontractors and before he got the money to his office that's how long it took about a year and he had the bigger wheels Chrysler, Kelsey-Hayes, Great Lakes Steel, McLeod Steel, all those big companies down there that's how he ran it but when the grandsons took over everybody else 30, 60, 90 day basis and they had to pay right now, a lot of the companies just dropped them just like that, and the company was going bankrupt so they laid me off. Let me see in '75, I think or '74 somewhere in there, laid me off down there, working on.

There's a fellow here Jim T. was a water works—I don't know I don't think he had no title at the time, but anyway he come over on a Saturday and needed someone to help him so I said, "Yeah, okay", "can you drive a truck?" "yep," "a tar back hoe," "yeah," I drove truck for the R.S. Company for about eight years on the city there and I was dispatcher for about five but anyway we worked on a Saturday—put in a water line helped Jim with that and then so he said "I got another one Monday, can you come over Monday?" "Yeah, okay." Albert was the boss and he said, "Eric, I need a truck driver," he says, "could you drive for a couple of weeks?" and I said, "Sure, sure" okay so I drove a truck, dump truck so 25 years later and I'm still there now that insurance policy over here 70 and out so I had to get out so that was all the work. (Eric, October 7, 2010)

In the same vein, another survivor described her work life:

The goodness and kindness of people in my everyday life really helped me to blossom as a human being. From a very early age my goal was to be a nurse but because I dropped out of school that was not possible. My career has been working as a receptionist, bookkeeper, and supervisor and finally, as an ophthalmic assistant for doctors in Sarnia and they all were very wonderful people. I have been fortunate in my life to have a loyal loving husband, six very dear children, seven delightful grandchildren and seven treasured great grandchildren. My choices guided by the Great Spirit served me well. (Geraldine, October 5, 2010)

Another survivor recounted his experience in the military:

I joined the Marine Corps when I was eighteen, just after I turned eighteen and a lot of people said "Oh they'll never take you—they'll never take you, you don't—you're not smart enough for—you didn't go to school" but during that time—during that period of time, they had a war going on in Korea and they needed a cannon fodder so they took me. And, I guess I wasn't so dumb after all. I made sergeant where a lot of people didn't . . . (Vernon, October 2, 2010)

Acceptance into a family was paramount to the survivors as they craved a sense of belonging. As young ones some had had the happy experience of returning to Walpole Island and becoming a part of a combined family while others felt rejected and alien from their birth family. As the latter may have been the case, some survivors sought out substitute families and lifestyles. Some embraced alcohol while others became workaholics. One survivor, after many years of drinking joined Alcoholics Anonymous as his new family. Others tried to pick up the culture again. Some also embraced organized religion. Many had to learn how to like themselves and relearn how to live a healthier way for the rest of their lives. They knew that they had to do something. One survivor remarked that:

There was nowhere to go, no one to talk to at that time and I thought well I got—I got a life to live. I have family and stuff and I want to change all that. I said I don't want to be living like I did at the residential school. I want to change that and I can you know so what little I started to do is find myself—what am I doing that's going to console other people. (Gladys, October 9, 2010)

However, what she found from other survivors was that "they said, 'I don't want to hear it' and I thought geez it's something that happened in your life and they're always bitter. They're bitter all the time" (Gladys, October 9, 2010).

The Shingwauk Project in Sault Ste. Marie facilitated the coming together of the Shingwauk Family for sharing, healing and learning.[14] All of the activities—for example reunions, healing circles, publications, videos, photo displays, curriculum development, historical tours, and the establishment of archive, library and heritage collections—were in keeping with the original vision of Chief Shingwauk in providing education for the Anishinaabek people, while maintaining their traditions and culture. But most important was reclaiming their identity as Indigenous people and recovering the most sacred: the language, ceremonies, and Indigenous knowledge.

The former students had worked to transform the site into an inviting, loving and safe environment. They came to realize how much the school experiment had affected their lives. For the Shingwauk survivors, by again becoming part of the Shingwauk Family, many of their needs were fulfilled. They were accepted back into their family, they gained a sense of belonging and made a commitment to this community as in essence their connection and conception of community had been restored (Leonard, June 9, 2008; Patrick, October 2, 2010; and Susie, October 2, 2010).

14 This is personal information that I observed from a volunteer position and later from a paid employee position..

As the survivors transitioned from young adults into their later years, what was paramount for them was to feel a keen sense of belonging. Getting married, finding work in a community or joining the military service accomplished this life purpose. Many survivors made a decision not to allow their life force to be destroyed. They found ways to move forward; each doing it in their own way. Some returned to their traditional ceremonies, some found healing and relationships through Alcoholics Anonymous, and some waited to see how others fared before starting their own. To me, a healing journey is a lifelong process that encompasses many layers of growth and understanding.

Even though the coping and survival skills learned at residential school numbed their feelings, their hearts were intact with the values and the teachings of the Seven Grandfathers as witnessed by their lives in present day. In the next chapter we will discover the many ways in which survivors chose to live out their later years and what responsibilities they embraced and challenges they overcame in reclaiming their spirit and becoming cultural warriors within their lives.

CHAPTER 8

"The Transformation" Survivors as Knowledge Holders

The journey continues in the northern door with the transformation to elderhood. From this direction we learn our ethical principles, traditional values, endurance and wisdom. We seek wisdom from the Creator, Traditional teachers and our Elders as spiritual teachers. This is also a time of reflecting, recovering, reclaiming, reconnecting and giving back to our family, clan, community and nation. The survivors I know want to ensure there was a positive contribution, a legacy that would endure, echo the positive, in spite of their horrific life experiences. For an Anishinaabek, this may also be the time to embrace being a Knowledge Holder and/or Elder.

    We open with a voice of a survivor who describes the necessity to change her life. Then follows a discussion about elderhood, defining the difference between Elders and elderhood, and I briefly describe some of the nutrients that feed our life force energy such as family, (especially grandchildren), and taking on leadership roles. Next I offer some survivor experiences as they make life changes and explore how they found ways to contribute to their community, reconnect with other survivors, and reclaim their lives.

Finally I examine how this reclaiming process "victorized"[1] their lives and, in turn, nourished their Anishinaabe life force energy or *mnidoo bemaasing bemaadiziwin* within them.

Gladys, a courageous survivor, explains the challenges and understanding that is required to undertake the reclamation process:

> Some of them but, not everybody okay—some tried to find something to help them along with their issues you know that they have. Everyone has different issues and I think some of them try to—like lately we've been having a lot of group—group sessions where you can talk about these things where years before that it was like you went there— you go home and forget, but it's all in here [points to the heart] and people learned to live with anger and things that they didn't know how to go on with their life to help themselves, to have a family because a lot of that was still in them and they didn't—and there was no one to tell anybody. Recently we've been having a little bit more group meetings here and there and other places, conferences, workshops and stuff and that kind of helps you bring your stuff out like today that was really good and that helps some of the people with their resilience like that. With mine I just kind of dealt with it myself and I thought—well I had to learn to like myself and to relearn that I couldn't live like that the rest of my life. I had to do something. (Gladys, October 9, 2010)

As witnessed by the above survivor quote, linking with other residential school survivors who had the similar mindset of Gladys

---

[1] Cynthia Wesley-Esquimaux uses this term to describe the process of reframing "our life narratives...[and] to celebrate our victory and our survival at home." Cynthia Wesley-Esquimaux, "Trauma to Resilience: Notes on Decolonization," in *Restoring the Balance: First Nations Women, Community, and Culture*, ed. Gail Guthrie Valaskakis et al. (Winnipeg: University of Manitoba Press, 2009), 26-27.

brought forth the needed support that was offered at the conferences, Shingwauk reunions, and workshops that re-kindled her life force energy, *mnidoo bemaasing bemaadiziwin*. We are further reminded and come to understand that the former residential school students were taking on the responsibilities in their lives without the benefits of the traditional rites of passages as Elder Doug Williams says:

> I feel sorry for the ones who are born and adopted right away or sent to residential school. They must have—I don't know how they can recover. That's a lifetime of having to pick up pieces that they should have gotten as a process of life.[2]

Anishinaabe Mino-bimaadiziwin (The Way of a Good Life)

Mino-bimaadiziwin means to live a good life and is rooted in our languages, relationships, family, traditions, ceremonies, spirituality, storytelling (morals), healing work and counselling (guidance). Based on who we are as Anishinaabek people, our way is to embrace the old ones. For their life experiences and wisdom are embedded within them and that is why we seek them out. For example, when I had questions about the Anishinaabe Creation Story, ceremony and the natural development of an individual, I turned to the Elders and presented them with tobacco and asked my questions. For me it is a natural process.

According to Elder Doug Williams it is during this transformational phase that we develop and experience in our lives and it is also when our physical and spiritual beings come together to a place of truth. During this time, we have moved past adulthood and are free to look inside ourselves as our lives take on a slower pace. This is a time to reflect, to give back, be teachers, and contribute. Once these two faces of truth come together, our physical and spiritual beings are

---

2 Elder Doug Williams, personal communication, July 11, 2012.

one—we are whole. Usually once you reach this stage of development you become a grandparent. In our traditional society this is a huge responsibility which shifts our priorities. We have an extra responsibility for this new life, this grandchild.

The first responsibility is to ask for a spirit name for the child. From my teachings there are two schools of thought on how this is done. This is the naming ceremony event which I talked about in Chapter One. Basil Johnston indicates that an Elder is sought out.[3] A traditionalist once told me that either the grandmother or an Elder could provide the spirit name for the grandchild. If an Elder provides the spirit name, the participation of the grandparent is still warranted as the old ones to whom Elder Doug Williams referred to, are the pure ones and they are needed to provide guidance and wisdom.[4]

Elders are pre-selected and prescribed by the Creator for the knowledge holder role. "Since life is cyclical, the Creator gave the older ones the responsibility of keeping the stories, traditions, customs, ceremonies and Traditional Teachings alive and this includes the responsibility of passing these teachings on through storytelling, generationally."[5] For example, in Anishinaabe tradition the Elders teach the young ones the teachings of the Seven Grandfathers.

"Storytelling is possibly the oldest and most valued of the arts and encompasses a kind of truth that goes beyond the restricted frameworks of positivism, empiricism, and common sense."[6] According to Marie Battiste and James Youngblood Henderson:

---

3   Basil Johnston, *Ojibway Ceremonies* (Lincoln: University of Nebraska Press, 1982), 182.
4   Elder Doug Williams, personal communication, July 11, 2012.
5   Elder Doug Williams, personal communication, March 19, 2008.
6   Julie Cruikshank, "Invention of Anthropology in British Columbia's Supreme Court: Oral Tradition as Evidence in Delgamuukw v. B.C.," in the *British Columbia Quarterly* 95, Autumn (1992): 34.

Stories are enfolding lessons. Not only do they transmit validated experience; they also renew, awaken, and honor spiritual forces. Hence, almost every ancient story does not explain; instead it focuses on processes of knowing. Stories discuss how to acquire these relationships on every level, how to properly use them, how to lose them. They also discuss the consequences attendant on the relationships. One is said to be lost without allies, and stories about allies are guides to the unseen as well as to the seen.[7]

There is a difference between elderhood and Elders. Elderhood is being used here to describe older individuals who may or may not become an Elder. The community members where the individual resides confers the honour and title of Elder on individuals. They are selected because they are role models who are highly respected, and revered. They possess deeper virtues, as they are trusting, accepting, and are honest and kind individuals who love people and radiate that love. They are selflessly devoted to the betterment of others, healthy, lead a spiritually based lifestyle in that "they teach it, and talk it and live it."[8] Elders experience their understanding of their role spiritually, "a profound sense of calling, and not a career or income-driven choice."[9] They fiercely protect Indigenous knowledge. They determine what should become public knowledge and what remains sacred. They are devoted to the service of Indigenous people and to their respective communities.

7   Marie Battiste and James Youngblood Henderson, *Protecting Indigenous Knowledge and Heritage: A Global Challenge* (Saskatoon: Purich Publishing Ltd., 2000), 77.
8   Jonathan H. Ellerby, *Working With Indigenous Elders: An Introductory Handbook for Institution-Based and Health Care Professionals Based on the Teachings of Winnipeg-Area Indigenous Elders and Cultural Teachers* (Winnipeg: Aboriginal Issues Press, 2005), 10.
9   Ibid., 11.

Jonathan H. Ellerby, in working with a number of Elders and cultural advisors in the Winnipeg area, suggests that there are "three general distinctions" for Elders: Elder/Teacher, Elder/Healer, and Community Elder.[10] While all Elders share a similar philosophy that encompasses pluralism and individual freedom within a collective, each serves within a somewhat different capacity. For example, if we investigate the role of the Community Elder, there are a number of distinguishing attributes. The Community Elder:

> reflects age and extensive life experience. In this case Elders are male or female Indigenous individuals that have lived a long life and presently maintain a healthy lifestyle and possess a wealth of practical knowledge. This knowledge may or may not be related to spiritual things and usually involves expertise based on experience. This type of Elder is often consulted, especially in communities, for assistance in drawing on local cultural practices and knowledge about a variety of topics like traditional diet, traditional hunting patterns and traditional child-rearing practices. This category of Elder, however, is generally *not* the sort associated with healing or institutional work.[11]

The Elder/Healer has a specialized sacred position that is more closely related to the identity of a traditional healer. Ellerby emphasizes that "some healers may not be elders, while all elders can be considered healers to some degree."[12] Elder/Healers focus on traditional healing specialities, practice traditional medicine in the form of ceremony by utilizing Indigenous pharmacology such as plants, and bark. You may recall earlier that Elder Doug Williams explained that when we would experience bad times in our lives and we would have to ask for help from the spirit world and we would re-enact

---

10 Ibid., 8.
11 Ibid.
12 Jonathan H. Ellerby, *Working With Indigenous Elders*, 9.

creation and re-enact birthing. Through ceremony we were able to rebalance both our physical and spiritual beings. These re-enactments Elder Doug Williams refers to are the naming, tobacco, walking-out, smudging, fasting, sweat lodge, and letting go ceremonies. For example, smudging is a purification ceremony that helps to cleanse our minds and hearts to be open to receive good messages, feelings, and thoughts. This also acts to cleanse our environment so that we can live a good life.

Fasting is also a cleansing ceremony whereby our bodies and minds are open to receive visions, dreaming and the assistance of an animal helper, our *baawaamin*. The sweat lodge ceremony is a re-creation of our being in our Mother's womb and together with the trees, the heated rocks as the power of the sun, and the Anishinaabe spirit will help us with whatever is bothering us when we are in a bad way. The cleansing, restoring, rediscovering, and reclaiming the Traditional healing methods are essential for balance and holistic health, but first we must contact helpers and then decide which time-tested practice would be right for the ones seeking assistance.

As a result of colonization and the residential school experience, there are Elders who are Christian and operate within a different paradigm. They exist:

> where Christianity has all but replaced traditional religious belief and practice, [although] the acknowledgement and utilization of Elders is maintained ... These individuals often fill the same roles as traditional Elders, providing counselling, advice, prayer, and healing rites.[13]

However, it cannot be assumed that an Indigenous Elder will never be a Christian Elder in belief or practice and one cannot assume that all Indigenous families will accept the authority or care of a Christian minister, chaplain or Christian Elder. One must always

---

13 Ibid., 13-14.

be respectful and ask what is the most appropriate in times of stress, trauma, pain, loss or change.

In Anishinaabe tradition, we honour these special Elders by first requesting the knowledge and offering a gift of tobacco. Most Elders will accept if they can. Most Elders are busy individuals and wear many hats. If they cannot help you, they will make suggestions of where one can seek the help they need in locating the information or resources.

We now know the challenge before the former residential school students who had come from a place of no control, to a place without the benefit of the ancestors or the knowledge of the Anishinaabe way of being. Some of the survivors sought change regarding their feelings and chose to go back and pick up the pieces.

Life Changes

If you recall the story of Gladys, she made a decision to change; she did not want to live like she lived at residential school. The other survivors she approached were not ready to move forward; they were bitter in an untrusting place. Like Susie Jones said, they are "still living the Shingwauk."[14] This inability to trust meant that the survivors could not move forward or move back, either lacked the knowledge or decided that they did not need to change. Gladys had her language and had kept it since she was a baby. She took control of her life and started reconnecting by going to workshops, talking circles and residential school reunions and today is a WIRSSG member and a teacher of *Anishinaabemowin*. However, others were lost, confused and in pain as Eric describes:

> A lot of them went the other way, went to the alcohol and all that cause I did meet two, three of them, they weren't—they

14 Susie Jones, personal communication, August 15, 2008.

didn't go back to the civilized world. I guess *zhaaganaash* people and I think a lot of them committed suicide too. I heard a lot of the people committed suicide that did come from—they couldn't make it or they were too scared to face what was out there and I don't know what the percentage would be but I did meet two or three of them and they weren't that well off. They went to bumming, alcoholism, drugs and all that, whatever's out there.

. . . there's a lot of people, that I come out, I probably know about half of them and—I like trying to figure out how they lived. The life they had after they came out of there. It seemed like they're—they didn't pick up too much like yeah, a lot of them—you look at the list, he never made it, he never made it. He didn't make it either and what he'd do? What'd he learn you know, was he a teacher after that, or did he take over some shop or, where did he go from there after he did come out? And, I think most of them, after they did come out, went back, tried to pick up the culture again.

. . . And to gain all that culture back it's really tough cause even now I make mistakes and people correct me and that's what I always said, I said, "Hey, if I'm wrong correct me," I said and, if you see anybody, correct them, I say, that's mistakes are knowledge. I keep telling you, mistakes are knowledge and that's your teachings from mistakes. That's what I keep telling people and I don't know if they listen to me but I've had two, three people come back and say "hey thank you" . . . me I think, I made it. I made it—had a big family . . . well see that's part of it right there so that's the way that went. (Eric, October 7, 2010)

Another survivor said in speaking about the loss:

So I can't say I had a terrible time there. I certainly missed my home but I also enjoyed the company. I was a social person when I went there. Today I don't think I am. I think Indian residential school changed me, and made me more withholding like if I have something to do, got a job to, you ask me to do, I'll do it but if I got to go there and be Miss Personality, I can't. When I look at our community sometimes, I think, even the people who didn't go there, due to residual impact of 100 years of Indian residential school experience, we're not as open and forthcoming as when I was a child. I see people now, we meet each other, we don't even say, "Hello" and, I mean, we know each other or we should, or we used to interact when we were little and to me that's, that's a residential school impact.

To me it's rude and I know it but do you think I can change myself now? It's very difficult to be the person I'm supposed to be—to be free and open . . . It's an awkward lack of trust. I cannot depend on somebody else is what I think I learned at Indian residential school. (Sylvia, October 3, 2010)

Geraldine, another survivor who found her strength said:

I think that strength was within me from probably in my genes from the time I was born you know. I think that's what has gotten me through because it was born within me and I had to find ways though to deal with that anger; you can't lash out, you can't you know, that's no way to live in this world so I used to do a lot of reading and I'd listen to music that was you know they, the musicians, they would have to do a lot of studying and practicing to get to be that good to play those instruments and I used to think how marvellous you know that they could achieve something and produce such beautiful music so I think that thinking thoughts like that that's what helped me to get my thinking straight because if I went by what I learned at residential school, my mind would be so warped but I think I was home long enough to get some grounding before I was subjected to that experience and this is—as an example my two sisters they were younger than I was, several years younger and they were totally devastated by their experience. They never recovered; they went into alcohol and drugs and they lost their children that they had born and yet we were from the same family but because they were younger when they went into that experience at Mohawk, that it destroyed them as people.

. . . they didn't live a long life. My one sister was in her thirties and my other sister she was just in her early fifties so none of them got to see their grandchildren or even their children grow up so it was so hurtful to me that they had such a life. I did what I could to protect them but because I worked most of the time I wasn't always available. I would learn second hand that they had been beaten up or something so and . . . it got to the point though where when I was at the school I was strong enough to hold my own with any of the people there of the students and I had warned them that if they ever touched my sisters that they were going to get it from me so they laid their hands off after that but it takes time to build up your own strength to fight the toughest girl in there. I was such a skinny thing that you know if I weighed 80 pounds and that was the size of me and I was short.

. . . I think those who didn't have that resiliency have succumbed and died and again from first-hand experience with my family and thinking back on the relatives my aunts and uncles, they all died at a young age too and I think it was the impact of residential schools you know. When I think back at the history of the family that I know and what kind of lives they led after coming out of that experience. None of them really survived to old age so I think those of us who are still here have got to be very strong.

I think it's the individual. It's their own staying power. For me, like I said during the opening remarks it was within me too . . . and some don't have that. I often think back . . . so I had to have been strong first of all—to withstand all that so my resiliency, I would have to say I was born and within me—so it would be in my genes.

I think each student's experience is different and even though I say I had a good experience at Mount Elgin there are other students in our community who did not have that same kind of experience. Their experience was gruelling and so it is from student to student to student, it's not the same story even though they might have gone to the same school. It all depends on who was the head at the time, the era that they went and even those who went to Mohawk some from the island will say well it wasn't that bad as far as abuse and punishment. The fact that we all share that we could not speak our language or we could not practice any of our traditional spirituality and we were all taken from our homes and our communities those are all common but each person had a different experience at the school and maybe their support system was different too probably because there were a lot of people from Walpole Island who went to Mohawk at the same time so they would be a support to each other and, in our community there were a few that went to Mohawk, but even some of them were quite aggressive too and tough, really tough. So, I just . . . each story is individual.

I can't speak it at all and since coming back to this community and that was only in 1995, I went to Ojibway classes but I found it so difficult and I thought that it would just all come flooding back but it didn't maybe I needed to stay with that for a period of years and then I would start maybe the memory would start coming back but I'm involved in a lot of things and I didn't have the time to devote to it and it's a difficult language to learn and, so I dropped out because I couldn't commit the time to it that I needed so, yeah that's all I ever spoke at home and that's one of the cautions that my parents said, "If you don't learn English, you're going to have a hard time at school" and I really resisted and I did have a hard time. (October 5, 2010)

All the survivors I interviewed made the decision to move beyond the grieving and loss stages and found ways to make a contribution to their community. This was their reclaiming and transformation. As Cynthia Wesley-Esquimaux states, "Today, First Nations peoples are turning their gaze away from the colonizer and back to the hoop in an effort to reclaim their culture and free themselves from that which they could not control.[15]

The Transformation

Many of the survivors living at Walpole Island, or survivors connected to the families at Walpole Island, embraced the Shingwauk Reunion(s). Many attended the inaugural 1981 Reunion in Sault Ste. Marie, Ontario, Canada and continued to attend follow up reunions in 1991, 1996, 2000, 2002, 2006, 2011 and 2012. As mentioned earlier, in 2000, several of the survivors at Walpole Island pooled their strengths and energies and held their own residential school conference. The conference was held at the elementary school and reflected several traditional healing workshops which included the "Ojibway Clan System Traditional Roles and Responsibilities," and "Ethnostress: The Disruption of Aboriginal Spirit." Other activities

---

15 Cynthia Wesley-Esquimaux, "Trauma to Resilience: Notes on Decolonization," 21.

such as residential school survivor talking circles and a drum and dance social were offered. At the conference, 50 survivors filled out an evaluation survey. They decided they wanted change (see Figure 10).

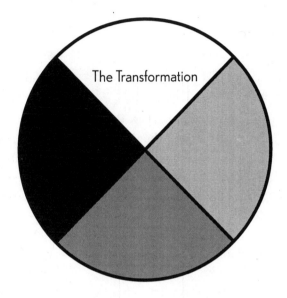

Figure 10. The Transformation

Please note that the colours that make up the Medicine Wheel are a crucial part of its extended meaning. The versions used in this text use the following colour formation: the North quadrant is white, the Eastern quadrant is yellow, the Southern quadrant is red, and the Western quadrant is black. The Medicine Wheels presented in this book have been approved by the Elders consulted for this work.

> Taking control of one's own life is a healing issue... We must exercise internal sovereignty, which is nothing more than taking control of our personal lives, our families, our clans, and our communities. To do that, we must return to our traditions, because they speak to right relationships, respect, solidarity, and survival.[16]

16 Robert Yazzie, "Indigenous Peoples and Postcolonial Colonialism," in *Reclaiming Indigenous Voice and Vision*, ed. by Marie Battiste (Vancouver: UBC Press, 2000), 47.

For me, all survivors of the residential schools possess individual gifts and many are leaders in their communities. For example, half of the 13 individuals I interviewed have been married for over 50 years and of those survivors four are married to other survivors and are the bedrock of their family:

> I've been married 50 years now, oh yeah so something must be working I don't know what and it's usually me—it's like I'm the anchor in the household. (Gladys, October 9, 2010)

Following the 2000 conference, they officially formed as the WIRSSG, and set out a plan on how best to acknowledge the former students' experience from their territory. The group constructed a Memorial Wall that listed the names of the former students and completed this project in 2002. The Memorial Wall is commemorated each year, followed by a luncheon.

The WIRSSG continues to function as an active group. Unfortunately, with many of the survivors passing into the spirit world, the WIRSSG is concerned because they know that their important work needs to continue and encompass the second and third generations on Walpole Island. WIRSSG representatives are invited to conferences and schools to speak about their experiences at residential schools and take an active role in educating the public on the legacy of residential schools.

In keeping with the role and responsibility of taking care of the children and the children of the seven generations, the Walpole Island residential school survivors became involved with the local high school. Alerted to the fact that the Walpole Island high school students were not graduating from high school, the survivors set out to remedy the situation by having built-in support for the students. One of the first volunteers to step forward was Sylvia, a Mushole Residential School survivor. To act as a resource and gathering place for the Walpole Islander students, the Harriet Jacobs Centre was established at Wallaceburg District Secondary School (WDSS) and is funded through the WIFN Secondary School Program. The high school students can now gather and have access to resources and resource personnel at the Centre.

In addition to the Centre, a mentorship program was inaugurated January 2008. The WIFN Future Elders Program was led by survivors, Susie and Sylvia and has a mission statement and many goals. The high school students had wanted an active group who shared their culture "with as many people they possibly could and organize special fundraisers to help people in the community."[17] One notable project included producing a video titled, *Celebrating Survival*, and is a collection of interviews about the experiences of the residential school survivors group living in their community. The secondary school students explain why the Future Elders name is used for this program:

> 'Elders' is a very special word in our community. We took the name Future Elders out of respect for our elders. They hold our stories, our culture, our visions, and our history. They're the people that we try to follow, the role models that we look up to, and the direction of the future that we hope for.[18]

On November 19, 2008, the Future Elders were awarded the Chatham-Kent YMCA Peace Medallion Award for community service. The Peace Medallion Award recognizes the achievements of individuals or groups who have made a significant contribution to fostering a culture of peace in the building of healthy and secure communities. This particular territory encapsulates the Chatham-Kent community. On November 25, 2009, the Walpole Island Residential School Survivors Group was awarded the YMCA Peace Medallion,

---

17   Wallaceburg District Secondary School, *Future Elders Program* brochure, Wallaceburg, Ontario (2009).
18   Ibid.

having been nominated by the WDSS Future Elders. The WIRSSG continues to meet on a regular basis, offers workshops, meetings and is involved with students who attend Western University.

Community Leadership

Many of the survivors are leaders in their community. "In fact, residential school survivors are often the very people creating and sustaining the key strategies and stories resisting potential encroachments in their communities. Their efforts are impressive."[19] The late Billy Diamond, a former Shingwauk residential school student is an example of a leader in his Quebec Cree community as he is recognized as a warrior for his people. Another example is my friend, a veteran, the late Ron Howard, Sr. who attended two Indian residential schools, Shingwauk and St. John's in Chapleau for a total of nine years. He joined the military at an early age, spending 10 years overseas, some time in Germany and eventually retired after serving 33 years while attaining the rank of master corporal. He was a member of Hiawatha First Nation and he ran for a position on Band Council.

Respected in the community, Ron, was an active pipe carrier, seen as a caring individual with leadership skills who has led the revitalization of the community powwow and was instrumental in creating the Serpent Mounds Trust. Ron related to me that being in Indian residential school made the students very shy and they felt alone in themselves and would not ask questions. He said "I never qualified for promotions because of my residential school experience..."[20] And, he feels that it was because of his inability to speak in front of a group at an early age that thwarted his ability to achieve a higher rank in the military.

19 John Borrows, *Drawing Out Law: A Spirit's Guide* (Toronto: University of Toronto Press, 2010b), 67.
20 Personal communication, February 3, 2008.

Another survivor, the late Patrick Isaac was a leader in the Walpole Island community. After leaving Shingwauk, he moved to the United States and in 1961 he returned to WIFN and worked as the Band Senior Administrator for 13 years from 1988-2002 and was responsible for administration including finances and human resources. In 2008, he served his third term as a Band Councillor and as part of his Councillor's duties, he sat on the following Board of Directors: the Ontario First Nations Technical Services Corporation and the Tecumseh Community Development Corporation. In addition, he had served on the Sydenham District Hospital Board and several sub-committees of the Ontario Hospital Association. His volunteer positions included being a trustee to the Three Fires Development Corporation, acting as a liaison with the Walpole Island Board of Education and sitting on seven sub-committees of Public Works.

Since 1991, Patrick had been a very active and involved executive committee member of the CSAA. A prolific orator and consummate communicator with his ear always to the ground and a passion for education, he had hoped to develop an Indigenous Bachelor of Arts in public administration. Patrick was fiercely protective and proud of his family and worked hard to maintain his commitment to them and to his community. He was extremely supportive of the healing processes that the Alumni have undertaken as their responsibility towards their Shingwauk Family. He was quick to accept a task and was always ready to voice a concern. Without his involvement with the Alumni, a strong voice would not have been heard and he worked hard to create an awareness of the impacts of residential schools and had exhibited compassion of the highest calibre when dealing with all people.

Another leader, Susie, was an Elder who also resided at WIFN. She was employed by the State of Michigan Department of Social Services for 18 years and occasionally acted as an expert witness for the State regarding litigation policy. Her volunteer work had been her hallmark beginning with her 12-year stint as a Board of Director on the Lapeer County Community Credit Union and served as a member of the Girl Scouts of America and the Lapeer County Citizen Probation Council for ten years. She served eight years on the Social Services Partnership Task Force and served as Board Director on the Indigenous Education Coalition.

Since 2000, she had been a member of the Early Years Task Force and from 2004-2006, she was a member of the Bkejwanong Attachment Awareness Team. She also has extensive experience achieving political positions in serving as a member of the Walpole Island Board of Education (1993-99) and the Lambton-Kent District School Board (representing four First Nations) since 2000. She also gained valuable experience as a WIFN Councillor from 2000-02 holding the Social Services, Health and Education portfolios. According to Susie, her most rewarding volunteer work has come from her life experience working in the area of the many branches of the Indian Residential School Syndrome. She had served on all 1991, 1996, 2000, 2002, 2006, 2011 and 2012 CSAA Reunion Advisory Committees. She continued to serve since 2004 on the CSAA Executive until her death in 2019. She was involved in no less than four Aboriginal Healing Foundation projects often acting in the capacity of advisor and "boss". She was a member of the Indian Residential School Eastern Gathering Advisory Team (2005-06) and since 1995 acted as the Bkejwanong Territory representative on residential school issues. Lastly, she served as an active member of the Shingwauk Education Trust, an Elder for Independent First Nations (as needed) and as a vocal participant of the 2007 Settlement Agreement Focus Group.

She travelled to Geneva to attend as a sitting member of the United Nations Forum on Indigenous Peoples where her main focus was to get Chief Shingwauk's name recorded in the plenary session's minutes. She was a tireless worker who worried about the future of the CSAA as she did not want to see the hard work that had gone on for the past 26 years dissipate and she noted as her goal in life was to help the survivors in her community (150 affected members) heal from the impacts of Indian Residential School and the subsequent generations.

Other survivors at WIFN served in active roles at the community level. For example, Garnet Dodge, Eric and Susie were all members of the Community Elders Advisory Council, and survivors Sylvia and Susie helped develop and draft the Band Election code.

Survivors are also viewed as role models and leaders in the recovery and restoration of the language. Language is an integral part of the reclamation process and restoring of the Anishinaabe identity. We are our language. Two of the survivors told me that it was the retaining of their language when they were young was what saved them at the school. They resisted and maintained:

> ... that's what I heard, get the savagery out of the people I guess that was one of their targets but anyway that's what pulled me through talking to other people, my language. (Eric, October 7, 2010)

Another survivor infers her views about language:

> Some people I've heard say, "They weren't going to take it away from me. They can tell me I can't talk it but they aren't taking it away from me" and I think that would have been my case if I would have spoke it when I was nine years old. (Sylvia, October 3, 2010)

In 1974, Elder Shirley Williams, a survivor of St. Joseph's Residential School and an *Anishinaabemowin* speaker and translator of the language, was challenged by the leaders in her home community to use language and culture as a resolution to the problem of suicide among the youth in her territory. The leaders felt that the children and youth lost their identity as the Anishinaabe culture and tradition was not being taught in the community schools. Shirley was spurred on to go back to school and make a contribution by teaching **Anishinaabemowin**. What she found was that there were no textbooks, no curricula and no materials for learning the language, so she developed her own and has since been a part of an annual language conference. She indicates that over the last 10 years that attendance at the annual language conference has increased dramatically along with the production of language materials such as compact disks, language tapes and books. Initially, the conference was planned as a coming together as a collective to work to increase the number of language speakers and save the languages. The primary goal in holding the language conference was to restore identity and pride in Aboriginal people.[21]

At Walpole Island, the **Anishinaabemowin** language is kept alive by survivors; Gladys, who teaches the language and Jennie Blackbird who acts as translator for the language. Keeping the language sacred within them helped the former students to keep a centred soul. They considered it as holding on to an important responsibility and built upon it to help restore cultural values and heritage, self-esteem and identity to the youth of their community. There is a real sense from the survivors that they care about the young ones in the community. They are concerned about the legacy of residential schools and the intergenerational effects. This is one of the reasons why they invited me to come into their community.

The men are disclosing at Walpole Island.[22] Many of the residential school students returned to their communities afflicted with Post-Traumatic Stress Disorder.[23] There is a rainbow of hope. Many of the survivors have gone on and assumed leadership roles in

---

21 Elder Shirley Williams, personal communication, September 15, 2011.
22 Susie Jones, personal communication, August 15, 2008.
23 Post Traumatic Stress Disorder refers to deep emotional wounds that results from exposure to an overwhelmingly stressful events, such as war, rape, or abuse. "It is a normal response by normal people to an abnormal situation." Glenn Schiraldi, *The Post-Traumatic Stress Disorder Sourcebook, Second Edition* (New York: McGraw Hill, 2009), 3.

their communities. They are no longer victims; they are Knowledge Holders and Elders as evidenced by the numerous invitations and requests to present and tell survivor life experiences at educational facilities. And, it is believed that the traditions and values of the Indigenous peoples are undergoing a recovery and reclaiming process.

Nurturing the Anishinaabe Life Force Energy or *"mnidoo bemaasing bemaadiziwin"*

Many of the survivors experienced a transformation with the birth of their grandchildren. As a grandmother myself, I sense it was the love of the grandchildren that brought forth pure joy. My own grandchildren are my "northern lights," for when I see them it is always a great opportunity to drink up the happiness and love. I experience a great feeling of contentment. As one survivor said, "We live for our grandchildren, they are our whole world."[24] The grandchildren are our future. As another survivor says:

> I think of family a lot and I know I'm not going to be around too much longer but I try to do things for them that . . . not so they'll remember me but so they'll know how to deal with things as they come on. (Vernon, October 2, 2010)

Elder Shirley Williams offered an understanding of the reclamation process to me as one of relearning, recovering, and reclaiming, (see Figure 11) as a survivor. When the young adults left the residential school, they had to relearn how to eat because there was never enough to food to eat. Often the resourceful students found ways to get food from the school pantry by either putting it in the girls' bloomers or by other means. Next, they had to recover their pride in who they are and reclaim their self-esteem as an individual. Many times I had heard that the residential school students were called

---

24 Anonymous communication.

"savages" (Eric, October 5, 2010) and heathens. Many of the students as adults had to learn how to recover trust, learn how to love and be kind and had to relearn how to like themselves, as they were taught to dislike "being an Indian." Lastly, the young adults had to relearn and recover the ceremonies which are instrumental to who we are, and as Susie Jones implied that it had to come from within.

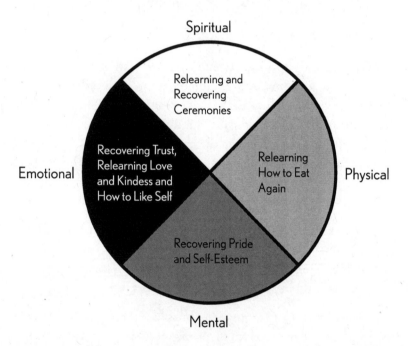

Figure 11. Relearning, Recovering, and Reclaiming

Please note that the colours that make up the Medicine Wheel are a crucial part of its extended meaning. The versions used in this text use the following colour formation: the North quadrant is white, the Eastern quadrant is yellow, the Southern quadrant is red, and the Western quadrant is black. The Medicine Wheels presented in this book have been approved by the Elders consulted for this work.

Some of the residential school survivors who are on their life journeys would say they did not read about the process to change in a how-to manual. Rather, they contacted helpers and decided for themselves which time-tested practice felt right for them. Specific supports such as the Shingwauk family or other substitute family enabled the coming together as a family to share their life experiences. "To a large extent, traditional healing draws its authority from the rootedness in a local community with a shared social life."[25]

> Instead of telling only the stories about trauma and victimization and pain, let us talk about our survival and our undeniable strengths. It is essential for us to articulate the strengths that we have, not only in a way that validates our survival, but in a way that validates and "victorizes" our ability to take control of our lives and be, in spite of past pain and present dysfunction.[26]

The literature is very clear that the reclaiming process is a difficult road to recovery.[27] This means that the person who needs to become whole—must come from a place of truth (those two faces coming together), and recognize that there needs to be a different path taken to change their life and create a different space of thought, mind and spirit and approach life with a new perspective and spirituality. "Recovering one's identity or spirit is central to healing. Spirit reconnects an individual to being a First Nations person,"[28] and reclaiming, rebalancing, and reconnecting with our Anishinaabe life force energy or *mnidoo bemaasing bemaadiziwin*. One example of a survivor feeding his life force energy or *mnidoo bemaasing bemaadiziwin* was to build a fire.

---

25 Laurence Kirmayer and Gail Guthrie Valaskakis, eds. *Healing Traditions: The Mental Health of Aboriginal Peoples in Canada* (Vancouver: University of British Columbia Press, 2009), 457.
26 Cynthia Wesley-Esquimaux,"Trauma to Resilience: Notes on Decolonization," 28.
27 See Assembly of First Nations 1994; Chansonneuve 2005; Kirmayer and Valaskakis 2009.
28 Assembly of First Nations, *Breaking the Silence: An Interpretive Study of Residential School Impact and Healing as Illustrated by the Stories of First Nations Individuals* (Ottawa, Ontario: First Nations Health Commission, 1994), 170.

I like the smell of wood smoke ... and it's a kind of a heat that warms my whole body and now I can feel it all the way into my bones and stuff. So I cut wood and I'll light my woodstove on fire just so I can sit there and feel that heat, makes me feel good...I just like the feel of it. I got a little bit of arthritis in my knees and stuff and that really takes it away good the wood stove does it—I don't know why. I was upset by the electric baseboard heaters that I got in the big house and I don't get the same thing off of them. (Louis, October 4, 2010)

Reclaiming for many of the survivors happens at the community level as a family. Elder Shirley Williams says, "it is the collective healing that is important and it takes seven generations."[29] Communities are trying to "re-establish a spiritual base for their communities with a foundation for healing."[30] Many of the survivors have gone on and assumed leadership roles in their communities. They are no longer victims; they are Knowledge Holders. And, it is believed that the traditions and values of the Indigenous peoples are undergoing a recovery and reclaiming process. The methods and practices for reclaiming are both an individual and collective Red Road.[31] The

---

29 Elder Shirley Williams, personal communication, September 15, 2010.
30 Assembly of First Nations, *Breaking the Silence*, 158.
31 Red road refers to an Indigenous path. For example, "The single most significant opportunity for me [in this therapeutic endeavor] is ... cultural identity.... We see ourselves as paving the Red Road to wellness.... Paving the Red Road speaks of an attempt to demystify indigenous processes and make it a lot easier to grapple with this "monster" called identity. Because I believe ... that a person who knows who and what they are simply makes healthier lifestyle decisions. So, we need to find ways to allow our people to embrace their own practices. To reclaim. To make the whole process of the cultural renaissance of the Red Man ... more palatable to the [Indigenous peoples] on the streets." Mike, "Healing Lodge" Administrator (2003 Interview) in Joseph Gone, "The Red Road to Wellness: Cultural Reclamation in a Native First Nations Community Treatment Center," in *American Journal of Community Psychology* 47, no. 1-2 (2011): 201, 187.

approaches such as the sweat lodge ceremony can be achieved as a collective whereby putting down tobacco, giving thanks and sharing with the water is individual. There is no standard way of how the processes work. One survivor said, "We could not speak. It wasn't until recent years we formed our voice and the courage to speak up" (Geraldine, October 5, 2010). My experience in learning as an *Anishinaabe-kwe* is that the reclaiming process I observed by the residential school survivors is a life journey. Wesley-Esquimaux calls it mining the diamonds.

> This is where the idea of "mining the diamonds" begins to have great utility for our lives. Yes, it (whatever it was for you) happened, and yes, it was disgusting and gross and even painful. The thing about it is that it happened, and that will never change. What can change is how we remember it, and what we do with that memory. We have to re-frame our life experiences so we can speak to them with the wisdom we have earned through our survival. We have to see those life events through new eyes, eyes that are older and wiser and can see past our own pain and into the distant past where it all began. This is where we will find the control that we did not have then, when we were small, alone, and helpless to stop what we didn't want, or to get the healthy attention that we needed from those around us. Today, we can take those memories, and reframe them into something that can help us now and add grace to our walk into the future. We can find our strengths, we can "victorize" our ability to keep standing and walking into tomorrow. Perhaps more importantly we can take those memories, enliven them as teaching tools to share and prevent what happened to us from continuing to happen to others, especially other small children.[32]

---

32 Cynthia Wesley-Esquimaux, "Mining Our Lives for the Diamonds," in *Indigenous Women: Our Strength, Our Story, Our Resilience*, edited by Wanda Gabriel, et al. (Kanehsatake Mohawk Territory, Quebec (pending book proposal 2012), 5.

Since the residential school experience has resulted in intergenerational trauma, part of the healing process is to make sure that there is an understanding and practice of traditional roles and responsibilities. No longer is there silence. Survivors are shouting and as I listen, they are saying, "This is my life experience and we want everyone to know it because we want the truth to come out!" Based on my interpretation of what I heard from the survivors, the analysis of the developmental process (see Figure 12) of the residential school survivors from childhood to elderhood is complete. This chapter brings us full circle and as the journey ends, I share some learnings and their significance.

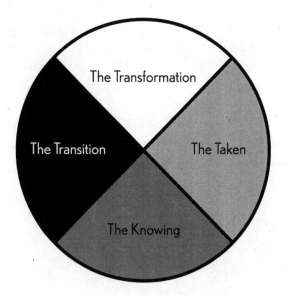

Figure 12. Survivors and Reigniting the Life Force Energy or *mnidoo bemaasing bemaadiziwin*

Please note that the colours that make up the Medicine Wheel are a crucial part of its extended meaning. The versions used in this text use the following colour formation: the North quadrant is white, the Eastern quadrant is yellow, the Southern quadrant is red, and the Western quadrant is black. The Medicine Wheels presented in this book have been approved by the Elders consulted for this work.

CHAPTER 9

The Path of Life Continues

At the root of Native American aboriginal concepts is the belief that the road conveys an eternal return. There is no end. At death, one returns in some way to the beginning. On the path of life, when one has reached old age, one knows what one knew when one was born, but only realizes and acknowledges it for the first time. The concept is at the root of aboriginal beliefs because like the road, the "sacred" had no beginning or end. This road is continuous and never ending.[1]

This chapter brings our journey full circle. The goal of this work was to listen to thirteen Indian residential school survivors from Walpole Island First Nation tell their life experiences. This work included giving voice to the survivors in their own words, and also listening, observing, journaling, reflecting, and interpreting how they understand resiliency. As mentioned earlier I believed that there is a positive energy, an endearing and enduring legacy that springs from the survivors. My journey began in 1991 when I was first introduced to a group of residential school survivors and, along that journey I learned Traditional Teachings and through revealed knowledge I have found that it was not the western concept of resiliency that I was getting from the survivors I interviewed but, in actuality, was

---

1   Peggy V. Beck and Anna Lee Walters, *The Sacred: Ways of Knowledge and Sources of Life* (Tsaile: Navajo Community College Press, 1977), 197.

life force energy or ***mnidoo bemaasing bemaadiziwin***. This is the essence of our being. Having come full circle, we now return to the bones and the bedrock or ***kanan miinwa nbagani-aasmaabkong***, the foundation of living or ***mino-bimaazidiwin***, and recall how the survivors nurtured their life force energy and reclaimed their spirit. Before closing this portion of this journey, I offer several learnings and the significance of those learnings for further work.

What We Are Made Of – The Essence of Our Being

I think that the essence of our being is the part of you that speaks to who you are. It can evolve from the time you're born into something that it was not when you were born or it could stay the same or I do believe that there's a part of you that will stay the same and that it could stay hidden for years and years and years. Now as much as I was assimilated and I will be the first to admit outside of the part I'm talking about, they did a very good job on me. I thought like a white man at the point when I left the school. I didn't know what it was to be an Indian.

When I got to Detroit, people would ask me, "Well what kind of an Indian are you?" I wouldn't know and so I picked the kind that I knew most about probably the kind I heard about in movies so I would say, "I'm a Cherokee" and I laugh now because I got the first two letters right ch but in doing genealogy I find out I might not even be as much Chippewa as I am Potawatomi but that part doesn't matter. It's not the tribe you belong to. It's not even being assimilated to the point where I was—but back to the question. When I left the school, I lived strictly in the white world for probably forty years before I ever returned to my community. All that time I thought white but when I went home, I was—the part of me that was Indian automatically came out. I loved to be on the reservation—reserve. I could relate to the people around me. I never thought I was better than they were even though I might have had a little bit more money than they did—than a lot of them did. A lot of people thought I had a lot more money than I really did which kind of made me laugh. I was no different than they were.

In my heart I was Indian and the assimilation that I had gone through almost disappeared from that point on until now. I still have some habits that I can't seem to get rid of but all the old ways—see my mother raised me as much as everybody raised me until I was four and a half, and she was strictly Indian. She never liked the English language even though she went to residential school. She always spoke Indian and that is the way she thought and up till a couple years ago, I didn't really think about it much what she thought, how she felt, what was she—I picked up a tape after my brother died, a tape that he had and I almost was apprehensive about playing it but I played it out of curiosity. It had my brother's name on it so I knew it was his and this is the only words on the whole tape. It's my brother saying to our mother, "I want to be Indian" and my mother said, "then learn the language" and I thought to myself after I heard it, it's those words that we use in our language that make us who we are, makes us Ojibway, Potawatomi or whatever and it's the meaning of the words that reflect the life that we lived and I think that even though I never lived in a wigwam, I never did all of those things, I was still Indian and I thought like an Indian and the more I got into education, I came to the belief that my thinking was right.

One of the other impacts I had was to read a book and understand how the loss of the land has affected us as a people and I do believe that my generation is the transition generation. My children are probably going to have a little inkling of it but my grandchildren will have none and that's the connection between the person and the land and that can only come from a North American Indian. I don't know if Australians have it. I don't know if other people have it that I've met from the South Pacific but I know we have it and it's the connection to the land that's spiritual and that can only come because you're an Indian. A European can't have it, a Middle Easterner coming here trying to understand our ways, he'll never gain that and so I believe that even with all the assimilation from residential schools, I believe that we are all still Indians and some even deny it but I don't think that they have searched their hearts and so that is where my belief comes from that I will always be an Indian.[2]

As Susie Jones states above, her spirituality can only come in being an Indian. Although she did not live in a wigwam, she is still connected to the land. Being Anishinaabe is spiritual and reaffirms that our cultural identity is vested within us no matter what occurs outside of our bodies. For the children who were forced to go to residential school, the natural process of the development of their cultural identity was disrupted, harming their life force energy or *mnidoo bemaasing bemaadiziwin*. This is the energy that I initially referred to as resiliency. I now recognize this as the essence of their being. For Anishinaabe, our foundation is the bones and the bedrock or *miinwa nbagani-aasmaabkong*. The Traditional Teachings of our ancestors is manifested within relationship and responsibility for living *mino-bimaazidiwin* and provides the protocol of acceptable social behaviour and Natural Law.

The Bones and the Bedrock or Kanan miinwa nbagani-aasmaabkong

The Anishinaabe Creation Story teaches us that we are dependent on Mother Earth, not the other way around. We are the last ones, earth beings, to be created and we rely on the plants, animals

---

2 Susie Jones, personal communication, January 14, 2012.

and the environment, and we are all related. Our responsibility goes outward in that our role in Creation is multi-layered and reflected in that first we are individuals connected to an extended family, one or more communities and globally, Mother Earth. The Original Instructions are a combination of our role as the stewards of the land and the expected behaviour rules encased within the Seven Grandfather Teachings as Natural Law or *Anishinaabenaakgonigewin*. As Garnet Angeconeb, a former student of Pelican Indian Residential School says:

> I think Indigenous people have a very special spiritual connection to the land absolutely, that's who we are, that's the way the Creator made us and you know we hear Elders talk about the Anishinaabe people being the stewards of the land, being the caretakers of the land and that's what we've been charged with—that's our responsibility as Anishinaabe people so we really need to honour that and not only honour that for ourselves but for our children in the future. What is it that we are going to leave for our grandchildren and our great grandchildren? So that is part of the sacred trust that we have that has been given to us to honour the land and one of the things about the healing movement of survivors and their families is that what has really worked is people going back to the land, land-based healing models where they actually live and work off the land the way our ancestors did and that's part of the healing therapy that many of our survivors are going through and so again it's not only connecting back to our families but we are also connecting back to the riches that the Creator gave us and that's the land and what it has to give us to sustain us in more ways than just our food.[3]

The core of Anishinaabe responsibility is relationship. The teachings, explained through storytelling are respectful ways of behaviour

3 Garnet Angeconeb, personal communication, July 2, 2011.

and understanding done in a gentle manner much like Mary (October 4, 2010) described in the story about her grandfather. This is one of the reasons why she loved him so much. Harrod contends that Indigenous people's memories "often exhibit an amazing consistency and tenacity . . . connect to traditions . . . it is evident that the chain of memory and transmission of oral traditions could be even older, involving the experiences of great-grandparents."[4] We carry with us life force energy or *mnidoo bemaasing bemaadiziwin* that springs from the notion of ancestral or blood memory or cellular memory and sparks with certain nutrients such as resistance and ceremonies.

Survivors have described this as ancestral information passed from generation to generation—innate, inborn and/or intuitive. Ancestral/blood memory appears to have a prominent place. Harold Cardinal once stated: "For being born an Aboriginal person you are born with special blessings and special gifts as a human being."[5] I wondered about the special gifts he spoke about. I found my guidance from the answers the survivors had given me when I asked them about their own resiliency. Some had pointed to the ancestors (Susie, October 2, 2010; Sylvia, October 3, 2010; Geraldine, October 5, 2010). Others insisted that it was part of their genetic make-up (Susie, October 2, 2010; Patrick, October 2, 2010) while some agreed that it was blood memory (Geraldine, October 5, 2010). "Native people must remember the 'strength of their blood, the same blood that ran through your ancestor's [sic] veins . . .'"[6] Former students explained as follows:

> I think that strength was within me from probably in my genes from the time I was born so I had to be strong first of all to withstand all that—so my resiliency, I would have

---

4 Howard L. Harrod, *The Animals Came Dancing* (Tucson: University of Arizona Press, 2000), xix.
5 Linda Jaine, ed. *Residential Schools: The Stolen Years*, (University of Saskatchewan: Extension Division Press, 1993), 23.
6 Aaron Denham, "Rethinking Historical Trauma: Narratives of Resilience," *Transcultural Psychiatry* 45, no.3 (2008): 406.

to say, was born within me so it would be in my genes. (Geraldine, October 5, 2010)

I think that your resiliency can come from a couple of sources. I've heard say that another person's resiliency comes from the teachings that she got from her parents and she presumed that we all had those teachings now—I did not have teachings from my parents. I might have from my grandfather who was mainly my caregiver but I do believe that resiliency can come from your bloodline only that I believe that it's genetically transmitted information not necessary genes that you have red hair, blue eyes and perfect teeth. I think that who you are comes from your bloodline. I just recently found out that I am the great, great granddaughter of a Grand Chief of the Great Lakes and I pondered upon that a lot and thought that—that genetically transmitted information could come from there. Now I don't have Traditional Teachings at all in my life—I'm Indian to the core. I know that and there was always a part of me and that even though my outer sphere was assimilated—the heart was still Indian and I know that has to come from somewhere. I believe that historically we have been resilient just as a people. (Susie, October 2, 2010)

Another survivor credits her late mother with passing on this information to her:

We are standing on the shoulders of those guys who survived four hundred years before we got here—my mother passing on the value of those people who came before. I think it has to do with what I was taught and being raised by Indian parents in an Indian community but also whatever is in me personally. I think the Creator has been good to all us Nishnobs and that blood memory is in me no matter what happens and my mother passed on the importance of being who we are and that we have the right to be. (Sylvia, October 3, 2010)

The former students have told me that there exists a strong link, a connection to the ancestors via blood memory, genetics, language, and survival techniques. As Elder Doug Williams reminded me:

> It's your heritage. It's our Anishinaabeness. Anishinaabe, there's a physical Anishnaabe then there's a Anishinaabe—spiritual Anishinaabe. We're a special people. The Elder Brother said that and the Creator said that through the Elder Brother, we're a spiritual people. How do you take spiritualness or spirituality from people who are spiritual? They couldn't do it.[7]

The inner spirit of an Anishinaabe individual is the life force energy or *mnidoo bemaasing bemaadiziwin*. "Further, an individual's spirit is seen as central to his/her ability to bounce back,"[8] and "it's not a blanket thing. I think it's ... individualist" (Patrick, October 2, 2010), and is "a living fire."[9] Herb Nabigon says, "The sacred fire represents the Creator who is inside every human being. Our responsibility is to keep that fire alive."[10] N. Scott Momaday describes the importance of bloodlines and memories and his own lived experiences with his mother and great-grandmother as, "Some of my mother's memories have become my own. This is the real burden of the blood; this is immortality."[11]

---

7 Elder Doug Williams, personal communication, July 11, 2012.
8 Colleen Dell et al., "Resiliency and Holistic Inhalant Abuse Treatment," *Journal of Aboriginal Health* 2, no. 1 (2005): 15.
9 Marlene Brant Castellano, "Updating Aboriginal Traditions of Knowledge," in *Indigenous Knowledges in Global Contexts: Multiple Readings of Our World*, ed. George J. Sefa Dei et al. (Toronto: University of Toronto Press, 2000), 34.
10 Herb Nabigon, *The Hollow Tree: Fighting Addiction with Traditional Native Healing* (Montreal: McGill-Queen's University Press, 2006), 87.
11 N. Scott Momaday, *The Names: A Memoir* (Tucson, Arizona: Sun Tracks/ The University of Arizona Press, 1976), 22.

Nurturing the Life Force Energy or *mnidoo bemaasing bemaadiziwin* in School

Through the interview process, the survivors identified several ways that they kept the life force energy or ***mnidoo bemaasing bemaadiziwin*** alive. One of the most significant ways of keeping love alive was by creating family. According to Susie Jones, "They took away our families and even separated us from our siblings at the school but we became a family ourselves to survive."[12] As the survivors reflected on their experiences, there were many references to the responsibility of looking after a sibling while at residential school, and later seeing to the wants of their family members.

A second way of keeping this life force energy alive was through the many acts of resistance such as stealing food and running away. For example, one of the survivors described his escape from the school and how that resistance energy spread amongst the children like a concentric circle. The escapees survived one week and when they were brought back, the boys were celebrated as "heroes" in the eyes of the other students. Later, the children would celebrate quietly and listen intently to the adventure stories regaled by the escapees. The "heroes" fed the euphoria and an energy of hope. To be sure, these boys were asked to tell and re-tell their adventures to an eager audience many times over. The survivors spoke of other acts of resistance including stealing little cakes from the neighbourhood convenience store, taking apples from the storage room and sharing them; "give me the core," with others especially the younger ones who needed the food to live. Also, despite the residential school administrators' best efforts to annihilate Indigenous languages, a number of the children were able to retain their mother tongue and eventually go on to teach the *Anishinaabemowin* language at the community level like Gladys.

Based on the bedrock and bones of our ancestors, the children who went to residential school, were able to tap into that spark of

---

12   Susie Jones, personal communication, February 3, 2008.

energy. The intuition borne in our people helped to protect them, and to know how to tap into their roots and resist the residential school policies like speaking the language in private places and practicing traditional ways. Those customs and Traditional Teachings in some cases lay dormant, sleeping, but never went away.

Reclaiming and Victory

Understanding and knowing what needs to be done is important. Reclaiming is essential as we learn from Garnet Angeconeb:

> It wasn't really stolen from us, it was set aside and we have to devote our energy into reclaiming what was set aside and today when I look at survivors, we're doing that. We're sitting around drums, people are celebrating their traditional lifestyles, people are into ceremonies and so on and that's coming back, that's coming back.
>
> Well, one of the things I find very interesting is I've travelled across Turtle Island and visited many First Nations in the last let's say thirteen years and I've watched a lot of survivor groups go back to their roots, go back to their traditions, the cultural ways, there seems to be a calling and so when you look at the healing movement, you know some people are immersed into the western style of healing, the western style therapy, and I would say the majority of survivors are immersed into their own ways, their own traditional ways cause there's a resurgence, there's a coming back and so that's a very important part of healing and I've really noticed that a lot of our people who went to residential schools are reclaiming their lives through Anishinaabe ways, through the Indigenous knowledge, through Indigenous practices and that's very healing for them and so I really believe in that that there is resiliency through Anishinaabe culture, Anishinaabe ways.[13]

13 Garnet Angeconeb, personal communication, July 2, 2011.

One survivor had felt that he never wanted anyone to be treated like he was treated at residential school and felt that having a huge family and a successful work life resonated his love for family (Eric, October 7, 2010). When I interviewed Eric, I sensed a tremendous amount of survivor pride. Wolin and Wolin defined a survivor's pride "as the well-deserved feeling of accomplishment that results from withstanding the pressures of hardship and prevailing in ways both large and small. It is a bittersweet mix of pain and triumph that is usually under the surface."[14] Being able to have children, especially grandchildren, provided contentment and a feeling of success for former students. When asked about their grandchildren, the former students' faces would light up with joy and one survivor admitted that he and his wife live for their grandchildren.

In 1981, some of the residential school survivors who attended Shingwauk residential school were re-born during the first reunion. From that first reunion, the Shingwauk Alumni took responsibility for their own collective healing. They met and planned subsequent reunions which included: lighting the sacred fire for the duration of the reunion days; holding talking circles; offering sweat lodge ceremonies; feasting; offering workshops; and holding a ghost supper and pipe ceremony.

Some of the spiritual energy that lay dormant within the residential school survivors because of colonization and/or abuse sprang to the forefront for them and they felt liberated from the impacts of residential school. Many of them disclosed their residential school abuse in talking circles and for the first time, the survivors spoke about the abuse out loud for others to bear witness to their life experiences. Others spoke of their experiences of running away from Shingwauk.

The importance of balance comes through when I hear the survivors speak about the need to talk to each other either in circles or in workshops. Most important is the need to try to regain the

14 Sybil Wolin and Steven J. Wolin, "Shaping a Brighter Future by Uncovering Survivor's Pride," *Reaching Today's Youth* 2, no. 3 (1998).

language and the ceremonies. In this particular environment, survivors feel comfortable and see each other as an extended family with the members in their community. Survivors are forming associations, leading and organizing and look to each other to fulfill their needs through action. As Wesley-Esquimaux, a descendent of two residential school survivors insists:

> We are on the move, and we are making a difference, and we will win many more battles. Over the next twenty years, we have the opportunity to profoundly influence the trajectory of our young people and our communities into the future. We have access to education and women are taking advantage of that wonderful opportunity and utilizing their knowledge to amazing effect. We have an incredibly young population that is ready to take on the world on their own terms and win. We have a stronger sense of who we are as a people and can teach the foundations of our beliefs and history in many circles. We can "mine our lives for the diamonds" and tell stories of strength, feminine grace, and an enduring power for living. I call it "victorizing" and that means calling forward the narratives of survival and tranforming them into stories of continuance and courage. We are still here, and we will be here tomorrow, and the day after that one.[15]

In keeping on the path of victorizing, as described by Wesley-Esquimaux, I have observed survivors from different First Nations meeting together and planning activities with all ways respected. This acceptance, I suspect is normal. The respect and the capacity to love were never lost on the survivors I interviewed. The recognition and awareness of what happened to the survivors and having the courage and bravery to tell and share with others very private life

---

15 Cynthia Wesley-Esquimaux, "Mining Our Lives for the Diamonds." In *Indigenous Women: Our Strength, Our Story, Our Resilience*, ed. Wanda Gabriel, et al. (Kanehsatake Mohawk Territory, Quebec (pending book proposal 2012), 7-8.

experiences are seen as beneficial to others who do not understand the intergenerational effects on seven generations after the residential school era. Since the residential school experiment goes beyond Canada's borders, the effects are felt globally. Indigenous nationhood, and the respectfulness exhibited to all tribes and Indigenous rites are included, rather than excluded and emphasizes the importance of reconnecting and reclaiming the traditional practices. Elder Shirley Williams said that prior to her going to residential school her father told her "don't forget who you are."[16]

Included in this role of responsibility is the passing on and re-generation of the Anishinaabe language, **Anishinaabemowin**. The survivors have been involved in translating and teaching the language, assisting youth with language retention and ceremonies. The ceremonies are performed in the language. I have heard the language spoken among the survivors and they are quick to let you know the translation if asked. For example, Elder Shirley Williams has acted as the translator for this work. I have heard and learned that as previously stated, we are our language and that culture is three things: land-based, language-based, and a social structure, and everything we do fits into one of these structures. If one is absent, then there is no culture.[17]

As Anishinaabe people we have survived an onslaught of assaults on us. When I interviewed the survivors, several examples of survival techniques were told to me. The survivors appeared to develop defensive mechanisms in order to survive including the inability to trust others. As one survivor said, "Resiliency I guess it would mean to me, being determined to survive no matter what and to not let anything stop me from doing that or try not to let anything stop me" (Mary, October 4, 2010). The survivors relayed to me that being at residential school toughened them up—making them ready to roll with the punches and adapt. As one survivor said, she was "thick skinned and hard headed." (Mary, October 4, 2010).

16 Elder Shirley Williams, personal communication, October 11, 2011.
17 Jan Longboat, personal communication, February 10, 2012.

For this work I viewed a video titled, *Last Call Indian*, a film by Sonia Bonspille Boileau. Sonia is the descendant of the late Mitchell Morris Bonspille who was a former student of the Shingwauk Indian Residential School. Along her quest to learn her heritage, she shared this additional important insight that is a testament to her grandfather's strength:

> My grandfather lived through things that probably would have been too difficult for me but I do hope his survival instincts live on inside me. I hope that that's what he has passed down and that in turn, it will be my legacy and the fact that I understand all this now should put an end to my worries.[18]

As Anishinaabe people we need to accept the tools and gifts we receive from the Creator when we are born. We need to believe in ourselves because within our spiritually, we possess great intuition. We must trust in this innate ability. We have our stories from time immemorial. We have our names, our teachings, our culture identity, and our Elders tell us the teachings. The ones that are innate are in our bones and pass through our bloodlines into future generations like the rivers that are ever flowing through Mother Earth as her blood. Our children are our legacies, our bloodlines. Whether we are community leaders who take an active role in ensuring a positive legacy or just sensitive human beings, we owe a responsibility to protect our names and pass on an enduring, respectful legacy to our families as they are the piece we leave behind.

Significant Learnings

My learnings throughout this work have been significant. To fully explain them is a challenge as I must reach back in my own mind and gather several parts of this life journey. My first learning is the

---

18 Sonia Bonspille Boileau, *Last Call Indian* (DVD) (Gatineau: Nish Media, 2010). Available from http://nishmedia.tv/view_television-productions.php?pid=98.

importance of reciprocal, fluid relationships fostered throughout my life; the recognition of the connectors associated with reigniting Anishinaabe life force energy for the residential school survivors and the nutrients that fed that life force energy.

Reciprocal, Fluid Relationships

The hallmark of this work is the family spider web-like connections that Leroy Little Bear writes about in *"Advancing Aboriginal Claims."*[19] The manifestation of these reciprocal, fluid relationships encompasses "all my relations."[20] Since observing, fostering and recognizing these web-like connectors and connections throughout my life, it is my belief that the understanding of the bones and the bedrock or **mnidoo bemaasing bemaadiziwin** came from the ancestors through revealed knowledge. Perhaps it was the trust that had been shared through all these relationships that assisted in opening a portal between me and the ancestors who fed me knowledge. The messages came when I was quiet, settling down, and getting ready to go to sleep. This is the time that the ancestors picked to send the knowledge and I had to be open to receive the knowledge. This is my experience and understanding of why the bones and the bedrock or **mnidoo bemaasing bemaadiziwin** are so important to know. My belief is that the Tobacco Ceremony facilitates my messages to the Creator, and this has facilitated revealed knowledge to come through to me.

In addition, it is my belief that the Elders, Traditional Teachers and Medicine people who have shared their Indigenous Knowledge and offered advice, have been placed on my life path. They have assisted and guided me in learning to pick up what was left by the path and carry this message on to the next generations. This leads to the first significance in that more work needs to be done by Indigenous

---

19 Leroy Little Bear, "Aboriginal Paradigms: Implications for Relationships to Land and Treaty Making," in *Advancing Aboriginal Claims*, ed. Kerry Wilkins (Saskatoon: Purich Publishing Ltd.), 29.
20 Ibid., 30.

peoples about Indigenous peoples because we know what needs to be done and how it should be done. Indigenous peoples know what they need as they live "within the land [as opposed to] on the land."[21]

This work began with a Western concept—resiliency—but along the journey, what was being described by the survivors was their life force energy or *mnidoo bemaasing bemaadiziwin*. But, if I did not know the Creation Story, the Original Instructions, the Medicine Wheel, responsibility and relationship, the bones and bedrock or *kanan miinwa nbagani-aasmaabkong* then I would not have recognized this and would not have the understanding of what was being presented to me. In other words, my journey as an *Anishinaabekwe* together with the Traditional Teachings which are integral to the Anishinaabe paradigm, enabled information to be revealed. Second, facilitating and conducting the work ourselves puts us in a unique position in that we are the ones who will invite individuals to come into our communities. These are individuals who most likely already have pre-existing relationships with us and are seen as trusted individuals who know of our history and have ties to our ancestors through reciprocal relationships. This approach is a big difference between those Western methods that presume there must be objectivity and no pre-existing relationship between the individual doing the work and the individuals who have consented to work with them. My work began with a Western approach however, after reading Kovach's work, it spoke and reached out to me. With Kovach's conceptual framework in hand, I went to an Elder and together with her assistance, we adapted and developed Kovach's Cree learning to an Anishinaabe teaching. In the same regard, my work, specifically the conceptual medicine wheel, may spark someone else's learning journey much like Kovach's work had done for me.

21 Mark Dockstator, "Toward an Understanding of Aboriginal Self-government: A Proposed Theoretical Model and Illustrative Factual Analysis," unpublished doctoral thesis, Toronto: York University (1993), 64.

Future work concerning the next seven generations must be approached from an optimistic and positive place for our people to accept it because we are so tired of hearing the negative[22] and the information must be useful to us. Part of this work was to highlight the many stories of struggle that have been turned into stories of strength. We know that the residential school students have taken the opportunity to speak out and tell their truth and talk about their life experiences at the national level at the Truth and Reconciliation Commission gatherings, and they want the citizens of Canada to be aware of this dark part of this land's history.

This work needs to emphasize strength-based research,[23] and to be more focused on discussion and conversation and not to come from a problem-based perspective like other studies concerning Indigenous peoples. The Walpole Island Residential School Survivors Group have put together memory books. The memory books ensure that survivor knowledge will be passed down to their succeeding generations with the idea that once one knows where they come from—they will be more accepting.

Strength-based work should seek information from a place of empowerment in every day understanding and community solutions that affects everyone concerned. For example, Wesley-Esquimaux and Smolewski, in retracing the history of the Indigenous peoples of Turtle Island and historical and intergenerational trauma, highlight that "the people carried their life ways forward in their hearts and spirits"[24] and go on to say:

> Today's Elders know that, although some aspects of the Aboriginal social self were deeply hurt and damaged, there

---

22 Susie Jones, personal communication, April 26, 2013.
23 See Wesley-Esquimaux and Smolewski, 2004; McCormick and Wong, 2005; Denham, 2008; Absolon, 2009; Brant Castellano, 2010.
24 Cynthia Wesley-Esquimaux and Magdalena Smolewski, *Historic Trauma and Aboriginal Healing* (Ottawa: The Aboriginal Healing Foundation, 2004), 85.

is yet another side of the Aboriginal psyche: the Aboriginal spiritual self that is full of positive energy, waiting to be revealed and used in the right way. The Elders see the effects of colonization and the subsequent collapse of Aboriginal social structures as central to the cause of the disintegration of Aboriginal communities, traditions and, in turn, individuals.[25]

This different approach is discussed by McCormick and Wong as post-traumatic growth, stress-related growth and tragic optimism.[26] Marlene Brant Castellano and Kathy Absolon highlight resilience strategies and would likely agree with Denham who indicates:

> Discussions concerning the consequences of colonialism and the challenges facing American Indian people frequently do not illustrate the strengths expressed by individuals and communities, as powerful stories, songs, histories and strategies for resilience are often present behind the realities of inequality, injustice and poverty.[27]

In addition, we need to cease looking at areas of interest from a problem-based perspective but rather from a "what's working" perspective. We should also come from a place where one size does not fit all. There are approximately 630 First Nations (Assembly of First Nations, 2013) on Turtle Island and each is an individual First Nation with its own history, territory and place. Best practices, which come through governmental agency reports, will not necessarily work for all or any Indigenous peoples. We have to be the ones who decide what we will do and how we will do it. The answers are within us and Elders are the glue which cannot be under-estimated.

---

25 Ibid., 92.
26 Roderick McCormick, and Paul T.P. Wong, "Adjustment and Coping in Aboriginal People," in *Handbook of Multicultural Perspectives on Stress and Coping*, (New York: Springer Science and Business Media Inc., 2005).
27 Aaron Denham, "Rethinking Historical Trauma: Narratives of Resilience," *Transcultural Psychiatry* 45, no. 3 (2008): 392.

The third significance is that gathering knowledge, learning and developing reciprocal relationships, is a lifelong process. As previously stated, my journey began as a teenager and continues to this day. Part of understanding of the development of this type of relationship encompasses knowing the protocol on how to respectfully approach Elders, Traditional Teachers, Medicine People, and the community. The development process includes recognizing the gifts of certain Elders and knowing what knowledge you are seeking and from whom. This important interaction should be done face-to-face so that the knowledge is successfully communicated. One should also know that doing this work takes a lot of time. For me, this journey has been 20 plus years of receiving Indigenous knowledge and working with the survivors.

The fourth significance concerns revealed knowledge which Lionel Kinunwa describes as cellular memory.[28] This is important as Western concepts do not convey an Indigenous paradigm and lens and revealed knowledge must be recognized as a valid method of acquiring knowledge. Rather than using English terms to describe our ways and understandings, we need to use our Anishinaabe meanings in Anishinaabe context. When Elder Shirley Williams translated the word resilience to me in *Anishinaabemowin* as *zongwaadiziwin* meaning "strength of life." I felt a sense of comfort and joy in that the translation held a different perspective and conjures up a keen feeling and sense of coming home for me. *Anishinaabemowin* comes from a different place than the English language and is a feeling language and holds more meaning.

> In the Anishinaabe way of life, when we are grateful to all our relations we say miigwech. As one survivor explains, this is more than saying thank you.
>
> I used to ask my dad, "How come a lot of Indian doesn't translate into English?" He says, "Because some of the words in Indian or some of things in Indian that you say are not

---

28 Patricia Steinhauer, "Situating Myself in Research," *Canadian Journal of Native Education* 25, no. 2 (2001): 184.

words, they're concepts. They're whole concepts and it means it covers a whole range of things that you'd have to talk about a whole lot in order to know what the actual thing means." When you say *miigwech*, he says, "you're not really saying thank you to this person." He says, "What you're actually doing is giving a little prayer to whatever being instilled that, that kindness in you." You know *miigwech*, that's what you are doing is sending that prayer to whoever made us have kindness or all the seven grandfathers inside of us, that's part of what *miigwech* means here it's a small prayer that just goes on and you're constantly doing it in all of your life. Almost everything in your life is about being grateful and I learned all this after my parents had separated. (Louis, October 4, 2010)

The next section discusses the learning and significance of how the survivors reignited their life force energy or ***mnidoo bemaasing bemaadiziwin*** through nutrients such as family, resistance, and the reclamation process.

Survivors Reigniting Their Life Force Energy

As stated earlier, I observed an energy that emitted from survivors which was first thought to be resiliency. Upon closer investigation, the observance was exposed as life force energy or ***mnidoo bemaasing bemaadiziwin***. With each survivor that I listened to, certain nutrients were revealed that fed their life force energy or ***mnidoo bemaasing bemaadiziwin***. The nutrients that kept their life force energy alive were family, resistance and the reclamation process.

Family

Since the students were taken as children from their family and community which for them were places of safety, love and caring, they created a family amongst each other. They called each other brother and sister and in certain instances, with the survivors who attended Shingwauk residential school, they called themselves Shingwauk Family. Recall in the Transition chapter, survivors spoke of getting married and having their own family. Other survivors joined a military family and one survivor spoke of Alcoholics Anonymous as his family. What was paramount was finding, feeling and knowing a sense of belonging.

Many acts of kindness were noted in how survivors relayed to me how the older ones would protect the younger ones and give them food to eat when they were hungry. The survivors like Geraldine also told me that they felt a huge responsibility to take care of their younger siblings and this responsibility was extended to the younger ones whether they were birth-related or not.

Survivors spoke eloquently about the importance of becoming a parent and having a family. One survivor explained why he had such a big family and it was because he wanted to feel the love and, other survivors said that when they became a grandparent—that they now live for their grandchildren. The grandchildren fed the life force energy or *mnidoo bemaasing bemaadiziwin*. Another factor that should be noted here is that out of the thirteen survivors interviewed, six survivors were married in excess of fifty years.

Resistance

There were many acts of resistance that fed the children's life force energy or *mnidoo bemaasing bemaadiziwin* while they lived at the residential schools. They were quite resourceful in acquiring food from the school pantry. This activity was usually a group undertaking as one student had to act as a lookout during this task to ensure that no one got caught. Speaking their Indigenous language even though they were told not to is another act of resistance. The students were able to preserve and speak the language despite fear of severe punishment. There are also many instances of students escaping the residential schools and when students were successfully on the lam, the remaining students at the school celebrated when there was no school staff around. This act of resistance was so powerful that the life force energy went out to the other students like a concentric circle, energizing and sending out joy and hope to the other students at the school.

Reclamation Process

The explanation of the reclamation process can be viewed from two perspectives. The first one is provided in Figure 11.[29] This Medicine Wheel, developed with assistance from Elder Shirley Williams, explains the relearning and recovering of nutrients that should have been known to the children if they had not been taken from their family and community. The second perspective was the cultural revitalization in recovering the ceremonies, gathering together, becoming leaders in their community and if they retained their language, some speakers became language teachers. The nutrients described here are the ones from this specific group of survivors and there may or may not be other survivors.

The fifth significance is that more work needs to be completed regarding the innate life force energy or ***mnidoo bemaasing bemaadiziwin*** or soul-spirit,[30] and what it means to other Indigenous peoples. One must be open to experiencing life force energy or ***mnidoo bemaasing bemaadiziwin*** and it needs to be sparked. For example, there is no expectation or assumption that Anishinaabe life force energy or ***mnidoo bemaasing bemaadiziwin***

---

29 See Chapter Eight, p. 228 for the figure titled *Relearning, Recovering, and Reclaiming*
30 Basil Johnston, *Ojibway Heritage* (Lincoln: University of Nebraska Press, 1976).

would be described in the same way. For me, it is rooted in each of us and consists of nutrients of teaching and meaning and a deeper coming to know. This includes "listening with heart" which I interpret as connecting with the spirits of the words of truth which I heard, and I think this process is sparse in the documents I read. As I had mentioned earlier perhaps something in my work will feed, spark someone else's life force energy, much like my life force energy was sparked when I first saw that circle being drawn on the school blackboard in class that day long ago. I was intrigued by the life force energy I observed emitting from the Shingwauk survivors. There also seems to me to be different degrees or strengths associated with life force energy which may be connected to our development within the life cycle. For example, consider the life experiences of Mike Cachagee and Elder Shirley Williams when they talk about soul travelling. They were both in different places in their lives at the time of this occurrence. Is soul travelling a nutrient that helps us continue our lives in a good way? Can soul travelling be achieved at only a deep, spiritual level?

Another observation is that experiencing and understanding life force energy or **mnidoo bemaasing bemaadiziwin** does not happen overnight. My awareness (see Figure 13) occurred many years ago, knowing that I was experiencing something important but not knowing what it was. Each subsequent instance, including my experiences with survivors, deepened my awareness of life force energy or **mnidoo bemaasing bemaadiziwin**. The Elders were instrumental in helping me understand my experiences, in that knowledge is learned and experiential. This means that one cannot read this work and understand life force energy or **mnidoo bemaasing bemaadiziwin**; it must be experienced, felt and understood through teachings.

Figure 13. Life Force Energy or **mnidoo bemaasing bemaadiziwin** within the context of Learning[31]

Please note that the colours that make up the Medicine Wheel are a crucial part of its extended meaning. The versions used in this text use the following colour formation: the North quadrant is white, the Eastern quadrant is yellow, the Southern quadrant is red, and the Western quadrant is black. The Medicine Wheels presented in this book have been approved by the Elders consulted for this work.

The sixth significance is that more work is required regarding innate life force energy or *mnidoo bemaasing bemaadiziwin* in the reclamation process as it pertains to other residential school survivors, and others in other instances of trauma. The healing process is a lifelong process and does not happen overnight. This information is not only relevant to Indigenous people but also non-Indigenous people. Glenn Richardson was likely coming into an awareness of it when he wrote about quanta, chai, spirit, god, or resilience.[32] Again, if we revisit the soul travelling life experiences that Elder Shirley Williams and Mike Cachagee so generously shared with us, we can

---

31 Modified version based on description by Mark Dockstator.
32 Glenn Richardson, "The Metatheory of Resilience and Resiliency," *Journal of Clinical Psychology*, 58 no. 3 (2002): 315.

ask the question, is there a degree or level of crisis reached equivalent to how deep we are able to go? While Mike was in his coma, he reached out to his grandmas, women he had never ever met yet he was able to communicate with them. The same happened to Shirley in that she vividly recalls the smell of the food cooking in her home when her soul travelled there. At ten years of age, Shirley was close to the spirit world and at Mike's advanced age, he was as well. As we age, do we lose the capacity to experience the spirit world? Do we lose that connection during our lifetime then reconnect at an older age? These are questions on which I do not wish to speculate here. Finally, the survivors are the ones who know their nutrients, and are now living their reclamation process.

The seventh significance is the realization that it is in the best interest of everyone including non-Indigenous peoples that efforts to revitalize respective cultures would lead to healthier communities. As Indigenous peoples, we will choose work that will build upon our important cultural concepts, for example, language, identity, and self-esteem, also these various cultural revitalization methods which are seen as nutrients for our people. Susie Jones says that:

> We have to conform to Western methods through the funding that we get but when we run our programs, we cannot run them the way we know we should run them. We use alternate methods such as fasting, sweat lodges, talking circles and the traditional ceremonies like vision quests. This is not new to us, we have always had them, it takes a village to raise a child and Grandma always encourages us to talk about stuff like that.[33]

The final, and most important significance, is that there are different paradigms engaged when using the word resiliency. Resiliency is an over-used concept, and in this particular work, the stacking of positive factors against negative factors does not result

---

33 Susie Jones, personal communication, April 26, 2013.

in resiliency concerning Indigenous peoples. Life force energy or *mnidoo bemaasing bemaadiziwin* comes from within and is interconnected with "all our relations."[34] In 2013, I observed its specialness and oneness in a school hallway when I witnessed Elder Shirley Williams, a residential school survivor, greet the late Ron Howard Sr., another survivor with the love and care of a brother and sister coming together. This is not resiliency but, rather, something that goes much deeper.

What does this knowledge that I have brought forward contribute to the ongoing articulation of Indigenous Knowledge? Two instances come to my mind. First, this work feeds the spiritual side of our culture and promotes or grows positive self-esteem and identity in us as a people. "Life force energy is not new knowledge to us but it is new to the common man."[35] Elder Doug Williams has said that we are spiritual people. Our development as a people has always been to follow in the footsteps of our ancestors in how we re-enact the ceremonies when we find ourselves out of balance. Our healing methods as Susie Jones pointed out is to come together as a family and tell our stories at reunions and gatherings. We seize those opportunities to seek that strength together and bond with the bones and the bedrock or *kanan miinwaa nbagani-aasmaabkong*. We come to know our traditional ways and manifest cultural revitalization to re-energize our life forces which is the way we are supposed to be.

We have to encourage people to start that journey that will energize that life force. Nobody's going to give it to you. You cannot buy it in a bottle. You cannot go to a certain place to get it. It starts within.[36]

The second instance concerns Indigenous Knowledge. Western knowledge operates from a different paradigm or paradigms, and Indigenous Knowledge is rarely accepted by the Western world,

---

34 Leroy Little Bear, "Aboriginal Paradigms," 29.
35 Susie Jones, personal communication, April 26, 2013.
36 Ibid.

particularly because of its connection to us. These Indigenous knowledge systems are often "defined as inferior, and in fact unscientific."[37] Susie Jones also talks about this resistance, "The world is stuck in a rut – there is a hump that we have to get over in talking about Indigenous Knowledge."[38] Susie insists that the white world has not opened itself up to anything that we know and they do not want to listen. That is why it is up to us to take that step and take that personal journey, with the help of the many supports available to us. No one needs to approach it alone. Throughout the years I have witnessed the changes even in peoples' faces and demeanours as they have continued their learning journey. For me this has been a very long and special journey but we all learn differently. What I have learned and the path I have taken and what I picked up along the trail, may or may not have meaning to someone else. We are individuals and have different learning techniques and methods. As I continue to learn, I will continue to talk to Elders and ask questions, talk to survivors, and talk to medicine people because this is not the end of my learning journey. I never want to stop learning and I encourage others to take the journey and find out for themselves and their families. For the Shingwauk Family, there was a collective learning and a collective healing process that surpassed the lines of being from different First Nations.

Coming To Know

I once went on a writing retreat in a beautiful territory of the *Anishinaabek* of Curve Lake, a sacred place of beauty, water and land. I went for a walk down to the water and gave an offering of tobacco and asked for guidance and support. The smell of the water opened my heart and the sun on my face fed me energy. I have been

---

37 George Sefa Dei et al. eds., *Indigenous Knowledges in Global Contexts: Multiple Readings of Our World* (Toronto: University of Toronto Press, 2000), vii.
38 Susie Jones, personal communication, April 26, 2013.

told that water is Mother Earth's blood. For me water has energy and is the keeper of life. Sometimes water is calm and other times, when disturbed, it can be thrashing about.

Looking around, I saw many different styles and forms of rocks and stones. This spectacle reminded me of Anishinaabe people. The rocks were small, stones really, and some large, all different shades of colour and had more than one mineral emanating from them. Some of the rocks were piled on other rocks offering support yet gathered all together doing their job. We, the Anishinaabe, are like this. We have many layers nurtured by our Anishinaabeness, our cultural identity, spirituality, maturity and our connection to the ancestors. Each of us has a role and a responsibility. I have found my role as a helper and acknowledge my responsibility and since then I have been trying to live that responsibility. I am not totally there yet as I still have a lot to learn. I only speak to what I know and what I have heard. No one can take it away from you, as Susie Jones suggests; we must look inside ourselves.[39]

This is my learning from knowing and working with individuals who have gone to residential school. They are seen as leaders and role models who are quick to challenge issues, speak up for what is right and take on numerous tasks sometimes all at once. They are concrete examples who defy the odds of what the Indian Residential School system set out to destroy—the essence of who they are and it is through their finding of their gifts, the love for their families (both Shingwauk and natural), they are reclaiming spirit. Their legacies are rich, felt most at the community level first, and transcend far beyond any monetary value. For what is the price of memory and identity—they are priceless!

During this time of writing about my responsibilities, I have accepted my faults and limitations but have found some gifts. One gift is the gift of writing that comes to me intuitively—as a gift from my maternal grandmother, the Creator and the ancestors. How

---

39 Susie Jones, personal communication, January 14, 2012.

blessed I feel to have been chosen to prepare this message. Second, to have been gifted with the sacredness of trust; the trust of the survivors who have allowed me to learn through my mistakes with love. Third, I am most grateful to complete this important task along with a community that made sure that I enjoyed a keen sense of belonging in becoming part of their family.

My prayer, if it is possible, is to lessen the pain and suffering of all residential school survivors and their extended families. I trust that the ones who have gone into the spirit world have patience and support us earth beings who look to them for guidance and support in much the same way as one of my friends, Mike Cachagee has told us in his experience in soul travelling. We have survived since time immemorial with nutrients that have been given to us by the Creator and are entrenched within our beings as Anishinaabek people as our Anishinaabe life force energy or *mnidoo bemaasing bemaadiziwin*, but the true perpetuation of the essence of our being comes from the ancestors.

What non-Indigenous researchers call resiliency is better reflected as an understanding of Anishinaabe life force energy or *mnidoo bemaasing bemaadiziwin,* which is so evident in the voices of the Walpole Island survivors. Having endured the many hardships and lessons learned, the survivors became strong—*zongwaadiziwin* which makes them who they are today. Thank you and *miigwech/megweetch.*

INDEX

#
1763 Royal Proclamation 82
1764 Treaty of Niagara 82
1842 Bagot Commission 85
1844 Bagot Commission
  recommendations 85
1857 Gradual Civilization Act 86
1869 Enfranchisement Act 86
1876 Indian Act 21, 24, 85, 87, 167
1994 report of the Assembly of First
  Nations 93

A
Aamjiwnaang First Nation 96
Aboriginal Healing and Wellness
  Program 47
Aboriginal Healing Foundation
  (AHF) 15, 29, 90, 103, 104, 108, 224,
  249
Aboriginal philosophy 50
Aboriginal population 124
Aboriginal psyche 250
Aboriginal rights and
  self-determination 96
Absolon, Kathy 5, 10, 17, 63, 64, 127,
  249, 250
Abuse 2, 17, 25, 29, 90, 94, 100, 126, 151,
  192, 217, 226, 240, 243
aggressive assimilation 86
Ahnee (Hi; Hello; Greetings) 150
Ajunnginiq Centre 112, 125, 126
Alcoholics Anonymous 203, 205, 253
Algoma University College 21, 98
All of Creation 18, 33, 40

Ancestors 2, 18, 22, 27, 32, 33, 44, 45, 57,
  58, 60, 61, 76, 79, 132, 213, 236, 237,
  238, 240, 241, 247, 248, 258, 260, 261
Angeconeb, Garnet 74, 237, 242
Anglican Church 98
Animal 13, 34, 35, 36, 37, 38, 39, 40, 44,
  52, 55, 79, 84, 132, 140, 141, 145, 164,
  176, 177, 212, 236, 238
animate 44, 50
Anishinaabe 5, 13, 14, 17, 18, 22, 23, 25,
  26, 27, 28, 29, 30, 31, 32, 33, 34, 35, 37,
  38, 39, 41, 43, 44, 45, 46, 47, 48, 49,
  51, 52, 53, 54, 55, 56, 57, 58, 60, 61, 62,
  63, 64, 65, 66, 70, 71, 72, 74, 75, 77,
  78, 79, 80, 83, 84, 96, 105, 106, 107,
  108, 110, 111, 123, 127, 130, 132, 133, 134,
  135, 136, 137, 139, 140, 141, 142, 152,
  154, 156, 157, 158, 159, 163, 165, 167, 182,
  186, 187, 188, 189, 190, 198, 200, 201,
  204, 206, 207, 208, 209, 212, 213, 225,
  226, 227, 229, 231, 236, 237, 240, 241,
  242, 245, 246, 247, 248, 251, 254,
  259, 260, 261, 271
Anishinaabe approach 130, 134
Anishinaabe children 141, 157
Anishinaabe Clan System 140
Anishinaabe country 38, 72
Anishinaabe Creation Story 33, 208,
  236
Anishinaabe culture 225, 242
Anishinaabe education 51, 52
Anishinaabe Elders 62, 75
Anishinaabe epistemology 31
Anishinaabe identity 22, 23, 225

Anishinaabe Knowledge 27, 60, 61, 66
Anishinaabe knowledge holder 60, 61
Anishinaabe knowledge seekers 66
Anishinaabe Medicine Wheel 27, 29, 43
Anishinaabe Mino Bemaadiziwin (the good way of life) 18
Anishinaabe mino-bimaadiziwin (the way of a good life) 13, 29, 137, 139, 159, 163, 188, 208
Anishinaabe ontology 31, 61, 62
Anishinaabe oral tradition 84
Anishinaabe paradigm 31, 57, 248
Anishinaabe people 27, 28, 33, 57, 62, 63, 64, 65, 66, 108, 139, 237, 245, 246, 260
Anishinaabe perspective 51, 134
Anishinaabe philosophy 31
Anishinaabe responsibilities 182
Anishinaabe smudging ceremony 25
Anishinaabe spirit 152
Anishinaabe spirit name 139, 163, 165, 209
Anishinaabe spirituality 152
Anishinaabe stages of life 136
Anishinaabe survivor 142
Anishinaabe Thought 5, 27, 30, 31, 32, 33, 35, 37, 39, 41, 43, 45, 47, 49, 51, 53, 55, 57
Anishinaabe tradition 71, 209, 213
Anishinaabe worldview 32, 58, 62
Anishinaabeg 75
Anishinaabek (plural of Anishinaabe) 18, 96, 107, 188, 190, 198, 200, 201, 204, 206, 208, 248, 259, 261
Anishinaabek children 18
Anishinaabek Creation story teachings 18
Anishinaabek maturation 188
Anishinaabek people 190, 198, 204, 208, 261
Anishinaabek territory 96

Anishinaabe-kwe (woman) 17, 22, 26, 27, 30, 34, 35, 44, 54, 70, 78, 79, 110, 127, 130, 139, 231, 271
Anishinaabemowin (Ojibway language) 13, 14, 22, 35, 54, 72, 137, 165, 213, 225, 226, 241, 245, 251
Anishinaabe-naakgonigewin (Natural Law) 13, 51
Anishinaabeness 132, 240, 260
Anishnaabemowin dialect 22
Antone, Robert 41
Antonovsky, Aaron 116, 117
Archibald, Jo-Ann 53, 54
Assembly of First Nations 25, 93, 98, 229, 230
Assimilate 84, 124, 234, 239
Assimilation 26, 86, 87, 88, 235, 236
Assimilation policy 88
Autonomy 114, 116

B

Baawaamin (animal helper) 13, 212
Bagot, Charles 85
Bailey, George 193
Baker, Patricia 175, 185
balance and good health 31
Balanced life 56
Band Council 222, 223
Band Councillor 223
Band Election code 225
band member 48, 97, 105
Band Senior Administrator 223
Barman, Jean 50, 134, 137
Battiste, Marie 23, 25, 49, 50, 134, 137, 209, 210, 219
Bawating 96
Bay of Fundy 132
Beboon (winter) 49
Beck, Peggy V. 233
Being 10, 13, 22, 23, 27, 32, 34, 37, 39, 40, 41, 42, 46, 48, 51, 52, 60, 72, 75, 81, 89, 114, 117, 133, 134, 135, 137, 139, 140, 153, 154, 158, 159, 163, 184, 190, 201,

202, 208, 212, 213, 234, 236, 238, 240,
    245, 246, 252, 255, 259, 261
Benard, Bonnie 116, 131
Benton-Banai, Edward 42, 43, 52, 140
BIA (Bureau of Indian Affairs) 196
Biidaaban Ntam Bi Yaad (the first one
    out, the light before the dawn) 139,
    271
Bineshiinh (the Thunderbird) 14, 48
Bird Clan of the Ojibway and Odawa
    First Nations of Canada 22
Bird, Ann 10, 14, 22, 35, 37, 44, 45, 48,
    49, 192, 226
birth family 190, 192
Bkejwanong 69, 103, 224
Bkejwanong Attachment Awareness
    Team 224
Bkejwanong Territory 69, 103, 224
Blackbird, Jennie 10, 226
Blondin-Perrin, Alice 94, 147, 190, 191
boarding school system 88
Boileau, Sonia Bonspille 95, 246
Boissoneau, Ron 98
Boldt, Menno 84, 86
Bonspille, Mitchell Morris 95, 246
Bopp, Judie 32
Bopp, Michael 32
Borrows, John 82, 84, 85, 222
Bravery 10, 27, 43, 68, 140, 157, 244
British Isles 88
British North America Act of 1867 86
Brock 96
Brown, Lee 32, 87, 89, 126, 127, 148, 168,
    169, 173, 178, 179, 184
Bruyere, Gord 127
Bryce, Peter 17
Bryce Report 17
bskaabi-mugwewin wiijkiiwendiwin
    (reciprocal relationships) 13, 67
Buhkwuijene, Henry 97
Butterfly, Christine 149

C

Cachagee, Clarence 155
Cachagee, Michael (Mike) 10, 74, 82,
    83, 101, 102, 149, 155, 157, 172, 175, 178,
    255, 256, 261
Cajete, Greg 63, 84
Calliou, Sharilyn 50, 137
Canadian government residential
    school system 168
Canadian history 21
Canadian Indian 28, 44
Canadian society 87, 97
Capitalism 85
Cardinal, Lewis 41, 63, 238
Carlisle Industrial School 87
Castellano, Marlene Brant 59, 60, 76,
    240, 249, 250
Cattle truck 89
Cellular memory 58, 60, 62, 76, 238, 251
Centred soul 25, 226
Ceremony 23, 25, 33, 45, 61, 63, 64, 65,
    68, 70, 79, 165, 186, 188, 189, 190, 195,
    208, 209, 211, 212, 231, 243, 247
Chansonneuve, Deborah 86, 229
Chapel 174
Chaplain 212
Chapleau (see St. John's Residential
    School) 100, 222
Chapleau Cree First Nation 82
Chatham-Kent YMCA Peace
    Medallion Award 221
Cherokee 41, 234
Cherokee Nation 41
CHEX TV 95
Chi 10, 113
Chief Shingwauk 28, 96, 98, 100, 224
Chief Shingwaukonce 96
Children 9, 10, 15, 17, 18, 20, 21, 22, 23,
    24, 43, 51, 52, 54, 55, 66, 69, 73, 75,
    81, 84, 85, 87, 88, 89, 90, 94, 97, 99,
    100, 102, 105, 114, 115, 122, 124, 125,
    129, 130, 133, 137, 139, 140, 141, 142,
    143, 144, 145, 148, 149, 150, 151, 152,

153, 154, 157, 158, 164, 165, 167, 168, 172, 173, 174, 175, 177, 178, 190, 196, 198, 199, 200, 203, 206, 216, 220, 225, 227, 231, 235, 236, 237, 241, 243, 246, 252, 253, 254, 271
Children of Shingwauk Alumni Association 15, 81, 100
chi-megweetch 9
Chippewa 234
Chrisjohn, Roland 25, 88
Christian 15, 83, 85, 187, 212
Christian Elder 212
Christian minister 212
Christianization 85
Christmas 147, 174
Church 82, 83, 85, 97, 98, 102, 161
Chute, Janet 96, 97
Circle 25, 29, 32, 34, 43, 45, 46, 49, 50, 51, 62, 68, 88, 93, 94, 99, 100, 102, 106, 109, 127, 134, 137, 156, 187, 204, 213, 219, 232, 233, 234, 241, 243, 244, 254, 255, 257
Citizenship 88
Civilization 85, 86, 87, 88
Clan 13, 22, 33, 48, 91, 137, 140, 182, 187, 200, 206, 218, 219
Clan System 140, 218
Cleansing ceremony 212
Coast Tsimshian First Nations 44
Collective wisdom 60
Colonial policy 81
Colonial society 86
Colonialism 81, 219, 250
Colonization 2, 25, 57, 81, 128, 207, 212, 218, 229, 243, 250
Colonizer 218
Community 9, 22, 24, 29, 41, 42, 47, 52, 58, 61, 62, 63, 64, 65, 66, 67, 69, 70, 73, 74, 76, 78, 101, 102, 103, 104, 106, 114, 119, 120, 121, 125, 127, 130, 152, 159, 165, 168, 169, 182, 183, 187, 190, 191, 192, 193, 196, 199, 200, 204, 205, 206, 207, 210, 211, 215, 217, 218, 221, 222, 223, 224, 225, 226, 229, 230, 233, 234, 239, 241, 244, 246, 249, 251, 252, 254, 260, 261, 271
Community Elder 211, 225
Community Elders Advisory Council 225
Community partner 70
Community powwow 222
Community resilience 120, 121
Community well-being 62
Community-based resiliency 114
Consent 10, 66, 73, 74, 82, 248
Constitution 85, 91, 92
Constitution Act, 1982 28
Constitution of Turtle Island 92
Cook-Lynn, Elizabeth 61
Cosmos 34, 52
Creation 18, 27, 33, 34, 35, 36, 37, 38, 40, 41, 42, 43, 44, 51, 52, 54, 55, 58, 59, 60, 75, 106, 123, 137, 140, 145, 150, 208, 212, 236, 237, 248
Creation Story 18, 27, 33, 34, 40, 51, 58, 137, 140, 208, 236, 248
Creator 9, 32, 34, 35, 36, 38, 39, 40, 42, 56, 75, 85, 94, 153, 182, 206, 209, 237, 239, 240, 246, 247, 260, 261
Creator's vision 40
Cree 62, 82, 134, 156, 222, 248
Critical consciousness 131
Cruikshank, Julie 209
CSAA Reunion Advisory Committees 224
Cultural abuse 90
Cultural distinctiveness 23
Cultural expectations 65
Cultural genocide 17, 18, 19, 88
Cultural identity 44, 92, 132, 157, 182, 236
Cultural practices 60, 91, 127, 211
Cultural protocols 65
Culture 2, 22, 25, 51, 52, 53, 56, 61, 87, 88, 91, 93, 96, 102, 122, 125, 132, 145, 196, 198, 203, 204, 207, 214, 218, 221, 225, 242, 245, 246, 257, 258
Cunningham, Dorothy 74, 145

Curve Lake 34, 259
Cyrulnik, Boris 112, 113, 121, 131

D

Daes, Erica-Irene 23
Dan Pine Sr. Healing Lodge 102
Dance 21, 22, 32, 33, 45, 74, 79, 144, 145, 178, 200, 208, 209, 219, 226, 238, 259, 261
Dandeneau, Stephane F. 120
Danziger Jr., Edmund J. 196, 198
Davin, Nicholas Flood 87
Death 44, 144, 175, 224, 233
Debassige, Brent 123, 124, 132
Decolonization 207, 218, 229
Deconstruction 85
Deep listening 72, 76
DeHann, Laura 118
Dei, George J. Sefa 59, 84, 89, 240, 259
Dell, Colleen 240
Deloria Jr., Vine 76, 77
Denham, Aaron 223, 238, 249, 250
Department of Health Promotion and Education 112
De-spiritualized 83
Developmental process 232
Diamond, Billy 222, 231, 244
Dockstator, Mark 49, 82, 248, 256
Doctrine of discovery 57, 84
Dodge, Garnet 225
Dodge, Uriah 104, 106
Dual obligation 65
Duran, Bonnie 92
Duran, Eduardo 92

E

Eagle Clan 48, 140
Earth being 39, 236, 261
Earth lodge 18
Easter 36, 47, 50, 51, 59, 66, 67, 137, 142, 170, 174, 188, 219, 224, 228, 232, 236, 256
Eastern door 51, 66, 137

Ebingishmok/Epingishmok (in the West direction) 14, 39, 40, 48
Economic system 92
Edet, Jeanne 17, 21, 29, 51, 52, 86, 87, 98, 179
Education 24, 33, 41, 49, 51, 52, 54, 56, 58, 62, 63, 68, 77, 85, 86, 87, 88, 89, 92, 94, 97, 112, 123, 124, 134, 137, 145, 204, 223, 224, 227, 235, 244, 251
Elder 10, 18, 22, 27, 32, 34, 41, 43, 46, 47, 48, 50, 51, 52, 54, 55, 56, 57, 59, 60, 62, 64, 66, 67, 74, 75, 76, 79, 81, 84, 85, 91, 92, 95, 98, 109, 110, 126, 132, 134, 136, 139, 140, 141, 142, 143, 145, 148, 154, 155, 156, 163, 164, 165, 167, 170, 182, 184, 188, 189, 191, 196, 200, 201, 206, 208, 209, 210, 211, 212, 213, 219, 221, 222, 223, 224, 225, 226, 227, 228, 230, 232, 237, 240, 245, 246, 247, 248, 249, 250, 251, 254, 255, 256, 258, 259
Elder Brother 141, 240
Elder/Healer 211
Elder/Teacher 211
Elderhood 136, 206, 210, 232
Ellerby, Jonathan H. 34, 57, 210, 211
Ellesmere Island 91
Energy 2, 3, 5, 10, 13, 14, 18, 20, 28, 29, 32, 43, 44, 46, 50, 57, 75, 76, 77, 79, 102, 108, 109, 111, 113, 114, 115, 117, 119, 121, 123, 125, 126, 127, 129, 130, 131, 132, 133, 134, 135, 137, 153, 154, 157, 158, 159, 182, 184, 186, 200, 201, 206, 207, 208, 227, 229, 232, 233, 234, 236, 238, 240, 241, 242, 243, 247, 248, 250, 252, 253, 254, 255, 256, 258, 259, 260, 261
English language 154, 235, 251
English schooling 97
Enlightenment 51, 137
Epingishmok/Epingomook (the place where the sun sets in the west) 13, 39, 40, 48
Epstein, Irwin 118

Ermine, Willie 42, 57, 117, 134, 164, 210, 245
Ethical principles 206
Ethics 34, 62, 65
Experiential knowledge 60
Extreme power relations 98

F

Faith-based practices 26
Family 7, 9, 28, 32, 34, 43, 45, 46, 47, 53, 63, 64, 65, 66, 68, 69, 70, 73, 78, 99, 101, 102, 114, 115, 117, 118, 119, 120, 122, 123, 127, 130, 137, 140, 143, 144, 145, 147, 149, 150, 151, 152, 154, 155, 159, 165, 168, 169, 172, 173, 174, 175, 182, 183, 187, 188, 190, 191, 192, 193, 194, 198, 200, 201, 203, 204, 206, 207, 208, 214, 216, 220, 223, 227, 229, 230, 237, 241, 243, 244, 247, 252, 253, 254, 258, 259, 261
Family circle 137, 187
Family resiliency 117, 118, 120
Family Strengths 118
Family systems 118
Fasting 140, 159, 167, 212, 257
Federal government 17, 21, 29, 86, 87, 98, 179
Federal government of Canada 17, 29
Feeling language (anishinabiwin) 54, 251
First Instructions (See Original Instructions) 41
First Nation 2, 9, 10, 15, 22, 23, 24, 25, 26, 27, 28, 34, 44, 48, 49, 50, 64, 69, 70, 82, 86, 87, 93, 95, 96, 98, 102, 104, 105, 111, 124, 127, 131, 134, 137, 144, 145, 193, 200, 207, 218, 222, 223, 224, 229, 230, 233, 242, 244, 250, 259, 271
First Nation communities 22, 102, 230
First Nation individuals 93
First Nation language 25
First Nation people 93

First Nations 2, 22, 23, 24, 25, 26, 28, 44, 49, 50, 86, 87, 93, 96, 98, 124, 131, 134, 137, 144, 145, 200, 207, 218, 223, 224, 229, 230, 242, 244, 250, 259
First Nations Ancestors 44
First Nations Day Schools 86, 145
First Nations children 145, 200
First Nations community 22
First Nations people 23, 218
First Nations populations 86
Fitzmaurice, Andrew 84
Fletcher, Billy 149
Flood 36, 37, 39, 87, 217
Fontaine, Phil 179
Foreign language 25
Formal school education 145
Fort Resolution, NW Territories 191
Fort William First Nation 96
Fortier, Mary 94
Fox Lake Reserve 82
Free trade 82
Freire, Paulo 131
Friesen, Val 53, 54
Full Moon Ceremony 159, 165, 190
Future Elders 95, 221, 222

G

Gaa-bi-zhewebak gchi-zhaazhe gchi-piitendaagwaad (our past matters) 13, 81
Gabriel, Wanda 231, 244
Gallagher, Colin 64
Garden River First Nation 98, 102
Garden River First Nation Community Centre 102
Garroutte, Eva Marie 41, 42
Gathering Strength – Canada's Aboriginal Action Plan 29
Gchi-Manitou (The Creator) 75
Gchi-mikinaak (or gchi-mackinac) (The Turtle) 37
Gchi-minising 109
Genocide 17, 18, 19, 88

Ghost 139, 243
Gifts 17, 18, 27, 32, 33, 34, 58, 82, 111, 220, 238, 246, 251, 260
Giiwedinoong 49
Giizhigo-kwe (Sky Woman) 13, 36, 37, 38, 39
Girl Scouts of America 224
Goffman, Erving 98
Gone, Joseph 9, 33, 38, 93, 130, 151, 152, 162, 171, 217, 224, 226, 230, 235, 260, 261
Google Scholar 108
Goulet, Jean-Guy 155
Government agents 21
Government of Canada 2, 17, 26, 29
Graham, W. M. 111
Grand Entry 23
Grandchild 10, 73, 99, 102, 200, 203, 206, 209, 216, 227, 235, 237, 243, 253
Granddaughter 53, 139, 239
Grandfather 27, 33, 34, 42, 51, 70, 74, 76, 78, 136, 137, 140, 141, 157, 163, 164, 165, 183, 205, 209, 237, 238, 239, 246, 252
Grandmother 13, 14, 34, 39, 44, 46, 53, 138, 139, 142, 143, 156, 157, 189, 209, 227, 240, 260, 271
Grandparent 51, 72, 189, 209, 238, 253
Grandson 202
Grant, Agnes 94, 99
Grasso, Anthony J. 118
Graveline, Fyre Jean 62
Great Lakes 202, 239
Great Lakes Steel 202
Great Spirit 181, 183, 203
Gunderson 122

H

Haig-Brown, Celia 87, 89, 126, 127, 148, 168, 169, 173, 178, 179, 184
Harriet Jacobs Centre 220
Harrod, Howard L. 238
Hart, Michael Anthony 101, 127
Haudensaunee 36

Hawaiian epistemology 62
Hawley 118
Healer 55, 211
Healing Circle 68, 93, 99, 100, 102, 106
Healing medicine 18
Healing process 25, 232, 256, 259
Heart 7, 14, 18, 25, 29, 40, 54, 55, 56, 57, 68, 79, 84, 94, 108, 135, 139, 144, 146, 147, 191, 205, 207, 212, 235, 236, 239, 249, 255, 259
Henderson, James Youngblood 23, 209, 210
Henry, Geronimo 74, 84, 88, 97, 157, 177
Hiawatha First Nation 222
High Arctic 126
Hill's ABCX Model 118
Historical stories 52
Holistic knowledge 60
Holling 122
Holmes, Leilani 84
Holy Order 145
Honesty 10, 27, 43, 54, 136, 140, 157
Horn, Shirley 74, 144, 178
Howard Sr., Ron 222, 258, 74
Hub 32
Hudson's Bay Coast 126
Human 13, 17, 18, 22, 32, 35, 36, 39, 40, 41, 44, 51, 52, 56, 114, 116, 117, 127, 128, 132, 139, 153, 167, 190, 202, 223, 238, 240, 246
Humility 26, 27, 43, 50, 79, 140, 164, 184

I

Ideas 58, 61, 117
Identity 18, 20, 22, 23, 25, 42, 44, 47, 52, 53, 62, 91, 92, 101, 116, 124, 125, 132, 154, 157, 182, 200, 204, 211, 225, 226, 229, 230, 236, 246, 257, 258, 260
Independent First Nations 224
Indian Act of 1876 21
Indian Affairs 88, 106, 111, 196
Indian agent 89, 138, 142

Indian industrial school system 87
Indian philosopher 77
Indian problem 88
Indian Residential School 17, 18, 24, 25, 26, 28, 29, 67, 71, 81, 83, 89, 94, 95, 96, 98, 99, 100, 103, 105, 126, 172, 192, 195, 215, 222, 224, 225, 233, 237, 271
Indian Residential School Conference 103
Indian Residential School Eastern Gathering Advisory Team 224
Indian Residential School Independent Assessment Process 192
Indian Residential School legacy 71
Indian Residential School Syndrome 224
Indian residential schools projects 17, 18, 19
Indigenous 2, 17, 18, 19, 21, 22, 23, 24, 25, 26, 28, 32, 33, 34, 37, 41, 49, 57, 58, 59, 60, 61, 62, 63, 65, 66, 69, 72, 74, 78, 80, 81, 82, 84, 85, 86, 87, 88, 89, 90, 92, 93, 107, 108, 113, 120, 122, 123, 125, 127, 130, 131, 133, 143, 144, 145, 148, 154, 204, 210, 211, 212, 219, 223, 224, 227, 230, 231, 237, 238, 240, 241, 242, 244, 245, 247, 248, 249, 250, 251, 253, 254, 256, 257, 258, 259, 261, 271
Indigenous Affairs and Northern Affairs Canada 85
Indigenous ancestors 33
Indigenous Celtic Tribes 88
Indigenous children 17, 18, 85, 87
Indigenous culture 93
Indigenous Elder 34, 57, 210, 211, 212
Indigenous Families 212
Indigenous knowledge 19, 23, 57, 58, 59, 60, 62, 72, 74, 89, 125, 204, 210, 240, 247, 251, 258, 259
Indigenous language 143, 148, 154, 241, 253
Indigenous methodologies 19, 62, 66

Indigenous people 2, 17, 18, 21, 23, 24, 25, 32, 37, 41, 58, 61, 65, 69, 78, 82, 84, 85, 88, 89, 90, 92, 120, 122, 125, 127, 130, 131, 133, 145, 204, 210, 219, 224, 227, 230, 237, 238, 248, 249, 250, 254, 256, 257, 258
Indigenous peoples' identity 18
Indigenous peoples' suicide crises 125
Indigenous perspective 41
Indigenous pharmacology 211
Indigenous practices 242
Indigenous process 93, 230
Indigenous scholarship 18
Indigenous testimonies 93
Indigenous testimony 93
Indigenous traditionalists 76, 133, 209
Indigenous traditions 25
Indigenous world views 92
Individual freedom 211
Individual resilience 117
Individual resiliency 120
Individual responsibility 62
Individualism 85
Indoctrination 145
Industrial school 87, 88
Inner energy 134
Inner fire 32
Inner space 134
Institutional work 211
Intergenerational impacts 29
Intergenerational trauma 232, 249
Intermarriage 140
Internal sovereignty 219
Interrelationships 44, 50
Intuition (cellular memory) 46, 55, 60, 62, 76, 242, 246
Inuit 22, 23, 28, 50, 69, 124, 125, 126
Inuit Tapiriit Kanatami 69, 126
Inuvialuit Region 126
Invader 82
Isaac, Colette 120
Isaac, Patrick 10, 223
Island Board of Education 224

J

Jack, Agnes 49, 94, 98, 99
Jackson, Don 98, 99
Jacobs, Dean 105, 220
Jaine, Linda 174, 179, 238
Johnston, Basil 48, 75, 94, 140, 142, 143, 147, 150, 158, 185, 189, 190, 209, 254
Jones, Susie 7, 10, 25, 70, 73, 74, 99, 104, 107, 108, 111, 133, 137, 145, 150, 174, 213, 226, 228, 236, 241, 249, 257, 258, 259, 260
Journey 5, 10, 20, 21, 23, 25, 27, 28, 29, 30, 31, 34, 46, 58, 66, 68, 76, 95, 100, 103, 106, 122, 137, 155, 159, 186, 205, 206, 228, 231, 232, 233, 234, 246, 248, 251, 258, 259

K

Kamloops Indian Residential School 94
Kanan (Bones) 5, 13, 27, 29, 31, 32, 33, 58, 76, 133, 158, 234, 236, 248, 258
Kanan miinwaa nbagani-aasmaabkong (The Bones and the Bedrock) 13, 32, 58, 76, 258
Kauai Longitudinal Study 115, 122
Kauai, HI 115, 122
Kelsey-Hayes 202
Kill the Indian 84, 157
Kinship 41, 53, 133
Kinship responsibility 53
Kinunwa, Lionel 76, 251
Kipling, Gregory 94, 124
Kirmayer, Laurence J. 120, 229
Kitiga Migizi, Pike doodem (see Doug Williams) 34
Knockwood, Isabelle 94, 172
Knowing 5, 18, 19, 29, 33, 40, 60, 64, 68, 73, 75, 87, 90, 149, 155, 159, 161, 163, 165, 167, 168, 169, 170, 171, 173, 175, 177, 179, 181, 183, 185, 195, 210, 242, 251, 253, 255, 260
Knowledge 2, 5, 6, 9, 10, 13, 18, 19, 23, 24, 25, 27, 28, 32, 33, 34, 42, 43, 46, 48, 51, 55, 56, 57, 58, 59, 60, 61, 62, 63, 64, 65, 66, 67, 69, 71, 72, 74, 75, 76, 77, 79, 80, 82, 84, 89, 92, 99, 101, 102, 111, 114, 116, 120, 125, 127, 128, 135, 140, 151, 155, 164, 183, 184, 185, 186, 191, 204, 206, 207, 209, 210, 211, 212, 213, 214, 215, 217, 219, 220, 221, 223, 225, 227, 229, 230, 231, 233, 240, 242, 244, 247, 249, 251, 255, 258, 259, 260
Knowledge Holder 60, 61, 206, 207, 209, 211, 213, 215, 217, 219, 221, 223, 225, 227, 229, 230, 231
Knowledge seekers 66
Knowledge transfer model 125
Knowlton, Stan 92
Kokum (or nookmis or gchi nookmis) (lit. "great grandmother"; but in reference to the Moon) 39
Korhonen, Marja 112, 125, 126
Kovach, Margaret 10, 62, 63, 64, 66, 248
Kulchyski, peter 87

L

Labour 88, 168
Labrador Coast 126
Lake Superior 22
Lampton-Kent District School Board 224
Land-based [Culture] 91, 237, 245
Land-based healing models 237
Lane Jr., Phil 32
Language 13, 22, 23, 25, 32, 49, 54, 56, 57, 60, 70, 72, 79, 91, 92, 93, 96, 102, 108, 109, 130, 133, 134, 135, 143, 148, 152, 153, 154, 155, 156, 157, 158, 165, 167, 193, 199, 204, 208, 213, 217, 218, 225, 226, 235, 240, 241, 242, 244, 245, 251, 253, 254, 257
Language-based [Culture] 91, 245
Lapeer County Citizen Probation Council 224
Lapeer County Community Credit Union 224

Leckie, Keith Ross 95
Lee, Scott 50
Legal system 92
Life and spirit 31
Life energy 18
Life force 2, 3, 5, 10, 14, 18, 20, 28, 29, 32,
   43, 46, 57, 77, 79, 102, 108, 109, 111,
   113, 115, 117, 119, 121, 123, 125, 127, 129,
   130, 131, 132, 133, 134, 135, 137, 153, 154,
   157, 158, 159, 182, 184, 186, 200, 201,
   205, 206, 207, 208, 227, 229, 232, 234,
   236, 238, 240, 241, 247, 252, 253, 254,
   255, 256, 258, 261
Life force energy 2, 3, 5, 10, 14, 18, 20,
   28, 29, 32, 43, 46, 57, 77, 79, 102, 108,
   109, 111, 113, 115, 117, 119, 121, 123, 125,
   127, 129, 130, 131, 132, 133, 135, 153, 154,
   157, 158, 159, 182, 184, 186, 200, 201,
   206, 207, 227, 229, 232, 234, 236, 238,
   241, 247, 252, 254, 255, 256, 258, 261
Life path 20, 29, 33, 34, 55, 75, 139, 247
Little Bear, Leroy 31, 43, 44, 50, 247,
   258
Local authority 75
locus of control 115, 117, 121
Longboat, Dan 40, 91, 94
Longboat, Jan Kahehti:io 91, 94, 245
Love 2, 9, 10, 17, 27, 34, 43, 45, 51, 56,
   64, 110, 138, 139, 140, 141, 157, 176, 198,
   210, 227, 228, 234, 238, 241, 243, 244,
   252, 253, 258, 260, 261

M

M'Chigeeng 155
Maam'pee Day'aaw'meh Kay'ah'beh
   (We Are Still Here) 104
Maawndoobiigenin kendaaswin
   (gathering knowledge) 13, 71
Manitoulin Island 22, 155
Manore, Jean 97
Maraun, Michael 25, 88
Matron 149, 153, 172
Matthew, Robert 94

Maybury-Lewis, David 89
McCormick, Roderick 249, 250
McCubbin, Hamilton I. 117, 118
McCubbin, Marilyn A. 117, 118
McCubbin's Resilience Model 118
McGowan, Dave 95
McLaren, Nadia 95
McLeod, Yvonne 56, 202
Means, Russell 22, 25, 32, 34, 36, 39, 52,
   57, 63, 65, 67, 79, 82, 91, 93, 103, 112,
   113, 120, 123, 127, 129, 178, 189, 196,
   208, 227, 229, 244, 252, 254, 255
Medicine 18, 19, 25, 27, 29, 43, 45, 46,
   47, 48, 49, 50, 58, 59, 60, 66, 67, 74,
   132, 136, 137, 142, 156, 157, 170, 188,
   211, 219, 228, 232, 247, 248, 251, 254,
   256, 259
Medicine people 27, 247, 251, 259
Medicine Wheel 19, 27, 29, 43, 45, 46,
   47, 48, 49, 50, 58, 59, 60, 66, 67, 137,
   142, 170, 188, 219, 228, 232, 248, 256
Megweetch 9, 10, 13, 261
Memorial wall 71, 95, 104, 105, 106, 220
Mental Abuse 90
Mental health 2, 115, 229
Metaphorical knowledge 60
Metaphorical language 60
Methodist 72, 85
Methodist education 85
Métis 2, 22, 23, 28, 62
Meyer, Manu Aluli 33, 61, 62, 63
Michilimackinac, MI 37
Michipicoten 10, 22, 48, 271
Michipicoten First Nation 10, 48
Migizi ow Kwe (Eagle Woman) 22
Mihesuah, Devon A. 53, 61
Miigwech/Meegweetch 13, 20, 251,
   252, 261
Miigweyan neyaab 13, 78
Miller, Dianne 41
Miller, James Rodger 85, 89, 94
Miller, Robert J. 82
Milloy, John S. 84, 85, 86, 88, 94, 168

Mind 10, 11, 18, 25, 33, 34, 40, 41, 48, 51, 52, 54, 56, 57, 60, 64, 73, 76, 93, 98, 99, 101, 104, 107, 110, 125, 131, 133, 139, 140, 143, 149, 153, 157, 174, 175, 183, 193, 207, 208, 212, 216, 229, 240, 246, 258, 260
Mino-bimaazidiwin (foundation of living) 234, 236
Mississaugas of Curve Lake First Nation 34
Mnidoo Bemaasing Bemaadiziwin (Life Force Energy) 2, 5, 10, 13, 14, 18, 20, 22, 24, 26, 28, 30, 32, 34, 36, 38, 40, 42, 43, 44, 46, 48, 50, 52, 54, 56, 60, 62, 64, 66, 68, 70, 72, 74, 76, 77, 78, 79, 80, 82, 84, 86, 88, 90, 92, 94, 96, 98, 100, 102, 104, 106, 108, 110, 111, 112, 114, 116, 118, 120, 122, 123, 124, 126, 128, 130, 132, 133, 134, 135, 136, 137, 138, 140, 142, 144, 146, 148, 150, 152, 153, 154, 156, 157, 158, 159, 160, 162, 164, 166, 168, 170, 172, 174, 176, 178, 180, 182, 184, 186, 188, 190, 192, 194, 196, 198, 200, 201, 202, 204, 208, 210, 212, 214, 216, 218, 220, 222, 224, 226, 227, 228, 229, 230, 232, 234, 236, 238, 240, 241, 242, 244, 246, 247, 248, 250, 252, 253, 254, 255, 256, 258, 260, 261, 264, 268, 270
Models of resiliency 120
Mohawk 72, 87, 91, 105, 106, 129, 157, 177, 216, 217, 231, 244
Mohawk Institute 72, 105, 129, 157, 177
Mohawk Institute Residential School 129
Momaday, N. Scott 240
Monture-Angus, Patricia 87
Moose Factory 83, 100
Mother 2, 10, 13, 14, 22, 27, 31, 33, 34, 39, 40, 41, 42, 44, 45, 46, 51, 53, 55, 67, 72, 74, 79, 84, 118, 129, 138, 139, 142, 143, 144, 146, 147, 149, 150, 155, 156, 157, 183, 189, 193, 196, 197, 198, 200, 209, 212, 227, 235, 236, 237, 239, 240, 241, 246, 260, 271
Mother Earth 2, 27, 31, 33, 34, 40, 41, 51, 55, 67, 79, 84, 155, 236, 237, 246, 260
Mother's womb 212
Motion 17, 31, 41, 44, 49, 50, 51, 54, 55, 68, 75, 92, 95, 110, 112, 114, 117, 121, 125, 146, 147, 154, 175, 176, 196, 199, 201, 222, 226
Mount Elgin 72, 217
Mountie (see RCMP) 138, 163
Mukqua (bear) 49
Muncey 161
Mushole (AKA the Mohawk Institute Residential School) 129, 179, 220
Mutual sovereignty 82
Myers, Brian 41
Mythological stories 52

N

Nabigon, Herb 32, 49, 56, 153, 240
NAIA (North American Indian Association) 15, 198
Naming 159, 209, 212
Nanaboozhoo (trickster) 14, 83
Narrative knowledge 60
Narrative language 60
Native American population 198
Native American Studies 61
Native ceremonies 44
Native Children 97
Native kids 130, 151
Native people 2, 41, 45, 48, 52, 87, 238
Native youth 97
Natural Law 13, 27, 51, 84, 236, 237
Natural process 72, 75, 131, 208, 236
Nbagani-aasmaabkong (The Bedrock) 13, 14, 29, 31, 32, 33, 43, 44, 58, 76, 133, 158, 234, 236, 248, 258
Nee-zho-day' (twin) 42
Network of relations 43, 119
New Structure for Social Services 104
Nichol, Rosemary 10, 87, 123

Nimii-puu (Nez Perce) Leader, Chief
   Joseph 44
Nipissing First Nation 96
Nishnob 239
Nokiiwin e-zhimaajiihkag 5, 14, 58
Nokiiwin zhiitaang (work preparation)
   70
Nonhuman 41
Non-Indigenous 25, 113, 130, 133, 256,
   257, 261
Non-Indigenous people 25, 257
Non-resilient communities 125
Non-traditional practices 26
North America 15, 23, 28, 37, 81, 86, 91,
   108, 198, 236
North American Indian 15, 198, 236
Northern door 56, 206
Nsastamowin mnidoo bemaasing
   bemaadiziwin (understanding life
   force energy) 108
Nunavik 126
Nunavut 69, 126
Nunavut Research Institute 69
Nurturing process 60

O
Odeh (heart; heartbeat; inner fire) 14,
   135
Ojibway 13, 14, 22, 42, 48, 52, 54, 140,
   189, 190, 209, 217, 218, 235, 254
Ojibway Clan System 218
Ontario Hospital Association 223
Ontario Provincial Police (OPP) 161
Ontario's Residential Schools 95
Ontology 31, 61, 62
Oppression 18, 121, 127, 128, 131
Oral histories 56
Oral History 53
Oral Tradition 34, 51, 52, 84, 209, 238
Original Instructions (AKA First
   Instructions) 27, 33, 34, 41, 42, 49,
   51, 54, 70, 85, 137, 237, 248
Other 23, 61

Outsider 64, 70
Ownership 66, 85, 87

P
Path of Life Continues 6, 29, 233, 235,
   237, 239, 241, 243, 245, 247, 249, 251,
   253, 255, 257, 259, 261
Peacemakers 36
Peer 73, 99, 122, 143, 148, 168, 174, 183,
   224
Pelican Indian Residential School 237
Personal knowledge 60
Personal stories 60
Philosophy 31, 44, 50, 57, 61, 92, 211
Physical abuse 126
Physical body 45
Physical existence 42
Pikwakanagan 96
Pine Sr., Dan 98, 102
Pitawanakwat, Lillian 56
Pittman, Bruce 95
Pluralism 211
Policy 26, 80, 81, 85, 87, 88, 112, 125, 202,
   223
Porter, Tom 143, 154
Positive self-concept 115
Post-Traumatic Stress Disorder
   (PTSD) 226
Potawatomi 234, 235
Poverty 114, 115, 120, 133, 197, 250
Poverty level 133
Power 20, 23, 32, 39, 41, 46, 50, 56, 77,
   98, 110, 111, 116, 121, 126, 127, 128, 143,
   147, 154, 155, 192, 212, 217, 244, 249,
   250, 254
Power relations 98
Powwow 22, 222
Practical knowledge 211
Pratt, Richard Henry 84, 87, 88, 157
Predator 158, 172
Pre-destined life 33
Preknowledge 48, 140
Pride 2, 23, 226, 227, 243

Problem solving 92, 116
Profit-LeBlanc, Louise 53
ProQuest Theses and Dissertations 108
Protective factors 112, 114, 116, 118, 120, 124, 125
Prucha, Francis Paul 84, 157
Public knowledge 57, 210
Public Works 223
Punishment 94, 130, 143, 144, 145, 157, 176, 217, 254
Purification ceremony 212

Q

Quanta 113, 256
Quebec Cree 222

R

R.S. Company 202
Racism 94, 128
Racist policy 87
Reciprocal relationships 13, 51, 67, 248, 251
Reclamation 20, 81, 90, 91, 93, 94, 207, 225, 227, 230, 252, 254, 256, 257
Red Road 230
Relational accountability 19, 62, 63, 64, 65, 70
Relationship 5, 13, 14, 19, 22, 23, 24, 26, 27, 28, 31, 32, 34, 40, 41, 42, 43, 44, 45, 50, 51, 52, 53, 56, 57, 58, 59, 61, 62, 63, 64, 65, 66, 67, 68, 69, 70, 71, 74, 79, 84, 85, 90, 101, 103, 114, 116, 118, 119, 124, 131, 133, 149, 150, 152, 165, 168, 177, 178, 189, 190, 200, 201, 205, 208, 210, 219, 236, 237, 247, 248, 251
Religious institutions 88
Report on the Memorial Wall Project 95, 105
Reservation 88, 197, 198, 199, 234
Reserve land 86
Residential school experience 25, 88, 90, 94, 111, 134, 152, 212, 222, 232
Residential school policy 88

Residential School Settlement Agreement 89
Residential school survivor 2, 3, 7, 22, 23, 24, 26, 27, 28, 29, 58, 67, 68, 70, 74, 79, 81, 94, 95, 103, 108, 111, 132, 133, 179, 192, 207, 219, 220, 221, 222, 228, 231, 232, 233, 243, 244, 247, 256, 258, 261, 271
Residential school system 19, 26, 29, 79, 84, 108, 132, 168, 172
Resilience 2, 14, 17, 18, 19, 20, 53, 67, 94, 107, 108, 109, 110, 112, 113, 114, 115, 116, 117, 118, 120, 121, 122, 124, 125, 126, 127, 128, 131, 132, 133, 134, 135, 181, 207, 218, 229, 231, 238, 244, 250, 251, 256
Resiliency 2, 3, 19, 20, 22, 27, 28, 70, 71, 72, 73, 78, 107, 108, 111, 112, 113, 114, 115, 116, 117, 118, 119, 120, 121, 122, 123, 124, 125, 126, 127, 128, 129, 131, 132, 133, 134, 135, 136, 157, 171, 216, 217, 233, 236, 238, 239, 240, 242, 245, 248, 252, 256, 257, 258, 261, 271
Resiliency Network 122
Resiliency research 114, 120, 122
Resiliency theory 107, 108, 112, 113, 114, 125, 135, 271
Resilient communities 125
Resilient reintegration 113
Resistance 5, 18, 20, 29, 65, 87, 89, 119, 120, 126, 127, 128, 148, 155, 158, 159, 161, 163, 165, 167, 169, 171, 173, 175, 177, 178, 179, 181, 182, 183, 184, 185, 238, 241, 252, 253, 254, 259
Resistance knowledge 127, 128
Respect 19, 20, 22, 23, 25, 27, 28, 34, 41, 43, 47, 48, 52, 54, 55, 56, 61, 62, 64, 65, 67, 68, 69, 70, 71, 73, 74, 75, 76, 78, 79, 82, 85, 100, 106, 135, 136, 140, 141, 152, 164, 165, 172, 182, 183, 200, 210, 213, 219, 221, 222, 237, 244, 245, 246, 251, 257
Responsibility 26, 27, 40, 41, 42, 43, 46, 48, 51, 53, 55, 56, 62, 63, 65, 66, 69,

Index   275

70, 73, 76, 100, 101, 103, 136, 141, 154, 165, 168, 170, 171, 172, 173, 190, 193, 209, 220, 223, 226, 236, 237, 240, 241, 243, 245, 246, 248, 253, 260
Restorative justice 93
Reunion committee 69, 99
Revealed knowledge 46, 59, 67, 72, 76, 77, 79, 135, 233, 247, 251
Reyhner, Jon 51, 52
Rez (see reserve) 177
Rice, Brian 49, 56, 84, 113, 260
Richardson, Boyce 82
Richardson, Glenn E. 112, 113, 114, 115, 121, 134, 256
Risk factors 114, 115, 123, 125
Rite of passage 164, 165
Ritual 17, 23, 26, 31, 32, 41, 42, 44, 49, 54, 56, 61, 76, 83, 90, 92, 97, 101, 110, 113, 118, 121, 123, 131, 132, 133, 135, 137, 140, 151, 152, 153, 154, 157, 159, 189, 190, 201, 206, 208, 210, 211, 212, 217, 229, 230, 236, 237, 240, 243, 246, 250, 255, 258, 260
Ross, Jack 49
Ross, Jane 49
Royal Canadian Mounted Police (RCMP) 15, 89
Royal Commission on Aboriginal Peoples, 1996 (RCAP) 15, 28, 84, 87, 90, 91, 108
Ryerson, Egerton 85

S

Sacred medicines 25
Sacredness of process 19
Saleebey, Dennis 114
Salt, David Andrew 122
Salutogenic model 117
Sands, Daniel 18, 181, 192
Sarnia, ON 96, 103, 203
Sault Locks 146
Sault Ste. Marie, ON 24, 71, 78, 96, 97, 98, 103, 204

Scarlet fever 178
Schiraldi, Glenn 226
Scholar's Portal 108
School authorities 152
School education 145
School Truck 89
Sehdev, Megha 120
Self 19, 22, 23, 31, 43, 47, 49, 52, 56, 58, 61, 62, 65, 67, 79, 82, 84, 96, 100, 113, 115, 116, 117, 120, 123, 125, 127, 131, 133, 134, 138, 140, 153, 154, 166, 167, 170, 171, 175, 185, 187, 192, 204, 207, 210, 215, 226, 227, 235, 248, 249, 250, 251, 257, 258, 259
Self-actualization 113
Self-concept 115
Self-efficacy 117, 120
Self-identification 23
Sense of purpose 116, 171
Serpent Mounds Trust 222
Settlement Agreement Focus Group 224
Settler 37, 82, 84, 85, 96
Seven Grandfathers Teachings 27, 33, 34, 42, 51, 70, 74, 76, 78, 136, 137, 140, 157, 163, 164, 165, 183, 205, 209, 237, 252
Sexual abuse 29, 192
Sexuality 165, 189
Shawnoodin, neebin (summer wind) 48
Shingwauk, Augustin 97
Shingwauk 15, 21, 22, 23, 24, 26, 28, 66, 68, 69, 72, 78, 81, 89, 94, 95, 96, 97, 98, 99, 100, 101, 102, 103, 105, 106, 122, 123, 144, 148, 149, 150, 152, 153, 169, 173, 174, 176, 177, 180, 181, 192, 193, 195, 197, 198, 199, 204, 208, 213, 218, 222, 223, 224, 229, 243, 246, 253, 255, 259, 260
Shingwauk Alumni 15, 22, 24, 66, 81, 100, 101, 102, 243
Shingwauk Alumni Association 15, 24, 81, 100

Shingwauk Archives 66, 148, 149, 152, 193
Shingwauk Education Trust 224
Shingwauk Family 68, 69, 102, 122, 123, 204, 223, 229, 259
Shingwauk Hall 97, 98
Shingwauk Home for Boys 96
Shingwauk Indian Residential School 24, 81, 95, 96, 98, 105, 195
Shingwauk Project 78, 97, 98, 106, 181, 204
Shingwauk Project Archive 78, 98, 181
Shingwauk Residential School 21, 23, 26, 122, 149, 173, 177, 192, 222, 243, 253
Shingwauk residential school survivors 23, 26
Shingwauk reunion 68, 69, 98, 99, 208
Shingwauk School 98, 99, 103, 105, 144, 150, 176
Shingwauk students 98
Shingwauk University 101
Shingwauk's sons 97
Shingwauk's vision 28, 89, 94, 95, 97, 98, 100, 101
Shiva, Vandana 89
Shoo-pii (Turtle Island or Great Turtle; North America) 13, 36, 37, 38, 39, 51, 80, 82, 91, 92, 96, 106, 107, 242, 249, 250
Shubenacadie Residential School 172
Sik-Ooh-Kotoki Friendship Society 92
Simpson, Leanne Betasamosake 40, 41, 81, 84, 92
Sir James Dunn Secondary School 98
Sky Woman 27, 36, 40
Smith, Jeff 53, 54
Smith, Linda Tuhiwai 63, 65, 66, 92, 93, 101
Smith, Ruth S. 115, 133
Smolewski 249
Social competence 116
Social Services 104, 224

Social structure 91, 245, 250
Socio-political oppression 18
Soul 10, 25, 87, 95, 100, 133, 134, 139, 154, 155, 157, 158, 226, 254, 255, 256, 257, 261
Soul travel 154, 155, 157, 255, 256, 257, 261
Southern door 52, 67, 159
Sovereignty 82, 83, 219
Spanish, ON 100, 109, 142, 150, 185
Special treatment 144, 145
Spirit 10, 17, 18, 19, 20, 23, 25, 26, 28, 29, 31, 32, 33, 34, 35, 36, 39, 40, 41, 42, 44, 48, 49, 50, 52, 53, 54, 55, 56, 60, 61, 67, 70, 71, 74, 76, 77, 83, 90, 92, 95, 97, 100, 101, 110, 113, 121, 123, 131, 132, 133, 134, 135, 137, 139, 140, 151, 152, 154, 155, 157, 158, 159, 163, 164, 165, 172, 181, 183, 201, 203, 205, 206, 208, 209, 210, 211, 212, 217, 218, 220, 222, 229, 230, 234, 236, 237, 240, 243, 246, 249, 250, 254, 255, 256, 257, 258, 260, 261
Spirit beings 42, 140
Spirit name 139, 163, 165, 209
Spirit naming 159
Spirit partner 36
Spirit world 33, 34, 36, 74, 77, 139, 211, 257, 261
Spirits 18, 35, 39, 40, 54, 71, 83, 134, 164, 249, 255
Spiritual abuse 90
Spiritual Anishinaabe 240
Spiritual existence 42
Spiritual teachers 56, 206
Spirituality 32, 44, 61, 123, 132, 133, 152, 157, 208, 217, 229, 236, 240, 260
St. Joseph's [Roman Catholic Mission] Residential School 109, 111, 222
Standing Buffalo Warrior 94
Standingready, Cliff 94
Steinhauer, Patricia 58, 60, 61, 63, 65, 76, 251

Sterling, Shirley 94
Stewardship 41, 42, 49
Story 17, 18, 19, 20, 21, 23, 24, 26, 27, 29, 32, 33, 34, 35, 36, 38, 40, 43, 51, 52, 53, 55, 56, 58, 60, 61, 66, 68, 73, 78, 79, 81, 82, 85, 89, 94, 95, 103, 104, 106, 109, 110, 123, 127, 128, 131, 137, 140, 141, 142, 152, 155, 180, 182, 183, 185, 192, 196, 208, 209, 210, 213, 216, 217, 221, 231, 236, 237, 238, 244, 248, 249, 250
Story maker 19
Storyteller 19, 53, 182
Storytelling 32, 34, 43, 51, 52, 60, 66, 140, 182, 208, 209, 237
Stout, Madeline Dion 94, 124
Sturgeon Lake First Nation 134
Substitute family 122, 123, 150, 168, 229
Suicide 125, 126, 214, 225
Suicide crises 125
Summer 48, 55, 152, 173, 174, 186, 187, 193
Survivor 2, 3, 6, 7, 11, 15, 17, 18, 19, 20, 21, 22, 23, 24, 25, 26, 27, 28, 29, 43, 58, 66, 67, 68, 69, 70, 71, 72, 73, 74, 75, 76, 78, 79, 81, 82, 89, 90, 93, 94, 95, 96, 99, 100, 101, 102, 103, 104, 107, 108, 109, 110, 111, 123, 124, 127, 128, 130, 131, 132, 133, 134, 135, 136, 137, 138, 139, 141, 142, 143, 144, 145, 146, 148, 149, 151, 152, 153, 155, 157, 158, 159, 163, 168, 169, 171, 172, 173, 174, 175, 178, 179, 180, 181, 182, 183, 184, 185, 186, 187, 190, 191, 192, 193, 194, 195, 196, 197, 198, 199, 200, 201, 202, 203, 204, 205, 206, 207, 209, 211, 213, 214, 215, 217, 218, 219, 220, 221, 222, 223, 225, 226, 227, 228, 229, 230, 231, 232, 233, 234, 237, 238, 239, 241, 242, 243, 244, 245, 247, 248, 249, 251, 252, 253, 254, 255, 256, 257, 258, 259, 261, 271
Suspended judgment 76, 77
Sweat lodge 23, 68, 100, 102, 212, 231, 243, 257
Sweat lodge ceremony 23, 68, 212, 231

T

Taboo 25
Taken 5, 24, 26, 29, 68, 72, 76, 78, 89, 91, 98, 99, 102, 106, 125, 137, 139, 141, 142, 143, 144, 145, 147, 149, 151, 153, 155, 157, 158, 173, 182, 190, 196, 200, 217, 223, 229, 249, 252, 254, 259
Teacher 27, 34, 52, 56, 76, 96, 138, 145, 180, 206, 208, 210, 211, 213, 214, 247, 251, 254
Tecumseh 96, 105, 223
Tecumseh Community Development Corporation 223
Terra Nullius (land belonging to no one) 84
The doctrine of discovery 57
The smudging 25, 68
Theories of resiliency 113
Theory of creation and re-creation 35
Thompson, Anne I. 117
Three Day Healing Circles 100
Thriving 116
Thunder Bay 96
Thunderbird, Shannon 14, 44, 45, 48
Timmins Native Friendship Centre 47
Titley, Brian 88, 111
To kill the Indian 157
Tobacco 46, 62, 64, 75, 79, 156, 208, 212, 213, 231, 247, 259
Tobacco Ceremony 247
Total institutions 98
Totem 140
Traditional Teacher 27, 56, 206, 247, 251
Traditional Teachings 2, 19, 27, 51, 67, 68, 71, 74, 135, 209, 233, 236, 239, 242, 248
Traditional Anishinaabe stages of life 136
Traditional ceremonies 25, 45, 205, 257
Traditional child-rearing practices 211
Traditional diet 211
Traditional Elders 212
Traditional healing methods 212

Traditional hunting patterns 211
Traditional indigenous practices 26
Traditional knowledge 34, 59
Traditional protocols 19, 34, 62, 65, 66, 69, 73, 75, 76, 164, 236, 251
Traditional Teachings 2, 19, 27, 51, 67, 71, 74, 135, 200, 209, 233, 236, 239, 242, 248
Traditional values 56, 206
Traditionalist 76, 133, 209
Trait trap 125
Transformation 6, 20, 23, 29, 44, 53, 182, 206, 207, 208, 209, 211, 213, 215, 217, 218, 219, 221, 223, 225, 227, 229, 231
Transition 6, 20, 29, 115, 118, 119, 185, 186, 187, 188, 189, 190, 191, 193, 194, 195, 197, 199, 201, 203, 205, 235, 253
Trauma 17, 18, 24, 86, 90, 112, 127, 139, 173, 174, 191, 198, 199, 207, 213, 218, 226, 229, 232, 238, 249, 250, 256
Treaty 2, 24, 31, 44, 82, 84, 85, 247
Treaty relationship 24
Tribal affiliation 86
Tribal survival 45
Tribal traditions 51
Truth 15, 17, 21, 22, 26, 27, 43, 44, 71, 76, 79, 90, 94, 95, 102, 128, 135, 136, 140, 157, 183, 192, 201, 208, 209, 229, 232, 249, 255
Truth and Reconciliation Commission (TRC) 15, 21, 71, 90, 128, 130, 134
Truth and Reconciliation Commission's 2012 Interim Report 90
Tuberculosis 175, 178
Tuktoyaktuk 126
Turmel, Theresa 2, 3, 17, 18, 19, 108, 271
Turtle Island (See Shoo-pii)

U

Union of Ontario Indians 96
Unresolved trauma 90
Unseen 45, 68, 210

Upper Canada Legislative Assembly 85

V

Valaskakis, Gail Guthrie 207, 229
van Breda, Adrian 114, 115, 116, 117, 118, 120, 121
Vanistendael, Stefan 112
Victim restoration 93
Victimhood 131
Vision 25, 28, 38, 40, 49, 54, 60, 66, 76, 84, 86, 88, 89, 90, 94, 95, 96, 97, 98, 100, 101, 103, 111, 139, 140, 155, 174, 179, 204, 212, 219, 221, 238, 246, 257

W

Waabin (winds coming from the four directions) 48
Waabun (morning) 48
Walker, Brian Harrison 122
Wallaceburg District Secondary School (WDSS) 15, 95, 220, 221, 222
Wallaceburg District Secondary School Future Elders Program 95
Walpole Island 9, 15, 22, 26, 27, 69, 70, 71, 72, 73, 78, 81, 95, 103, 104, 105, 111, 173, 177, 194, 197, 203, 217, 218, 220, 221, 223, 226, 233, 249, 261, 271
Walpole Island children 105
Walpole Island First Nation 9, 15, 22, 26, 27, 69, 70, 95, 104, 105, 111, 233, 271
Walpole Island First Nation Chief and Council 70
Walpole Island Residential School Survivors Group (WIRSSG) 15, 24, 27, 28, 29, 67, 68, 69, 70, 71, 73, 81, 95, 103, 106, 108, 133, 213, 220, 222
Walters, Anna Lee 233
War of 1812-14 96
Wasakajec/Wesakejig (the trickster) 14, 83
Washburn, Carol 50
Water Beings 27, 40

Wawa, ON 22, 56, 97
Wawanosh Home 97
WDSS Future Elders 222
Weber-Pillwax, Cora 63, 65
Weedjeewaugun (companion;
 Companion on the Path of Life;
 he who goes with; she who walks
 with) 14, 189
Well-being 40, 62, 117
Welsh 88
Werner, Emmy 115, 122, 133
Wesley-Esquimaux, Cynthia 207, 218,
 229, 231, 244, 249
Western door 55, 186
Western knowledge 258
Western society 61
White people 14, 83, 192
Whitemen 88
Whiteye, Enos 94
Whitley, Rob 120
WIFN Future Elders Program 221
WIFN Secondary School Program 221
Wigwam 96, 133, 235, 236
Wiijiiwaagan (going to be joined;
 betrothed) 14, 189
Wiijikiiwendiwin miininwaa
 kendaaswin 58
Wikwemikong 22
Wildcat, Daniel 77
Wilkins, Kerry 31, 247
Williams, Doug 10, 34, 48, 49, 55, 75,
 76, 85, 134, 135, 139, 140, 141, 164, 167,
 188, 189, 201, 208, 209, 211, 212, 240
Williams, Shirley Ida 10, 20, 22, 54, 67,
 75, 109, 110, 132, 143, 145, 148, 154, 155,
 165, 167, 184, 189, 191, 196, 225, 226,
 227, 230, 245, 251, 254, 255, 256, 258
Williams Jr., Robert A. 84
Wilshere, John 122
Wilson, Angela Cavender 52, 53
Wilson, Edward 97
Wilson, Shawn 33, 61, 63, 64, 65, 70
Wisdom 27, 32, 33, 43, 56, 60, 61, 140,
 183, 206, 208, 209, 231

Wisps of snow 83
Witchcraft 167
Wolin, Steven J. 243
Wolin, Sybil 243
Wong, Paul T.P. 249, 250
Worldview 22, 30, 31, 32, 34, 58, 62, 133

Y
Yazzie, Robert 219
YMCA Peace Medallion 221
Young, Sherri 25, 88
Young ones 10, 54, 131, 141, 149, 150, 154,
 158, 183, 203, 209, 226
Young Women's Christian Association
 (YWCA) 15, 187

Z
Zhaaganaash (white people) 14, 22, 88,
 192, 214
Zhichigan zhitaang (project
 preparation) 14
Ziiqwan (a spirit) 14, 48
Zongwaadiziwin (strength of life) 14,
 68, 251, 261

REFERENCES

Aboriginal Healing Foundation. n.d. "FAQs." http://www.ahf.ca/faqs.
Aboriginal Healing Foundation. n.d. "Mission." Accessed August 21, 2011. http://www.ahf.ca/about-us/mission.
Absolon, Kathy. "Navigating the Landscape of Practice: Dbaagmowin of a Helper." In Raven Sinclair, Michael Anthony Hart, and Gord Bruyere (Eds.) *Wicihitowin: Aboriginal Social Work in Canada*, 172-199. Winnipeg: Fernwood Publishing, 2009.
Antone, Robert A., Diane Miller, and Brian A. Myers. *The Power Within People: A Community Organizing Perspective*. Brantford: Hurryprint, 1986.
Antonovsky, Aaron. "The Salutogenic Model as a Theory to Guide Health Promotion." *Health Promotion International* 11no.1 (1996): 11-18.
Archibald, Jo-Ann, ed. *Courageous spirits: Aboriginal Heroes of Our Children Teachers' Guide*. Penticton: Theytus Books, Ltd., 1993.
Assembly of First Nations. *Description of the Assembly of First Nations*. Ottawa, Ontario, 2013, http://www.afn.ca/index.php/en/about-afn/description-of-the-afn
Assembly of First Nations. *Breaking the Silence: An Interpretive Study of Residential School Impact and Healing as Illustrated by the Stories of First Nations Individuals*. Ottawa, Ontario: First Nations Health Commission, 1994.
Auger, Donald J. *Tipaachimowinan Stories from Residential School*. Nishnawbe Aski Nation and the Aboriginal Healing Foundation, 2005.
Baker, Patricia. "A Place of History, a Place of Healing." *The Sault Star*, April 26, 2008, Section E1.
Baker, Patricia. 2008. "Learning the hard way: Michael Cachagee reveals scars of residential school experience." *The Sault Star*, October 15, 2008, http://www.thepost.on.ca/ArticleDisplay.aspx?archive=true&e=733104.
Barnard, Charles. "Resiliency: A Shift in Perception." *American Journal of Family Therapy*, 22 no.2 (1994): 135-144.
Battiste, Marie, ed. *Reclaiming Indigenous Voice and Vision*. Vancouver: UBC Press, 2000.
Battiste, Marie. *First Nations Education in Canada: The Circle Unfolds*. British Columbia: University of British Columbia Press, 1995.
Battiste, Marie and James Youngblood Henderson. *Protecting Indigenous Knowledge and Heritage: A Global Challenge*. Saskatoon: Purich Publishing Ltd., 2000.

Beck, Peggy V., and Anna Lee Walters. *The Sacred: Ways of Knowledge and Sources of Life*. Tsaile (Navajo Nation): Navajo Community College Press, 1977.

Benard, Bonnie. *Resiliency: What We Have Learned*. San Francisco: WestEd, 2004.

Benton-Banai, Edward. *The Mishomis Book: The Voice of the Ojibway*. Minneapolis: University of Minnesota Press, 1988.

Blondin-Perrin, Alice. *My Heart Shook Like a Drum: What I Learned at the Indian Mission Schools, Northwest Territories*. Ottawa: Borealis Press, 2009.

Boileau, Sonia Bonspille, writer and director. *Last Call Indian* (DVD). Gatineau: Nish Media, 2010, http://nishmedia.tv/view_television-productions.php?pid=98

Boldt, Menno. *Surviving as Indians: The Challenge of Self-Government*. Toronto: University of Toronto Press, 1993.

Borrows, John. *Canada's Indigenous Constitution*. Toronto: University of Toronto Press. 2010a.

Borrows, John. *Drawing Out Law: A Spirit's Guide*. Toronto: University of Toronto Press, 2010b.

Borrows, John. "Wampum at Niagara: The Royal Proclamation, Canadian Legal History, and Self-Government." In *Aboriginal and Treaty Rights in Canada: Essays on Law, Equity, and Respect and Difference*, edited by Michael Asch, 155-172. British Columbia: UBC Press, 1997.

Brant Castellano, Marlene. "Healing Residential School Trauma: The Case for Evidence-Based Policy and Community-Led Programs." *Native Social Work Journal*. 7 (November 2010.): 11-31.

Brant Castellano, Marlene. "Updating Aboriginal Traditions of Knowledge." In *Indigenous Knowledges in Global Contexts: Multiple Readings of Our World*, edited by George J. Sefa Dei, Budd L. Hall, and Dorothy Goldin Rosenberg, 21-36. Toronto: University of Toronto Press, 2000.

Cajete, Greg. *Native Science: Natural Laws of Interdependence*. Santa Fe: Clear Light Publishers, 2000.

Cajete, Greg. *Look to the Mountain: An Ecology of Indigenous Education*. Skyland: Kivaki Press, 1994.

Calliou, Brian. "Methodology for researching oral histories in the Aboriginal community." *Native Studies Review* 15 no.1 (2004): 73-105.

Calliou, Sharilyn. "Peacekeeping actions at home: A medicine wheel model for a peacekeeping pedagogy." In *First Nations Education in Canada: The Circle Unfolds*, edited by Marie Battiste and Jean Barman, 47-72. Vancouver: UBC Press, 1995.

Cardinal, Lewis. "What is an Indigenous Perspective?" *The Canadian Journal of Native Education* 25 no. 2 (2001)1: 80-183.

Chansonneuve, Deborah. *Reclaiming Connections: Understanding Residential School Trauma among Aboriginal People*. Ottawa: Aboriginal Healing Foundation, 2005.

Chrisjohn, Roland, Sherri Young, and Michael Maraun. *The Circle Game: Shadows and Substance in the Indian Residential School Experience in Canada*. Penticton: Theytus Books, Ltd., 2006.

Chute, Janet. *The Legacy of Shingwaukonse: A Century of Native Leadership*. Toronto: University of Toronto Press, 1998.

Cook-Lynn, Elizabeth. "American Indian Intellectualism and the New Indian Story." In *Natives and Academics: Researching and Writing About American Indians*, edited by Devon Abbott Mihesuah. Lincoln: University of Nebraska, 1998.

Couture, Joseph E. "The Role of Native Elders: Emergent Issues." In *Visions of the Heart, Canadian Aboriginal Issues*, edited by David Alan Long and Olive Patricia Dickason, 41-56. Toronto: Harcourt Brace Canada, 1996.

Cruikshank, Julie. "Invention of Anthropology in British Columbia's Supreme Court: Oral Tradition as Evidence in Delgamuukw v. B.C." in the *British Columbia Quarterly*, 95 (Autumn 1992): 25-42.

Cyrulnik, Boris. *Resilience: How Your Inner Strength Can Set You Free From the Past* Toronto: Penguin Books, 2009.

Danziger, Edmund Jefferson Jr. *Survival and Regeneration: Detroit's American Indian Community*. Detroit: Wayne State University Press, 1991.

Debassige, Brent. *Navigating the Rapids and Stumbling Through the Bush: A Study in Understanding Resiliency Through the Lens of Anishnaabe*. Unpublished MA Thesis. Kingston: Queen's University, 2002.

Dell, Colleen, Debra E. Dell, and Carol Hopkins. "Resiliency and Holistic Inhalant Abuse Treatment." *Journal of Aboriginal Health* 2.1(2005): 4-15.

Deloria Jr, Vine. "American Indian metaphysics.' In *Power and place: Indian education in America*, edited by Vine Deloria Jr. and Daniel Wildcat, 1-6. Golden: American Indian Graduate Center and Fulcrum Publishing, 2001.

Denham, Aaron R. "Rethinking Historical Trauma: Narratives of Resilience." *Transcultural Psychiatry*. 45 no. 3 (2008): 391-414.

Dockstator, Mark. "Toward an Understanding of Aboriginal Self-government: A Proposed Theoretical Model and Illustrative Factual Analysis." Unpublished thesis. Toronto: York University, 1993.

Dodge, Uriah. *Gaagnig Pane Chiyaayong: Forever We Will Remain. A Report on the Memorial Wall Project*. Walpole Island First Nation, 2002.

Duran, Eduardo and Bonnie Duran. *Native American Postcolonial Psychology*. Albany: State University of New York Press, 1995.

Ellerby, Jonathan. H. *Working With Indigenous Elders: An Introductory Handbook for Institution-Based and Health Care Professionals Based on the Teachings of Winnipeg-Area Indigenous Elders and Cultural Teachers*. Winnipeg: Aboriginal Issues Press, 2005.

Ermine, Willie. "Aboriginal Epistemology." In *First Nations Education in Canada: The Circle Unfolds*, edited by Marie Battiste and Jean Barman, 101-112. Vancouver: UBC Press, 1995.

Fitzmaurice, Andrew. "The genealogy of terra nullius." *Australian Historical Studies*, 38, 129 (2007): 1-15.
Fortier, Mary. *A Survivor's Story of the Boarding School Syndrome*. Belleville: Epic Publishin, 2002.
Gallagher, Colin. "Quit Thinking Like a Scientist." In *Native Voices in Research*, edited by Jill Oakes, Rick Riewe, K. Wilde, A. Edmunds, and A. Dubois, 183-190. Winnipeg, Manitoba: Aboriginal Issues Press, 2003.
Garroutte, Eva Marie. *Real Indians: Identity and the survival of Native America*. Berkeley: University of California Press, 2003.
Geniusz, Wendy Makoons. *Our knowledge is not primitive: Decolonising botanical Anishinaabe teachings*. Syracuse: Syracuse University Press, 2009.
Giago, Tim. *Children Left Behind: The Dark Legacy of Indian Mission Boarding Schools*. Santa Fe: Clear Light Publishing, 2006.
Goffman, Erving. *Asylums: Essays on the social situation of mental patients and other inmates*. Garden City: Anchor Books, 1961.
Gone, Joseph P. "The Red Road to Wellness: Cultural Reclamation in a Native First Nations Community Treatment Center." In *American Journal of Community Psychology* 47 (1-2, 2011):187-202.
Goulet, Jean-Guy *Ways of Knowing: Experience, Knowledge, and Power Among the Dene Tha.*Vancouver: UBC Press, 1998.
Grant, Agnes. *No End of Grief: Indian Residential Schools in Canada*. Winnipeg: Pemmican Publications, 1996.
Graveline, Fyre Jean. *Circle Works: Transforming Eurocentric Consciousness*. Halifax: Fernwood Publishing, 1998.
Gunderson, Lance. H, ed. *Panarchy: Understanding Transformations in Human and Natural Systems*. Washington: Island Press, 2002.
Haig-Brown, Celia. *Resistance and Renewal: Surviving the Indian Residential School*. Vancouver: Arsenal Pulp Press, 1988.
Harrod, Howard L. *The Animals Came Dancing*. Tucson: University of Arizona Press, 2000.
Hawley, Dale R., and Laura De Haan. "Toward a Definition of Family Resilience: Integrating Life-span and Family Perspectives." *Family Process*, 35 no.3 (1996): 283-298.
HeavyRunner, Iris. and Joann Sebastian Morris. "Traditional Native Culture and Resilience." *Center for Applied Research and Educational Improvement (CAREI) Newsletter*. University of Minnesota, Spring, 5 no.1 (1997): 1-5.
Holmes, L. "Heart Knowledge, Blood Memory, and the Voice of the Land: Implications of Research Among Hawaiian Elders." In *Indigenous Knowledges in Global Contexts: Multiple Readings of Our World*, edited by George J. Sefa Dei, Budd L. Hall, and Dorothy Goldin Rosenberg, 37-53. Toronto: University of Toronto Press, 2000.

Indian and Northern Affairs Canada. *Words First: An Evolving Terminology Relating to Aboriginal Peoples in Canada.* 2004. Retrieved from http://www.collectionscanada.gc.ca/webarchives/20071114225835/ http://www.ainc-inac.gc.ca/pr/pub/wfrmrslt_e.asp?term=10

Inuit Tapiriit Kanatami and Nunavut Research Institute. *Negotiating Research Relationships with Inuit Communities: A Guide for Researchers.* Ottawa, Ontario and Iqaluit, Nunavut, 2007.

Inuit Tapiriit Kanatami "About Inuit." https://www.itk.ca/about-inuit.

Jack, Agness. 2006. *Behind Closed Doors: Stories from the Kamloops Indian Residential School.* Michigan: The University of Michigan, Secwepemc Cultural Education Society, n.d..

Jackson, D. "The Shingwauk Project Archives: The Residential School Legacy and the Canadian Narrative", A talk prepared for the Archives Association of Ontario Annual Conference, Algoma University, Sault Ste. Marie, Ontario, 2005.

Jaenen, Cornelius J. "Education for Francization: The Case for New France in the Seventeenth Century." In *Indian Education in Canada, Volume 1: The Legacy,* edited by Jean Barman, Yvonne Hébert, and Don McCaskill. Vancouver: University of British Columbia Press, 1986.

Jaine, Linda, ed. *Residential Schools: The Stolen Years.* University of Saskatchewan: Extension Division Press, 1993.

Johnston, Basil. *Indian School Days.* Toronto: Key Porter, 1988.

Johnston, Basil. *Ojibway Ceremonies.* Lincoln: University of Nebraska Press, 1982.

Johnston, Basil. *Ojibway Heritage.* Lincoln: University of Nebraska Press, 1976.

Kirmayer, Laurence, Megha Sehdev, and Collette Isaac. "Community Resilience: Models, Metaphors and Measures." *Journal of Aboriginal Health.* 5 no.1 (2009):62-117.

Kirmayer, Laurence, and Gail Guthrie Valaskakis, eds. *Healing Traditions: The Mental Health of Aboriginal Peoples in Canada.* Vancouver: University of British Columbia Press, 2009.

Knockwood, Isabelle. *Out of the Depths: The Experiences of Mi'kmaw Children at the Indian Residential School at Shubenacadie, Nova Scotia.* Lockeport: Roseway Publishing, 1992.

Knowlton Stan. Spoken at Sik-ooh-Kotoki Friendship Society, Lethbridge, Alberta, as part of RCAP proceedings, May 25, 1993

Korhonen, Marja. *Resilience: Overcoming Challenges and Moving on Positively.* Ottawa: National Aboriginal Health Organization (NAHO), Ajunnginiq Centre, 2007.

Kovach, Margaret. *Indigenous Methodologies: Characteristics, Conversations and Contexts.* Toronto: University of Toronto Press, Inc., 2009.

Kulchyski, Peter. *The Red Indians.* Winnipeg: Arbeiter Ring Publishing, 2007.

Lalonde, Christopher. "Identity Formation and Cultural Resilience in Aboriginal Communities." In *Promoting Resilience in Child Welfare,* 52-71 Victoria, British Columbia: University of Victoria, 2004.

Lane Jr., Phile, Judie Bopp, Michael Bopp, Lee Brown, and Elders *The Sacred Tree*. Lethbridge: Four Worlds International Institute, 1984.

Leckie, Keith Ross, writer. *Where the Spirit Lives* [VHS]. Canada: Amazing Spirit Productions Ltd., 1989.

Lee, Scott Cloud, and Carol AnnWashburn. *The Circle is Sacred: Stalking the Spirit-Powered Life*. San Francisco: Council Oak Books, 2003.

Legacy of Hope Foundation. *Where Are the Children? Healing the Legacy of the Residential Schools* (Exhibition). Ottawa, Ontario, 2001.

Little Bear, Leroy. "Aboriginal Paradigms: Implications for Relationships to Land and Treaty Making." In *Advancing Aboriginal Claims*, edited by Kerry Wilkins, 26-38. Saskatoon: Purich Publishing Ltd., 2004.

Little Bear, Leroy. "Jagged Worldviews Colliding." In *Reclaiming Indigenous Voice and Vision*, edited by Marie Battiste, 77-85. Vancouver: UBC Press, 2000.

Longboat, Dan. Lecture October 1, 2008, Trent University.

Longboat, Jan Kahehti:io. *Idawadadi: December 1999 - March 2010: Coming Home, Stories of Residential School Survivors with Contributions by Aboriginal Women*. Ottawa: Aboriginal Healing Foundation, 2010.

Manore, Jean. "A vision of trust: The legal, moral, and spiritual foundations of Shingwauk Hall." *Native Studies Review*, 9 no.2 (1993-1994.): 1-22.

Maybury-Lewis, David. *Indigenous Peoples, ethnic groups, and the state*. Needham Heights: Allyn and Bacon, 1997.

McCormick, Roderick. and Paul T.P. Wong. "Adjustment and Coping in Aboriginal People." In *Handbook of Multicultural Perspectives on Stress and Coping*, 513-531 New York: Springer Science and Business Media Inc., 2005.

McCubbin, Marilyn A., and Hamilton I. McCubbin. "Resiliency in Families: A Conceptual Model of Family Adjustment and Adaptation in Response to Stress and Crises." In *Family Assessment: Resiliency, Coping and Adaptation: Inventories for Research and Practice*, edited by Hamilton I. McCubbin, Anne I. Thompson, and Marilyn A. McCubbin, 1-64. Madison: University of Wisconsin, 1996.

McCubbin, Marilyn A., and Hamilton I. McCubbin. "Research Utilization in Social Work Practice of Family Treatment." In *Research Utilization in the Social Sciences: Innovations for Practice and Administration*, edited by Anthony J. Grasso, and Irwin Epstein, 149-192. New York City: Haworth Press Inc., 1992.

McGowan, Dave, producer. *Silent Thunder: The Search for Truth and Reconciliation* (documentary). (Peterborough: CHEX Television, 2012).

McLaren, Nadia, director. *Muffins for Granny*. (Toronto: Mongrel Media, 2008), DVD.

McLeod, Yvonne. "Change Makers: Empowering Ourselves Thro' the Education and Culture of Aboriginal Languages: A Collaborative Team Effort." *Canadian Journal of Native Education*, 27 no.1 (2003): 108-126.

Meyer, Manu Aluli. "Acultural Assumptions of Empiricism: A Native Hawaiian Critique." *Canadian Journal of Native Education*, 25 no. 2 (2001): 188-200.

Miller, James Rodger. *Shingwauk's Vision: A History of Native Residential Schools*. Toronto: University of Toronto Press, 1996.

Miller, James Rodger. *Skyscrapers Hide the Heavens: A History of Indian-White Relations in Canada*. Toronto: University of Toronto Press, 1989.

Miller, Robert J. *Native America, Discovered and Conquered: Thomas Jefferson, Lewis and Clark, and Manifest Destiny*. Lincoln: University of Nebraska Press, 2008.

Milloy, John S. *A National Crime: The Canadian Government and the Residential School System 1879 to 1986*. Winnipeg: University of Manitoba Press, 1999.

Momaday, N. Scott. *The Names, A Memoir*. Tucson, Arizona: Sun Tracks/The University of Arizona Press, 1976.

Monture-Angus, Patricia. *Thunder In My Soul: A Mohawk Woman Speaks*. Halifax: Fernwood Publishing, 1995.

Nabigon, Herb. *The Hollow Tree: Fighting Addiction with Traditional Native Healing*. Montreal: McGill-Queen's University Press, 2006.

Nichol, Rosemary A. *Factors contributing to resilience in Aboriginal persons who attended residential schools*. Unpublished MA Thesis. Winnipeg: University of Manitoba, 2000.

Nin.da.waab.jib. *Minishenhying Anishnaabe-aki: Walpole Island: The Soul of Indian Territory*. Walpole Island: Walpole Island Band Council, 1987.

Nock, David A. *Victorian Missionary and Canadian Indian Policy: Cultural Synthesis vs. Cultural Replacement*. Waterloo: Wilfrid Laurier University Press, 1988.

Patterson, Joän M. "Understanding family resilience." *Journal of Clinical Psychology*, 58 no.3 (2002.): 233-246.

Pitawanakwat, Lillian. *Ojibwe/Powawatomi (Anishinabe) teaching*. 2006. Retrieved from http://www.fourdirectionsteachings.com/transcripts/ojibwe.pdf

Pratt, Richard Henry. *Battlefield and Classroom: Four Decades With the American Indian, 1867-1904*. Norman: University of Oklahoma Press, 2003.

Pratt, Richard Henry. "The Advantages of Mingling Indians with Whites." In *Americanizing the American Indians: Writings by the "Friends of the Indian" 1880–1900*, edited by Francis Paul Prucha, 260-271. Cambridge: Harvard University Press, 1973.

Reyhner, Jon, and Jeanne Eder. *American Indian Education: A History*. United States of America: University of Oklahoma Press, Norman Publishing, 2004.

Rice, Brian. *Seeing the World with Aboriginal Eyes: A Four Directional Perspective on Human and Non-human Values, Cultures and Relationships on Turtle Island*. Winnipeg: Aboriginal Issues Press, 2005.

Richardson, Boyce. *People of Terra Nullius: The Trail and Rebirth in Aboriginal Canada*. Seattle: University of Washington Press, 1993.

Richardson, Glenn E. "The Metatheory of Resilience and Resiliency." *Journal of Clinical Psychology*, 58 no.3 (2002): 307-321.

Rogers, Shelagh, Mike Degagne, and Jonathan Dewar. 2012. *Speaking my truth: Reflections on Reconciliation and Residential School*. Ottawa: Aboriginal Healing Foundation.

Ross, Jane, and Jack Ross. "Keep the Circle Strong: Native Health Promotion." *Journal of Speech Language Pathology and Audiology*, 16 no.3 (1992): 291-302.

Royal Commission on Aboriginal Peoples. *Report of the Royal Commission on Aboriginal Peoples Volume 1: Looking Forward, Looking Back.* Ottawa: Canada Communication Group, 1996a.

Royal Commission on Aboriginal Peoples. *Report of the Royal Commission on Aboriginal Peoples Volume 2: Restructuring the Relationship.* Ottawa: Canada Communication Group, 1996b. http://www.collectionscanada.gc.ca/webarchives/20071124125834/http://www.ainc-inac.gc.ca/ch/rcap/sg/shm2_e.html

Saleebey, Dennis. "The Strengths Perspectives in Social Work Practice: Extensions and Cautions." *Social Work* 41 no. 3 (2003): 296-305.

Sands, Donald. *As Your God is My Witness: Rebuttal to Bernice Logan.* The Shingwauk Project Archives (2010-004-006, (006)). Residential School Centre, Algoma University, Sault Ste. Marie, Ontario, 1996.

Schiraldi, Glenn. *The Post-Traumatic Stress Disorder Sourcebook, Second Edition.* New York: McGraw Hill, 2009.

George J. Sefa Dei, Budd L. Hall, and Dorothy Goldin Rosenberg, editors. *Indigenous Knowledges in Global Contexts: Multiple Readings of Our World.* Toronto: University of Toronto Press, 2000

Sherman, Paula. "Indawendiwan: Spiritual Ecology as the Foundation of Omamiwinini Relations." PhD diss., Trent University, 2007. Retrieved from http://search.proquest.com/docview/304763315?accountid=14391

Shingwauk Trust. n.d. http://www.shingwauk.auc.ca/shingwauktrust/shingwauktrust2.html

Shingwauk. n.d. "Welcome" Retrieved from http://www.shingwauk.auc.ca/welcome_index.html

Shiva, Vandana. "Foreword: Cultural Diversity and the Politics of Knowledge." In *Indigenous Knowledges in Global Contexts: Multiple Readings of Our World*, edited by George J. Sefa Dei, Budd L. Hall, and Dorothy Goldin Rosenberg. Toronto: University of Toronto Press, 2000.

Simpson, Leanne Betasamosake. *Dancing On Our Turtle's Back: Stories of Nishnaabeg Re-creation, Resurgence, and a New Emergence.* Winnipeg: Arbeiter Ring Publishing, 2011.

Simpson, Leanne Betasamosake. *Lighting the Eighth Fire: The Liberation, Resurgence, and Protection of Indigenous Nations.* Winnipeg: Arbeiter Ring Publishing, 2008.

Smith, Derek G, ed. *Canadian Indians and the Law: Selected Documents, 1663-1972.* Toronto: McClelland and Stewart, 1975.

Smith, Linda Tuhiwai. *Decolonizing Methodologies: Research and Indigenous peoples.* New York: Zed Books, 1999.

Special Supplement about Algoma University. 1992. *The Sault Star*, June 18, 1992. Sault Ste. Marie, Ontario: Sun Media.

Standingready, Cliff, Standing Buffalo Warrior. *Children of the Creator.* Port Perry, Ontario: Boys Press, 2010.

Steinhauer, Patricia. "Situating Myself in Research." *Canadian Journal of Native Education,* 25 no.2 (2001): 183-188.

Sterling, Shirley. *My Name is Seepeetza.* Toronto: Groundwood Books, 1992.

Stoecker, Randy. *Research Methods for Community Change: A Project-Based Approach.* Thousand Oaks, California: Sage Publications, Inc., 2005.

Stout, Madeleine Dion. and Gregory Kipling. *Aboriginal People, Resilience and the Residential School Legacy.* Ottawa: Aboriginal Healing Foundation, 2003.

Thunderbird, Shannon. n.d. "Symbols and Meanings." http://www.shannonthunderbird.com/symbols_and_meanings.htm

Titley, E. Brian. *A Narrow Vision: Duncan Campbell Scott and the Administration of Indian Affairs in Canada.* Vancouver: UBC Press, 1986.

Truth and Reconciliation Commission of Canada. 2011. "Principles." Accessed August 22, 2011, from http://www.trc.ca/websites/trcinstitution/index.php?p=7#Principles

Truth and Reconciliation Commission of Canada. 2012. *Truth and Reconciliation Commission of Canada: Interim report.* http://www.trc.ca/websites/trcinstitution/index.php?p=580

Truth and Reconciliation Commission of Canada (2012). *Canada, Aboriginal Peoples, and Residential Schools: They Came for the Children.*

Union of the Ontario Indians. 2010. *Welcome to Anishinabek Territory.* Communication department, North Bay: Creative Impressions.

Van Breda, Adrian D. 2001. *Resilience Theory: A Literature Review.* Accessed at http://vanbreda.org/adrian/resilience/resilience2.pdf

Van Kirk, Sylvia. 1996. *Many Tender Ties: Women in the Fur Trade, 1670-1870.* Winnipeg: Watson and Dwyer.

Waldram, James Burgess. *Aboriginal Healing in Canada: Studies in Therapeutic Meaning and Practice.* Ottawa: Aboriginal healing Foundation Research Series, 2008.

Waldram, James Burgess, Ann Herring, and T. Kue Young. *Aboriginal Health in Canada: Historical, Cultural, and Epidemiological Perspectives.* Toronto: University of Toronto Press, 2006.

Walker, Brian, and David Salt. *Resilience Thinking: Sustaining Ecosystems and People in a Changing World.* Washington: Island Press, 2006.

Wallaceburg District Secondary School. *Future Elders Program* brochure. Wallaceburg, Ontario, 2009.

Wallaceburg District Secondary School Future Elders Program. (Directors). *Celebrating Survival: A Tribute to the Residential School Survivors of Walpole Island First Nation* (2009), DVD.

Warry, Wayne. *Unfinished Dreams: Community Healing and the Reality of Aboriginal Self-government.* Toronto: University of Toronto Press, 1998.

Weber-Pillwax, Cora. "Coming to an Understanding: A panel presentation: What is Indigenous Research?" *Canadian Journal of Native Education*, 26 no.2 (2001): 166-174.

Werner, Emmy E. "Risk, Resilience, and Recovery: Perspectives From the Kauai Longitudinal Study." *Development and Psychopathy*, 5 (1993):503-515.

Werner, Emmy E. and Ruth S. Smith. *Kauai's children come of age*. Honolulu: University of Hawaii Press, 1977.

Wesley-Esquimaux, Cynthia. and Magdalena Smolewski. *Historic Trauma and Aboriginal Healing*. Ottawa: The Aboriginal Healing Foundation, 2004.

Wesley-Esquimaux, Cynthia. "Mining Our Lives for the Diamonds." *First Peoples Child & Family Review*, 8 no.2 (2013). https://fpcfr.com/index.php/FPCFR/article/view/210.

Wesley-Esquimaux, Cynthia. "Trauma to Resilience: Notes on Decolonization." In *Restoring the Balance: First Nations Women, Community, and Culture*, edited by Gail Guthrie Valaskakis et al, 13-34. Winnipeg: University of Manitoba Press, 2009.

Whiteye, Enos Bud. *A Dark Legacy: A Primer on Indian Residential Schools in Canada*. Walpole Island, Ontario, 2002.

Wilkes, Glenda. "Introduction: A Second Generation of Resilience Research." *Journal of Clinical Psychology*, 58 no.3 (2002): 229-232.

Williams Jr., Robert A. *Linking Arms Together: American Indian Treaty Visions of Law and Peace, 1600-1800*. New York: Oxford University Press, 1997.

Williams, Shirley. n.d. "Living Healing Quilt Project." http://quiltinggallery.com/2009/01/22/anishinaabe-kwes-resilience/.

Williams, Shirley. n.d. http://wherearethechildren.ca/en/blackboard/page-8.html.

Williams, Shirley. "The Development of Ojibway language Materials." *Canadian Journal of Native Education*, 27 no.1 (2003): 79-88.

Wilshere, Donald John. "The Experiences of Seven Alumni Who Attended Shingwauk Residential School as Children 1929-1964." MA thesis, Lakehead University, 1999.

Wilson, Angela Cavender. "American Indian History or Non-Indian Perceptions of American Indian History?" In *Natives and Academics: Researching and Writing About American Indians*, edited by Devon Abott Mihesuah. Lincoln: University of Nebraska Press, 1998.

Wilson, Angela Cavender. "Grandmother to Granddaughter: Generations of Oral History in a Dakota Family." In *Natives and Academics: Researching and Writing about American Indians*, edited by Devon Abott Mihesuah. Lincoln: University of Nebraska Press, 1998.

Wilson, Shawn. *Research is Ceremony: Indigenous Research Methods*. Halifax: Fernwood Publishing, 2008.

Wolin, Sybil, and Steven J. Wolin. "Shaping a Brighter Future by Uncovering Survivor's Pride." *Reaching Today's Youth*. Vol. 2 no.3 (1998).

Yazzie, Robert. "Indigenous Peoples and Postcolonial Colonialism." In *Reclaiming Indigenous Voice and Vision*, edited by Marie Battiste. Vancouver: UBC Press, 2000.

Younging, Gregory, Jonathan Dewar, and Mike DeGagne. *Response, Responsibility, and Renewal: Canada's Truth and Reconciliation Journey*. Ottawa: Aboriginal Healing Foundation, 2009.

Archives:

G.J., Shingwauk Archives, Fonds No. 2010-082/001(002).
C.W., Shingwauk Archives, Fonds No. 2010-047/001(010).
M.C., Shingwauk Archives, Fonds No. 2010-047/001(008).
M.C., Shingwauk Archives, Fonds No. 2010-082/001(002).

BIO

Dr. Theresa Turmel *(Biidaaban Ntam bi yaad)* is an Anishinaabe-kwe from Michipicoten First Nation. She completed her Ph.D. in Indigenous Studies from Trent University in 2013. Her doctoral dissertation, *'Forever We Will Remain: Reflections and Memories: 'Resiliency' Concerning the Walpole Island Residential School Survivors Group'*, was the product of twenty plus years of a participatory, community-based partnership with the residential school survivors from Walpole Island First Nation. Her most significant research work has been working with Indian residential school survivors in a special project capacity with a critical analysis of resiliency theory. She is currently diligently researching and writing her second book, a thorough investigation of missing and murdered Indigenous women and girls from an Anishinaabe-kwe perspective. In her personal life, Theresa is the proud mother of three adult children, John, Danielle and Chantal and extremely proud grandmother of Ariel, Alexandra, Dylahn, Emma-Leigh and Ben and has been married to husband Mike for the past thirty-six years.